Tragedy without Triumph
The Coalition in Office 2013-22

Connor Court Publishing

Published by Connor Court Publishing Pty Ltd, 2024.

CONNOR COURT PUBLISHING PTY LTD
PO Box 7257
Redland Bay QLD 4165
sales@connorcourt.com
www.connorcourtpublishing.com.au

ISBN: 9781923224087

Cover design by Ian James.

Front cover photos taken from Wikipedia Commons.

Published in Australia.

Table of Contents

Introduction

Tragedy without Triumph:
The Coalition in Office 2013-22

Scott Prasser

What is this book about?

The sixth volume of Sir Winston's Churchill's Nobel Prize winning series, *The Second World War* was entitled *Triumph and Tragedy*. His argument was that although it was a triumph because of the "overwhelming victory of the grand Alliance", it was also a tragedy because it had "failed so far to bring general peace to our anxious world" (Churchill 1954/2005: xiii). Adding to the "tragedy" was US President Roosevelt's death in April before the war had ended and the expansion of the Soviet Union into western Europe with its terrible consequences. At a personal level, there was Churchill's surprise electoral defeat in July 1945.

By contrast, this volume argues that the Federal Coalition, despite three election wins, 2013, 2016, and 2019, and nine years in office, was a tragedy with little triumph. And to be clear, when we discuss Coalition governments, we are really discussing the Liberal Party, the dominant partner and leader of this long running and politically successful particular Australian political configuration known as "the Coalition" which will be referred to throughout this volume (Lovell and Blyth 2022).

The Coalition Government during this period was a "tragedy" not just in terms of the usual policy mistakes, ministerial bungles or indiscretions, failing to implement some election promises or as its time in office extended, of losing its policy and political momentum. After all, most governments can be the target of such complaints. The previous Labor administration, in office for a shorter period (2007-2013), was condemned for similar reasons (Kitney 2013; Wanna 2010).

Rather, this volume proposes that the real "tragedy" of the Coalition, particularly for the Liberals, was its failure in both its overall policy direction and governing style to act in ways consistent with its heritage, espoused principles and supporters' expectations, including the general public that has so often endorsed the Coalition with their vote and elected them to office. This is not about whether the Liberals in office lacked ideological purity in failing to pursue certain unrealistic policies judged essential by right of centre think tanks. The Liberals have never been a doctrinaire party based on adherence to a rigid platform. At the same time, neither has it been a totally pragmatic one only concerned short term political fixes. It has worked within a broad discernible, if sometimes ill-defined, complex philosophical framework (Starr et al 1978; Tiver 1978). And if Australian politics is not supposed to be ideological, it has nevertheless at times been about a "battle of ideas" reflecting differences between the major parties based on different principles, processes, language and desired policy outcomes (Kemp 1988; Kelly 1992; Kelly 2011: Kelly 2014). Nor is this a discussion about the old, now largely discredited initiative-resistance debate – that Labor was the party of policy initiative and the non-Labor parties one of resistance and reaction (Mayer 1966; and for a revisit see Botterill and Fenna 2020).

Perhaps former Labor Prime Minister Paul Keating framed the issue more precisely when on the eve of his 1996 election defeat by the Howard led opposition, he observed that, "When the government changes, the country changes" (Keating 2014: 207).

That's the issue. Did nine years of Liberal/Coalition government make a distinct difference in how the nation functioned, in what was valued? Was, for instance, policy driven more by political expediency aimed at getting re-elected, appeasing the interest groups at any price, and committing repeated policy 'U' turns on key issues? Was there little attempt to progress policies that were needed, that is genuine "reform" which according to Gary Banks' means actions that "makes things better" for the whole of society (Banks 2012).

Former prime minister John Howard claimed that his administrations "brought a philosophical road map to government" in how issues and policies were addressed (Howard 2011: 670). Sometimes this was to its electoral detriment like when the Howard Government embarked on further industrial relations reforms after it gained control of the Senate following the 2004 election (Carney 2022). Labelled by some as an extreme and ideological policy (Brett 2007) and later even seen by its own supporters as the "poisoned chalice" that caused its 2007 election defeat (Robb 2007), it seemed to have gone too far. Perhaps! Others argue the further reforms in this area were both needed and legitimate given changing economic circumstances (Lewis 2008). After all, the first tranche of industrial relations changes introduced in 1996 had been heavily compromised by Senate amendments proposed by the Labor opposition and minor parties, especially by the then Australian Democrats (Singleton 1997). To not pursue further changes at this juncture would have been a betrayal of the Liberal Party's (and Howard's) long term policy commitments, promises, and core beliefs (Kelly 2014: 110-14). It also reflected Howard's resolve to avoid the complaints made against Fraser Coalition Government which despite its large majority and control of the Senate (1975-81) was later condemned by many of its own members (Brown 1984), the Liberal Party (Valder 1983) and other key commentators (Henderson 1985) of failing to implement a more distinct Liberal agenda, and to have succumbed too easily to short term politics and interest group pressures.

The issue then is whether this most recent Liberal/Coalition regime had anything like a "philosophical roadmap" or overarching narrative and framework that provided a sense of policy coherence across the disparate portfolios of a modern national government? Was there a liberal or conservative framework at play? Or was this Coalition more like the Fraser period, which also ended catastrophically? This is what contributors to this volume have been asked to do. It is therefore different from some of the other regular assessments of governments where such clear frameworks have not been imposed (see McCaffrie et al 2023 for latest example). Nor was it possible to cover every policy area. Instead, key issues and areas pertinent to Coalition governments are reviewed. These issues are explored across the Coalition's electoral results, prime ministerial performances, institutional arrangements, selected policy areas such as economic policy, welfare, indigenous affairs, religious freedom, and the Coalition government's management of a major issue like the pandemic.

What's in the book?

This book is divided into four sections.

Part 1 Overview begins with **Malcolm Mackerras** (Chapter 1) giving attention to prime ministerial performance including their electoral results. He traces the Coalition's initial 2013 election success to the subsequent decline by the 2016 election and then onto the 2019 and 2022 elections. All this was further infected by the Coalition's lack of a Senate majority and their tinkering prior to the 2016 election that in his opinion, only made matters worse in terms of giving opportunity for more minor and micro parties and independents to be elected. **Greg Melleuish** (Chapter 2) follows and discusses Menzies' liberalism assessing just what was the Coalition's narrative during these nine years in office. He concludes that it was hard to find across the three prime ministers of Abbott, Turnbull or Morrison anything like a political narrative that was understandable, consistent or convincing, to explain what the Coalition direction was or why it should be elected. **Graeme Starr's** historical overview (Chapter 3) written in 2021 before he passed away and while the Coalition was still in office, draws on what he describes as Menzies' 1944 Forgotten Speech. That was when Menzies identified all that was wrong with the non-Labor parties and cause at the time. Starr compares Menzies' assessment then to the Liberal Party's current situation. He asks the sobering question, "what would Menzies think of the Liberal Party today"? You can read his assessment.

Part 2: The Coalition and Institutions begins with **John Halligan's** (Chapter 4) detailed assessment of the Coalition in relation to its management of executive government, parliament and the public service. It is not a flattering analysis but an accurate one highlighting all too clearly the Coalition's haphazard and reactive way of managing these key institutions. The legacy left, perhaps best reflected in the findings of the 2023 *Royal Commission into the Robodebt Scheme*, is not a memorable one. Overall, it showed a poor preparation before coming to office, ideological blinkers and lacking a clear enunciation of operating principles. **Scott Prasser and Andrea Wallace** (Chapter 5) give attention to the Coalition's deployment of public inquiries including eight royal commissions – an unprecedented number for a Coalition government. Although public inquiries were appointed like previous government for both legitimate and politically expedient reasons there were mistakes in some of the members appointed and topics targeted. These reinforced perceptions of the Coalition as being particularly political and ideological. That there were so many royal commissions reflected what journalist Paul Kelly (2020) called the "cult of the royal commission" – whereby declining trust in existing institutions has resulted in an over-recourse to royal commissions that are being asked to resolve both policy and political problems.

Part 3: Managing the policies opens with **Robert Carling's** Chapter 6 on economic policy where attention is given to the Coalition's difficulties in controlling spending, returning the budget to surplus, managing federal-state financial relations and delivering tax cuts. What makes this chapter so important is that managing the economy is what Coalition governments are supposed to be good at – but this chapter argues it was not such a great success. Ongoing economic reforms to foster productivity improvements were half-heartedly pursued and usually dropped in the face of policy disagreement within government and resistance from outside.

Aynsley Kellow (Chapter 7) considers climate and energy policy, which gains so much attention, but which is greatly misunderstood. It is an area marked increasingly by reactive politics and flawed policy. He points out that the Coalition won power in 2013 largely because of their key point of difference from the then Labor government concerning climate change but squandered this political capital in committing to "Net Zero" at the 26th Conference of the Parties to the Framework Convention on Climate Change in Glasgow in 2021. Kellow argues the Coalition lost sight of both its core principles but also its political nous in a policy area in which they were just too willing to "vacate the field".

David Lee (Chapter 8) reviews the Morrison Government's management of the pandemic. He concludes that although not as bad as some have argued, after all Australia fared better than many other nations in terms rate of deaths and economic impacts, it was still, at best, a mixed result. Certain necessary actions were done swiftly but in other cases the Morrison Government allowed the states to have too much leeway and genuflected too much at the federalism ideal as distinct to considering electoral politics. Within some circles the massive increases in expenditure (see Chapter 6) which a Liberal Treasurer unleased at this time, were seen as excessive and in contradiction of the Coalition's traditional approaches, thus undermined one of its core strengths.

Mark Spencer (Chapter 9) considers the broken promise of the religious freedom legislation. It provides perhaps the most symbolic failure of the Coalition's political temerity, policy confusion, electoral misreading and inept management of any issue. The legislation was long promised and much anticipated to ensure long accepted religious freedom. It would be especially important for Australia's large Christian school community. It was never delivered. In so doing, the Coalition managed to upset those who had long been its allies. They were both disappointed and perplexed. Disappointed that a promise had not been delivered and perplexed as to why. In essence, the Liberals in office for nine years, failed to address changes to the anti-discrimination legislation made by the Gillard Labor Government that had triggered this concern. It was a clear case of policy failure, lack of nerve and inability to frame an issue in a modern and appealing way especially for younger voters.

Patrick McClure (Chapter 10) on welfare policy exposes how the resort to this former and well-regarded expert to chair another major inquiry into the welfare system in the hope to duplicate the success of his earlier review for the Howard Government, generally failed. The turmoil inside government – changing ministers and prime ministers, lack of clarity about principles and policy goals and indifference from the powerful Prime Minister's Office, were all contributing factors. It was a case of being a "missed opportunity" where a Liberal government could have made considerable headway.

Gary Johns (Chapter 11) considers indigenous issues and shows once again how the Coalition failed to develop any point of difference to what they had inherited from Labor in this sensitive and complex area. They had no strategy as to how they might manage policy change that seemed to be set on a fixed course. There was an all too willingness by the Coalition government and ministers in that portfolio to accept that status quo. Johns' assessment is the Coalition could not even hold the line at what they inherited but rather continued down the same policy track. The change to a Coalition government brought no change in this area of public policy.

Part 4: Conclusions – where next for the Coalition? opens with **Michael Sexton's** (Chapter 12) pessimistic analysis of how the Liberal Party, once the party of the establishment, has itself been disestablished from the key institutions of business, education, the public service, and professional and community bodies. There can be no long-term future for the Liberal Party, and thus the Coalition, unless this very real problem is addressed. Finally, **Scott Prasser** (Chapter 13) asks what were the Coalition's nine years in office all for – and more importantly what lessons can be learnt from this recent history for a future, and possibly, for the next Coalition government?

References

Banks, G., "Successful Reform: Past Lessons, Future Challenges", in Banks, G., (ed), *Advancing the Reform Agenda: Selected Speeches,* Productivity Commission: Canberra: Commonwealth of Australia, December 2012, 103-20

Botterill, L.A., and Fenna, A., "Initiative-Resistance and the Australian Party Systems", *Australian Journal of Politics and History*, 66(1) 2020, 63-77

Brett, J., "Exit Right: The Unravelling of John Howard", *Quarterly Essay,* Melbourne: Black Inc, 2007, 1-96

Brown, N., "Two Years as a Minister in the Fraser Government", Speech to Liberal Speakers' Group Annual General Meeting, Brisbane 12 March 1985

Carney, S., "The 'continuing work' of industrial relations", in Frame, T., (ed), *The Desire for Change, 2004-2007: The Howard Government Volume IV*, Sydney: UNSW Press, 2021, 59-72

Churchill, W.S., *The Second World War – Volume VI, Triumph and Tragedy*, London: Penguin Classics, 2005

Henderson, G., "The Liberals: Why another period of lost opportunity would be the end", *The Australian*, 24 January 1987

Howard, J., *John Howard: Lazarus Rising*, Sydney: HarperCollinsPublishers, 2011

Keating, P., quoted in "Why would they go to the photocopiers", in Warhaft, S., (ed), *Well may they say: The Speeches that made Australia*, Melbourne: Text Publishing, 2014

Kelly, P., *The End of Certainty: The Story of the 1980s*, St Leonards: Allen and Unwin, 1992

Kelly, P., *The March of Patriots: The Struggle for Modern Australia*, Carlton: Melbourne University Press, 2011

Kelly, P., *Triumph and Demise: The Broken Promise of a Labor Generation*, Carlton: Melbourne University Press, 2014

Kelly, P., "The cult that won false hopes in 2020", *The Australian*, 23 December 2020

Kemp, D.A., *Foundations for Australian Political Analysis: Politics and Authority*, Melbourne: Oxford University Press, 1988, 252-63

Kitney, G., "Why Labor is leaving so little to remember it by," *Australian Financial Review*, 7-8 September 2013

Lewis, P., "Industrial Relations and the Labour Market", in Aulich, C., and Wettenhall, R., (eds), *Howard's Fourth Government: Australian Commonwealth Administration, 2004-2007*, Sydney: UNSW Press, 2008

Lovell, D.W., and Blyth, A., (eds), *The Art of Coalition: The Howard Government Experience 1996-2007*, Sydney: UNSW Press, 2022

Mayer, H., "Parties: Initiative and Resistance", in Mayer, H., (ed), *Australian Politics: A Reader*, Melbourne: Cheshire, 1966

McCaffrie, B., Grattan, M., Wallace, C., (eds), *The Morrison Government: Governing through Crisis, 2019-2022*, Sydney: UNSW Press, 2023 (this is the fourteenth volume in this series)

McClure, P., "Hearts and heads: The challenge of welfare reform", in Frame, T., (ed), *The Desire for Change, 2004-2007: The Howard Government Volume IV*, Sydney: UNSW Press, 2021, 177-93

Prasser, S., Nethercote, J.R., and Warhurst, J., (eds), *The Menzies Era: A Reappraisal of Government, Politics and Policy*, Sydney: Hale and Iremonger, 1995, 44-54

Prasser, S., "Coalition held back yet again by its unpreparedness", *The Australian*, 25 August, 2010

Prasser, S., and Clune, D., *The Whitlam Era: A Reappraisal of Government, Politics and Policy*, Redland Bay: Connor Court Publishing, 2022

Robb, A., quoted in O'Malley, S., and Dunkley, S., "We went too far, Libs reformer says of WorkChoices", *Canberra Times*, 14 December 2007

Singleton., G., "Industrial Relations: Pragmatic Change", in Prasser, S., and Starr, G., (eds), *Policy and Change: The Howard Mandate*, Sydney: Hale and Iremonger, 1997, 192-2017

Starr, G., Richmond, K., and Maddox, G., *Political Parties in Australia*, Richmond: Heinemann Educational Australia, 1978, 11-101

Tiffen, R., *Disposable Leaders*, Sydney: New South/UNSW Press, 2017

Tiver, P., *The Liberal Party: Principles and Performance*, Milton: The Jacaranda Press, 1978

Valder, J., (Chair), Liberal Party of Australia, Report of the Committee of Review (Valder Review), *Facing the Facts*, September, Canberra, September 1983

Wanna, J., "Issues and agendas for the term," in Aulich, C., and Evans, M., (eds) *The Rudd Government: Australian Commonwealth Administration 2007-2010*, Canberra: ANU Press, 2010, 17-32

Part 1: Overview

1

Abbott, Turnbull and Morrison and Australian Voters

Malcolm Mackerras

Introduction

The three men covered in this chapter are best described as "average" prime ministers – and my ranking of all past holders of that office in order of greatness is done regularly. As at March 2024 Australia has 30 former prime ministers. Greatness is not necessarily measured by length of time in office. Nevertheless, I do rate as greatest the man longest in that office, Sir Robert Menzies. Coming in at number 30 is Frank Forde whose eight days marks him as the shortest to serve as prime minister. The best illustration of how I sometimes discount length of time in office is given by the fact that I rank John Curtin as Australia's second greatest prime minister – yet he is placed at only number 12 in terms of days served – just one rung ahead of Scott Morrison. See Table 1.

My full statement on this subject can be found on my blog at www. malcolmmackerras.com. It shows the five flawed post-Howard former prime ministers in this order of greatness: 16 Scott Morrison (2018-22), 17 Julia Gillard (2010-13), 18 Kevin Rudd (2007-10 and 2013), 19 Malcolm Turnbull (2015-18) and 20 Tony Abbott (2013-15). All five won a single general election. Morrison heads that list, however, in recognition of his three other achievements: his successful instigation and negotiation of the AUKUS defence arrangement, his successful handling of the coronavirus pandemic and the fact that, alone among the five, his party allowed him to contest the election next after his winning contest. Gillard, Rudd, Turnbull and Abbott led her/his party to one election win, only to be denied the chance of a second term. Morrison too was denied that second term by public opinion, expressed in votes cast at the ballot box: the others suffered the humiliation of being denied it by the party's mere reading of public opinion.

We all have our own views on these subjects – and mine are of no special value. For that reason, I turn now to undisputed statistics, beginning with Table 1 showing the number of days in office of the 29 men and one woman to hold Australia's highest political office in the past. That table is followed by Table 2 giving the statistics of the aggregate national two-party preferred vote at recent elections. These are the statistics of the *actual* two-party preferred votes which have been counted out fully and officially since 1983. There is now no need to make *estimates* of such a statistic as was the case at elections from 1910 to 1980.

A chapter titled "Abbott, Turnbull and Morrison and Australian Voters" attempts to ask and answer two questions: "Which of these three men performed best with Australian voters?" and "Which man performed the worst?" This chapter attempts to measure the three men to answer those questions. It turns out that Morrison answers the first question and Abbott the second. As in several things Malcolm lies in the middle. He performed better with Australian voters than Abbott but not as well as Morrison. I argue my case for that view in the pages below.

Motivation for leadership changes

There will never be universal agreement as to what really motivates a party when it decides to kick out one leader to be replaced by another. Nevertheless, one interesting view has been presented by Malcolm Turnbull in his 2020 autobiography *A Bigger Picture* published by Hardie Grant. It is self-serving but enlightening none-the-less. Virtually every account of the transition from Abbott to Turnbull reveals it was opinion poll driven. Let me note what Turnbull records himself on page 261 as saying at a press conference at Parliament House, Canberra, on Monday 14 September 2015:

> We also need a new style of leadership in the way we deal with others, whether it is our fellow members of parliament, whether it is the Australian people. We need to restore traditional cabinet government. There must be an end to policy on the run and captain's calls. We need to be truly consultative with colleagues, members of parliament, senators and the wider public. We need an open government that recognises there is an enormous sum of wisdom both within our colleagues in this building and, of course, further afield.
>
> But above all we must remember that we have a great example of good cabinet government. John Howard's government most of us served in, and yet few would say that the cabinet government of Mr Abbott bears any similarity to the style of Mr Howard.

But then Turnbull lets slip the real reason why he succeeded in persuading the Liberal Party that he should replace Abbott as Prime Minister. He describes it as "the most mundane observation that I came to regret.". In truth it summed up the party's reasoning: "We have lost 30 Newspolls in a row. It is clear that the people have made up their minds about Mr Abbott's leadership." Now we know the reason for the change! Turnbull was sworn in as Prime Minister the following day, on Tuesday 15 September 2015.

A look back at Abbott's popularity

It is my contention that Abbott was the successful leader of the Liberal Party who performed worst with Australian voters. As Opposition leader he was successful to the point of making significant gains for the Liberal Party in August 2010. Yet those gains were mostly in Queensland where the replacement of Rudd by Gillard rankled with the voting public. Abbott then went on to win in September 2013, but his victory applied only in the House of Representatives election.

Abbott's supporters try to make out that his 2013 victory was on the same scale as was Howard's in 1996. A glance at Table 2 and Table 3 for the lower house seems to support that contention – Howard 53.63 per cent of the two-party preferred vote in 1996 versus 53.49 per cent for Abbott. Howard's Liberal Party won 76 of 148 House seats in 1996, Abbott 75 of 150 in 2013.

However, when one compares the Senate performance one understands how unpopular Abbott was. Table 10 tells us that Howard in 1996 won 20 of the 40 seats with 44 per cent of the vote, but Table 12 tells us that Abbott only managed 37 per cent of the vote in 2013-14, winning only 17 of the 40 seats. So, voters were willing to kick out the Rudd-Gillard-Rudd government but not willing to give Abbott a Senate on which he could rely. Later in this chapter I demolish the argument put by Abbott's supporters that his poor Senate performance was mainly due to the activities of the famous "preference whisperer", Glenn Druery.

In terms of popularity with the general public Abbott performed fairly well for eight months, September to December 2013 and January to April 2014. That reasonable level of popularity culminated in a good win for the Liberal Party in the special half-Senate re-election in Western Australia on 5 April 2014. The Liberal Party secured the election of three senators, David Johnston, Michaelia Cash and Linda Reynolds, with a Coalition vote of 474,038. Labor secured the election of only one senator, Joe Bullock, with a vote of 275,094 while the Greens secured the election of one senator, Scott Ludlam, with a vote of 199,122.

The total formal vote was 1,277,804 and the quota 182,544. That meant Johnston, Bullock and Ludlam were elected on the first count with surplus votes of 251,116 for Johnston, 86,479 for Bullock and 16,301 for Ludlam. Surplus distribution gave the fourth seat to Cash. Then the distribution of further surplus votes took place along with the transfer of votes from the obvious losers, all seventy of them. That gave the fifth seat to Zhenya Wang of the Palmer United Party. Wang began with 156,352 primary votes (0.86 of a quota) but finished with 201,846 at which point he was elected to the fifth seat.

The final count for the sixth seat produced this result:

Linda Reynolds (Liberal)   188,169 votes   Surplus 5,625 votes

Louise Pratt (Labor)   176,042

That was a very pleasing result for the Liberal Party.

It should be mentioned that the original, voided, election was on 7 September 2013 and Johnston, Cash, Reynolds, Bullock and Ludlam were declared elected. The problem lay with the sixth seat. During the counting stage it appeared likely that Pratt would be re-elected to a seat she had held since 1 July 2008. The problem was whether that seat should go to Pratt, Wang or Wayne Dropulich of the Sports Party. Anyway, the problem was solved by Mr. Justice Kenneth Hayne in his judgment handed down on 18 February 2014 in the case known as *Australian Electoral Commission v Johnston: Wang v Johnston: Mead v Johnston {2014} HCA 5.* For more detail see Table 12.

The days that destroyed Abbott: 13 May 2014 and Australia Day 2015

There is general agreement among historians that the 2014 budget was the biggest element in the destruction of Abbott as Prime Minister. That budget, handed down by Treasurer Joe Hockey on Tuesday 13 May 2014, displayed every element of lack of political judgment for which Abbott and his office became unfavourably noted. While Turnbull is not an impartial commentator, I must agree with these comments on pages 216 and 217 of his autobiography (Turnbull 2020):

> People often say the 2014 budget wrecked the Abbott government, but it has to be said the polls were bad leading up to it. The floating of the so-called deficit levy and an increase in the pension age to 70 were going down like lead balloons. . .

> The budget was seen as mean, unfair and dishonest. What made it worse was Abbott's white line fever-induced promise shortly before polling day: 'No cuts to health, schools, ABC or SBS.' The budget broke all those promises and the hike in the top marginal

rate (for three years only) did nothing to assuage the public's anguish.

The other day that destroyed Abbott was Australia Day 2015 when he made the Duke of Edinburgh an Australian knight. In his chapter "Arise, Sir Phil the Greek" Turnbull (233) writes

> While I was flying across the Pacific to officiate at 'G'day USA' events on the West Coast, my parliamentary colleagues were going to one Australia Day function after another and by the end of the day most of them were punch-drunk as their constituents berated them for the sheer craziness of our leader. Reinstating knights and dames was wacky enough, but Prince Philip? Hadn't Abbott pledged that knighthoods and damehoods would be reserved for 'pre-eminent Australians'?

On Monday 9 February there was a Liberal Party spill for the leadership. Turnbull (240) writes:

> The News Corp papers that morning were interesting – staunchly defending Abbott, with Simon Benson on the front page of *The Daily Telegraph* predicting a 'voter revolt' if Abbott was dumped. Yet the Newspoll was showing me far ahead as preferred Liberal leader over Abbott 64:25 and, most ominously, the government behind Labor 43-57 and Abbott behind Shorten as preferred PM 30:48.

> The spill was defeated 61 votes to 39. This was much worse than Abbott had anticipated. His office had been briefing the press gallery there were only 15 likely votes for a spill (out of a party room of 102).

On 21 July 2015 the Liberal member for Canning (WA) died unexpectedly. That produced a by-election on Saturday 19 September. As noted above Turnbull replaced Abbott on Tuesday 15 September. It will never be known how Canning would have voted had Abbott survived the second challenge, but my belief is that Labor would have won Canning in such an event. Consequently, as a result of the change in leadership earlier that week the Liberal candidate, Andrew Hastie, won Canning easily. Turnbull's leadership was off to a very good start. It is also my belief that Labor would have won the 2016 general election had not the Liberal leadership change occurred in September 2015.

Turnbull and Morrison compared

My opinion on Abbott is clear from the above. Of the three men he was, in my judgment, the one coming lowest in terms of prime ministerial greatness and of performing with Australian voters. It is also a fact that he served the shortest time in the office of prime minister. See Table 1.

Turnbull's sole general election win in July 2016 was very peculiar. It was dominated by his strong desire for a double dissolution. His ambition to achieve industrial relations reform was commendable but that meant the need for a winter election which was politically unwise. The result was a poor win and one that was far below expectations. The campaign proved his campaigning skills to be distinctly poor. The result left Abbott supporters claiming that Abbott would have performed better – a plausible view on the statistics, though not to anyone who had followed Abbott's career.

There was a "Super Saturday" of by-elections on 28 July 2018 caused by the resignation of members in the seats of Longman (Queensland), Fremantle and Perth (WA), Mayo (SA) and Braddon (Tasmania). Apart from Perth the resignations were forced by sitting members needing to avoid High Court disqualification under the Court's peculiar citizenship rulings. Commentator Peter Van Onselen correctly predicted all five results from the start – as did yours truly. There was no reason to think the Liberal Party would perform well in any of the contests, but Turnbull talked up his party's chances – thereby showing poor political judgment.

Nevertheless, the replacement of Turnbull by Morrison on 24 August 2018 (less than a month after "Super Saturday") was not opinion poll driven. It was mainly ideological, though partly driven by the party's depression at Turnbull's poor judgment and campaigning abilities. Morrison won the 2019 election unexpectedly. Would Turnbull have won it? Without any confidence in this counter factual I say Turnbull would not have won it.

Having won that election Morrison remained reasonably popular for the remainder of 2019 and for the whole of 2020. His popularity was indicated by the good result for the Liberal Party at the by-election for Eden-Monaro (NSW) on 4 July 2020. His candidate, Fiona Kotvojs, did not win the seat but came very close and achieved two swings in her favour, at the 2019 general election and at the 2020 by-election.

The defeat of Morrison at the 2022 election was generally expected and quite heavy. For the Liberal Party it was the second worst defeat for a government, the worst having been in March 1983 when the Fraser government was ousted. There is no reason to believe that any other leader could have won.

Abbott, Turnbull and Senate "democratic reforms"

When Abbott won in 2013 the Liberal Party noticed that his House of Representatives win was roughly as good as Howard's first in 1996. Compare Table 3 with Table 6 and notice the 1996 and 2013 entries in Table 2. However, they also noticed the poor Abbott Senate performance compared with Howard's. Compare Table 10 with Table 12. They must have known that a sensible analysis would yield the judgment that a substantial increase in minor party votes reflected itself in Senate seats for minor parties of a kind not existing back in 1996.

However, that was not the way they wanted these results to be seen. In that wish they were helped by media propaganda on election night and in subsequent commentary in the weeks thereafter. The narrative went that the Liberal Party had been cheated out of Senate seats by "micro parties gaming the system". The result was that the Federal Joint Standing Committee on Electoral Matters established a special committee which reported in May 2014. Its report, titled "Interim report on the inquiry into the conduct of the 2013 Federal Election: Senate voting practices" searched high and low to find evidence to support the proposition but could find only one case: Motoring Enthusiast Party Victorian candidate Ricky Muir had stolen her seat off Senator Helen Kroger (Liberal) by hiring the "preference whisperer" Glenn

Druery. The case for "democratic reforms" was provided by that one example.

My view was (and continues to be) that these proposed "democratic reforms" were nothing more than a further rigging of the system, the process of which was started by the Hawke government in 1984 implementing above-the-line voting. My view is that above-the-line voting corrupts the system of the Single Transferable Vote by turning it from being candidate-based (as intended by section 7 of the Constitution) into a party-based system as wanted by the machines of big political parties.

Prime Minister Abbott did nothing about that report, reasoning along the lines "be careful what you wish for." However, when Turnbull replaced Abbott, he decided that his place in history should be, among other things, to implement industrial relations reform. For that he needed a double dissolution, but such could not be held under the old system. He, therefore, decided to proceed full speed ahead and that resulted in the enactment in the autumn of 2016 of the *Commonwealth Electoral Amendment Act 2016* which increased the number of contrivances in the system from three to four. The group voting ticket was labelled the villain of the piece under the old system, so it was scrapped. In its place were inserted two new contrivances.

My tables attached tell the story. Half-Senate elections under the new system yield a worse reflection of the will of the people than under the old system. On the other hand, Table 13 tells us that the first election in 2016 yielded a good reflection. That was because of it being consequent upon a double dissolution, so 12 senators were elected in each state. Among several consequences was the resurrection of the political career of Pauline Hanson.

The Senate ballot paper is now thoroughly dishonest. It manipulates the citizen into voting in ways wanted by the machines of big political parties. There are four contrivances, none of which can be justified according to any democratic principle. They are the thick black line that runs through the ballot paper, the party boxes above that ballot dividing line, the deceitful instructions to voters for the ATL vote and the deceitful instructions for the BTL vote.

The instructions ARE deceitful. When the ATL instruction reads "by numbering at least 6 of these boxes in the order of your choice" it conceals from the voter the fact that a single first preference for a party stated above the line is required by law to be counted as a formal vote. When the BTL instruction reads "by numbering at least 12 of these boxes in the order of your choice" it conceals from the voter that a vote between candidates 1, 2, 3, 4, 5 and 6 is required by law to be counted as a formal vote. So, why this deceit? Why this voter manipulation? There is a simple answer. The machines of big political parties want a guarantee that their senators will be elected in the correct order – the order decided by the machines. This disgraceful system has given them what they want.

My conclusion on these three men

During my lifetime the Labor Party has had only one leader very successful at winning elections, Bob Hawke. On the other hand, the Liberal Party has had three, Bob Menzies, Malcolm Fraser and John Howard. Compared with those three giants these three latest examples of power without purpose look rather small. Nevertheless, I stay with my view that Scott Morrison was the leader most successful at winning the support of his party and of the Australian people.

Table 1: Days in Office of Australia's 30 Former Prime Ministers

1	Robert Menzies (Liberal)	6,740
2	John Howard (Liberal)	4,285
3	Bob Hawke (Labor)	3,207
4	Malcolm Fraser (Liberal)	2,678
5	Billy Hughes (Labor/Nationalist)	2,663
6	Joseph Lyons (United Australia Party)	2,649
7	Stanley Bruce (Nationalist)	2,448
8	Andrew Fisher (Labor)	1,761
9	Ben Chifley (Labor)	1,621
10	Paul Keating (Labor)	1,544
11	Alfred Deakin (Protectionist/Liberal)	1,445
12	John Curtin (Labor)	1,368
13	Scott Morrison (Liberal)	1,365
14	John Gorton (Liberal)	1,156
15	Julia Gillard (Labor)	1,100
16	Malcolm Turnbull (Liberal)	1,075
17	Gough Whitlam (Labor)	1,072
18	Kevin Rudd (Labor)	1,019
19	Edmund Barton (Protectionist)	997
20	James Scullin (Labor)	807
21	Tony Abbott (Liberal)	728
22	Harold Holt (Liberal)	691
23	William McMahon (Liberal)	637
24	Joseph Cook (Liberal)	451
25	George Reid (Free Trade)	322
26	Chris Watson (Labor)	114
27	Arthur Fadden (Country Party)	40
28	John McEwen (Country Party)	23
29	Earle Page (Country Party)	20
30	Frank Forde (Labor)	8

Source: Article by Troy Bramston in the *Weekend Australian* for 28 and 29 May 2022, page 7 titled "Fastest transition of power in our history". Earlier information is from Bramston's article "Malcolm in the middle", *Weekend Australian* for 25 and 26 August 2018, page 21.

Table 2: Aggregate Two-Party Preferred Percentages, House of Representatives, 1980-2022

Election	% Labor	% Lib-Nat	% Swing
18 October1980	49.60	50.40	4.20 to Labor
5 March 1983	53.23	46.77	3.63 to Labor
1 December 1984	51.77	48.23	1.46 to Lib-Nat
11 July 1987	50.83	49.17	0.94 to Lib-Nat
24 March 1990	49.90	50.10	0.93 to Lib-Nat
13 March 1993	51.44	48.56	1.54 to Labor
2 March 1996	46.37	53.63	5.07 to Lib-Nat
3 October 1998	50.98	49.02	4.61 to Labor
10 November 2001	49.05	50.95	1.93 to Lib-Nat
9 October 2004	47.26	52.74	1.79 to Lib-Nat
24 November 2007	52.70	47.30	5.44 to Labor
21 August 2010	50.12	49.88	2.58 to Lib-Nat
7 September 2013	46.51	53.49	3.61 to Lib-Nat
2 July 2016	49.64	50.36	3.13 to Labor
18 May 2019	48.47	51.53	1.17 to Lib-Nat
21 May 2022	52.13	47.87	3.66 to Labor

Note that in the above table the 1980 statistics *are my estimates.* All the later statistics are official calculations done by the Australian Electoral Commission.

Table 3: Seats Won in House of Representatives, 2 March 1996: Howard's First Win

State/Territory	Labor	Liberal	Nationals	Independent	Total
New South Wales	20	19	10	1	50
Victoria	16	19	2	-	37
Queensland	2	17	6	1	26
Western Australia	3	8	-	3	14
South Australia	2	10	-	-	12
Tasmania	3	2	-	-	5
Australian Capital Territory	3	-	-	-	3
Northern Territory	-	1	-	-	1
Total	49	76	18	5	148

Table 4: Seats Won in House of Representatives, 24 November 2007: Rudd's Win

State/Territory	Labor	Liberal	Nationals	Independent	Total
New South Wales	28	15	5	1	49
Victoria	21	14	2	-	37
Queensland	15	10	3	1	29
Western Australia	4	11	-	-	15
South Australia	6	5	-	-	11
Tasmania	5	-	-	-	5
Australian Capital Territory	2	-	-	-	2
Northern Territory	2	-	-	-	2
Total	83	55	10	2	150

Table 5: Seats Won in House of Representatives, 21 August 2010: Gillard's Win

State/Territory	Labor	Liberal	Nationals	Greens	Independent	Total
New South Wales	26	16	4	-	2	48
Victoria	22	12	2	1	-	37
Queensland	8	16	5	-	1	30
Western Australia	3	11	1	-	-	15
South Australia	6	5	-	-	-	11
Tasmania	4	-	-	-	1	5
Australian Capital Territory	2	-	-	-	-	2
Northern Territory	1	1	-	-	-	2
Total	72	61	12	1	4	150

Table 6: Seats Won in House of Representatives, 7 September 2013: Abbotts's Win

State/Territory	Labor	Liberal	Nationals	Greens	Independent*	Total
New South Wales	18	23	7	-	-	48
Victoria	19	14	2	1	1	37
Queensland	6	16	6	-	2	30
Western Australia	3	12	-	-	-	15
South Australia	5	6	-	-	-	11
Tasmania	1	3	-	-	1	5
ACT	2	-	-	-	-	2
Northern Territory	1	1	-	-	-	2
Total	55	75	15	1	4	150

*Including Katter's Australian Party and Palmer United Party, both in Queensland.

Table 7: Seats Won in House of Representatives, 2 July 2016: Turnbull's Win

State/Territory	Labor	Liberal	Nationals	Greens	Independent*	Total
New South Wales	24	16	7	-	-	47
Victoria	18	14	3	1	1	37
Queensland	8	15	6	-	1	30
Western Australia	5	11	-	-	-	16
South Australia	6	4	-	-	1	11
Tasmania	4	-	-	-	1	5
ACT	2	-	-	-	-	2
Northern Territory	2	-	-	-	-	2
Total	69	60	16	1	4	150

**Including Katter's Australian Party (Kennedy, Queensland) and Nick Xenophon Team (Rebekha Sharkie, Mayo, SA).

Table 8: Seats Won in House of Representatives, 18 May 2019: Morrison's Win

State/Territory	Labor	Liberal	Nationals	Greens	Independent*	Total
New South Wales	24	15	7	-	1	47
Victoria	21	12	3	1	1	38
Queensland	6	17	6	-	1	30
Western Australia	5	11	-	-	-	16
South Australia	5	4	-	-	1	10
Tasmania	2	2	-	-	1	5
ACT	3	-	-	-	-	3
Northern Territory	2	-	-	-	-	2
Total	68	61	16	1	5	151

* Including Katter's Australian Party (Kennedy, Queensland) and Centre Alliance (Rebekha Sharkie, Mayo, SA).

Table 9: Seats Won in House of Representatives, 21 May 2022: Albanese's Win

State/Territory	Labor	Liberal	Nationals	Greens	Independent*	Total
New South Wales	26	9	7	-	5	47
Victoria	24	8	3	1	3	39
Queensland	5	15	6	3	1	30
Western Australia	9	5	-	-	1	15
South Australia	6	3	-	-	1	10
Tasmania	2	2	-	-	1	5
ACT	3	-	-	-	-	3
Northern Territory	2	-	-	-	-	2
Total	77	42	16	4	12	151

* Including Katter in Kennedy (Queensland), Haines in Indi (Victoria), Sharkie in Mayo (SA) and Wilkie in Clark (Tasmania). In New South Wales one independent is Dai Le in Fowler but four of the five seats (Mackellar, North Sydney, Warringah and Wentworth) were won by so-called "teal" independents as were two of the three in Victoria (Goldstein and Kooyong). The sole independent in Western Australia is another "teal" (Chaney), elected in Curtin. Indi and Warringah had also elected independents in 2019, with Indi electing an independent in 2013 and 2016.

Table 10: Half-Senate Election, 1996

Date of Election 2 March						
Further Information Seats filled: 40 Total enrolment: 11,740,568			Formal votes cast: 10,899,037 (96.5%) Informal votes: 395,442 (3.5%) Total votes: 11,294,479			
Party	Votes		Change since 1993	Seats		Over-under Representation
	Number	%		Number	%	
Liberal-National	4,792,682	44.0	+1.0	20	50.0	+6.0
Labor	3,940,150	36.2	-7.3	14	35.0	-1.2
Democrats	1,179,357	10.8	+5.5	5	12.5	+1.7
Greens	369,040	3.4	+0.1	1	2.5	-0.9
Others	617,808	5.6	+0.7	-	-	-5.6

Source: Page 106 under the heading "Results of Senate elections" in *Australian Political Facts: Second Edition* by Ian McAllister, Malcolm Mackerras and Carolyn Brown Boldiston , Macmillan, 1997.

Table 11: Half-Senate Election, 2010

Date of Election: 21 August							
Further Information Seats filled: 40 Total enrolment: 14,086,869			Formal votes cast: 12,722,233 (96.3%) Informal votes: 495,160 (3.7%) Total votes: 13,217,393				
Party	Votes		Change since 2007	Change since 2004	Seats		Over-under Representation
	Number	%			Number	%	
Liberal-National	4,914,205	38.6	-1.3	-6.5	18	45.0	+6.4
Labor	4,469,734	35.1	-5.2	+0.1	15	37.5	+2.4
Greens	1,667,315	13.1	+4.0	+5.4	6	15.0	+1.9
Democratic Labor Party	134,987	1.1	+0.2	+0.6	1	2.5	+1.4
Others	1,535,992	12.1	+2.3	+0.4	-	-	-12.1

Note: The above statistics come directly from the Australian Election Commission. They also come from page 274 of the *Parliamentary Handbook of the Commonwealth of Australia 2011* produced by the Parliamentary Library.

Table 12: Half-Senate Elections, 2013 and 2014

Dates of Election 7 September 2013 for the seven eastern jurisdictions 5 April 2014 for Western Australia							
Further Information Seats filled: 40 Total enrolment: 14,749,709			Formal votes cast: 13,380,545 (97.1%) Informal votes: 403,380 (2.9%) Total votes: 13,783,925				

Party	Votes		Change since 2010	Change since 2007	Seats		Over-under Repre-sentation
	Number	%			Number	%	
Liberal-National	4,951,196	37.0	-1.6	-2.9	17	42.5	+5.5
Labor	3,965,284	29.6	-5.5	-10.7	12	30.0	+0.4
Greens	1,234,592	9.2	-3.9	+0.2	4	10.0	+0.8
Palmer United	751,121	5.6	+5.6	+5.6	3	7.5	+1.9
Liberal Democrats	502,180	3.8	+2.0	+3.7	1	2.5	-1.3
Nick Xenophon Group	258,376	1.9	+1.9	+0.7	1	2.5	+0.6
Family First	149,994	1.1	-1.0	-0.5	1	2.5	+1.4
Motoring Enthusiasts	66,807	0.5	+0.5	+0.5	1	2.5	+2.0
Others	1,500,995	11.3	+2.0	+3.4	-	-	-11.3

Note (1):   The above statistics do not come directly from the AEC. Rather they are a re-working from pages 274 to 281 of the *Parliamentary Handbook of the Commonwealth of Australia 2014* produced by the Parliamentary Library. The pages are introduced by this note on page 274:

"The following section presents national, State and Territory results for the 2013-14 Senate elections. Note that the High Court, sitting as the Court of Disputed Returns, declared void the 7 September 2013 Senate result in Western Australia following the loss of 1,375 ballot papers. Subsequently a special half-Senate election was held in that state on 5 April 2014, the results of which are shown here."

Note (2):   If Victorian Senator Helen Kroger had won and Ricky Muir had lost, the Liberal-National seat-number would have been 18, or 45 per cent of seats. The Coalition's over-representation, therefore, would have been 8 per cent.

Table 13: Senate General Election, 2016

Date of Election: 2 July						
Further Information Seats filled: 76 Total enrolment: 15,676,659			Formal votes cast: 13,838,900 (96.1%) Informal votes: 567,806 (3.9%) Total votes: 14,406,706			

Party	Votes		Change since 2013-14	Seats		Over-under Representation
	Number	%		Number	%	
Liberal-National	4,868,246	35.2	-1.8	30	39.5	+4.3
Labor	4,123,084	29.8	+0.2	26	34.2	+4.4
Greens	1,197,657	8.6	-0.6	9	11.8	+3.2
Pauline Hanson's One Nation	593,013	4.3	+3.8	4	5.3	+1.0
Nick Xenophon's Team	456,369	3.3	+1.4	3	4.0	+0.7
Liberal Democrats	298,915	2.2	-1.6	1	1.3	-0.9
Derryn Hinch's Justice Party	266,607	1.9	+1.9	1	1.3	-0.6
Family First	191,112	1.4	+0.3	1	1.3	-0.1
Jacquie Lambie Network	69,074	0.5	+0.5	1	1.3	+0.8
Others	1,774,823	12.8	-4.1	-	-	-12.8

Note: The above statistics come directly from the Australian Electoral Commission.

Table 14: Senate General Election as Half-Senate Election, 2016

Date of Election: 31 August[a]					
Further Information Seats filled: 36 Other information: See Table 13					
	Votes		Seats	Over-under Representation	
Party	Number	%	Number	%	
Liberal-National	4,868,246	35.2	17	47.2	+12.0
Labor	4,123,084	29.8	13	36.1	+6.3
Greens	1,197,657	8.6	3	8.3	-0.3
Nick Xenophon's Team	456,369	3.3	2	5.6	+1.3
Pauline Hanson's One Nation	593,013	4.3	1	2.8	-0.5
Others	2,600,531	18.8			-18.8
Total Formal	13,838,900	100.0	36	100.0	

(a) That was the date of the Senate resolution reading as follows:

That, pursuant to section 13 of the Constitution, the senators chosen for each state be divided into two classes, as follows:

Senators listed at positions 7 to 12 on the certificate of election of senators for each state shall be allocated to the first class and receive 3-year terms.

Senators listed at positions 1 to 6 on the certificate of election of senators for each state shall be allocated to the second class and receive 6-year terms.

My comment: in effect that was a case of the Senate conducting its own half-Senate election but doing so in accordance with what the Senate majority perceived to be the will of the voters. The resolution was carried by 50 votes to 15.

Table 15: Half-Senate Election, 2019

Date of Election: 18 May					
Further Information					
Seats filled:	40				
Total enrolment:	16,419,543				
Formal votes cast:	14,604,925 (96.2%)				
Informal votes:	579,160 (3.8%)				
Total votes:	15,184,085				

	Votes		Seats		Over-under Representation
Party	Number	%	Number	%	
Liberal-National	5,548,142	38.0	19	47.5	+9.5
Labor	4,204,313	28.8	13	32.5	+3.7
Greens	1,488,427	10.2	6	15.0	+4.8
Pauline Hanson's One Nation	788,203	5.4	1	2.5	-2.9
Jacquie Lambie Network	31,383	0.2	1	2.5	+2.3
Others	2,544,455	17.4			-17.4
Total Formal	14,604,925	100.0	40	100.0	

A crude way to calculate disproportionality would be to add together 9.5, 3.7, 4.8, 2.9, 2.3 and 17.4 to produce a "distortion rate" of 40.6. In other words disproportionality would be shown to have been greatest in 2019 consequent upon the so-called "democratic reforms" of 2016. The purpose of that enactment was to make Senate election results less fair than previously because, with exception of Jacquie Lambie, independents were cut out. The only minor party allowed to win a seat in any state was the party with very substantial support.

Table 16: 46th Parliament, Comparing Whole Senate Seats with 2016 Votes

Dates of Election: 2 July 2016, 31 August 2016 and 18 May 2019					
Further Information Seats filled: 76 Total enrolment: See Tables 14 and 15					
	Votes		Seats		Over-under Representation
Party	Number	%	Number	%	
Liberal-National	4,868,246	35.2	36	47.4	+12.2
Labor	4,123,087	29.8	26	34.2	+4.4
Greens	1,197,657	8.6	9	11.8	+3.2
Pauline Hanson's One Nation	593,013	4.3	2	2.6	-1.7
NXT – Centre Alliance	456,369	3.3	2	2.6	-0.7
Jacquie Lambie Network	69,074	0.5	1	1.3	+0.8
Others	2,531,457	18.3			-18.3
Total Formal	13,838,900	100.0	76	100.0	

Comparing the above table with Table 13 it will be noticed that Labor and Greens stay the same at 26 and 9 respectively. By contrast the Coalition has gained six seats, two from Pauline Hanson's One Nation and one each from Centre Alliance, David Leyonhjelm, Derryn Hinch and Bob Day.

Table 17: Half-Senate Election, 2022

Date of Election: 21 May

Further Information
Seats filled: 40
Total enrolment: 17,213,433
Formal votes cast: 15,040,658 (96.6%)
Informal votes: 532,003 (3.4%)
Total votes: 15,572,661

Party	Votes Number	%	Seats Number	%	Over-under Representation
Liberal-National	5,148,028	34.2	15	37.5	+3.3
Labor	4,525,598	30.1	15	37.5	+7.4
Greens	1,903,403	12.7	6	15.0	+2.3
Pauline Hanson's One Nation	644,744	4.3	1	2.5	-1.8
United Australian Party	520,520	3.5	1	2.5	-1.0
Jacquie Lambie Network	31,203	0.2	1	2.5	+2.3
Others	2,267,162	15.0	1	2.5	-12.5
Total Formal	15,040,658	100.0	40	100.0	

That the so-called "democratic reforms" of 2016 made Senate results less fair than previously is shown by Table 15 and Table 16. Liberal-National has been the greatest beneficiary followed by the Greens and the Jacquie Lambie Network. Where 2022 differs from 2019 is that Labor too has started to get some benefit.

References

Joint Standing Committee on Electoral Matters, Electoral Matters, *Interim Report on the inquiry into the conduct of the 2013 Federal Election: Senate voting practices*, Canberra: Commonwealth Parliament, 2014

Turnbull, M., *A Bigger Picture*, Melbourne: Hardie Grant, 2020

2

The Coalition Government 2013-2022 and the end of Menzian Liberalism

Greg Melleuish

Introduction

How are we to explain the performance of the Coalition Government between 2013 and 2022. With a majority of thirty members in the House of Representatives after the 2013 election (see Mackerras, Chapter 2), almost as much as it had achieved under Howard in 1996, one might have expected a strong government with achievements to match its longevity. It survived for nine years, two years fewer than Howard and four years longer than the government of Malcolm Fraser but those nine years saw three prime ministers and a seemingly endless crisis.

It is worth noting that the narrative that emerges about a successful prime minister, such as Menzies or Howard, does so only in retrospect. It could have happened differently; Menzies was in dire trouble in 1953 and won the 1961 election by only a few hundred votes, while Howard gambled with the GST going into the 1998 election. One must admit that both Menzies and Howard rode their luck, as did Labor Prime Minister Bob Hawke in the 1980s. There is a Machiavellian precept that a leader needs to conquer fortune and that the way to do so is through direct and forthright action. The objective is to be respected and to avoid, at all costs, contempt (Machiavelli 1988: Chapter 19, 85).

To act in a forthright fashion, one also needs a strong sense of purpose and to have one's actions grounded in a set of principles. This does not mean being ideologically rigid, as any political leader needs to be able to act flexibly and pragmatically. It does mean possessing a vision of what one is seeking to achieve; gaining and holding power as ends in themselves is not the road to good government. Politics is an art and that art includes knowing the limits of what one can achieve; to put principles into practice a good leader will trim their aspirations without betraying those principles. When governments take power they inherit a whole set of policies, some of which may have been around for very many years. "Settled policies" possess an institutional inertia that makes them very hard to change; for example, the notorious White Australia policy was dismantled slowly over more than a decade. Radical changes usually require some sort of crisis. The decision to float the Australian dollar was made because of a financial emergency and was opposed by the Secretary of the Treasury, John Stone, himself an advocate of free markets. Hawke (ABC Labor in Power 1993) admitted at the time that "little Australia'" had to follow the rest of the world, in other words, bow to what Machiavelli termed necessity.

One big issue with most Australian political narratives of recent times is that they tend to focus on the moral and personality failings of particular politicians. This tendency can be traced back at least the prime ministership of John Howard when he was reviled and demonised by many progressive commentators and the consequence was a complete failure to understand his success. One can see a similar process occurring with Kevin Rudd where there was an extraordinary focus, especially by his enemies on his own side of politics, on his character deficiencies. Both Tony Abbott and Scott Morrison were routinely demonised during their time as prime minister. This is not to say that these political leaders did not have some character deficiencies as we all do. Rather, it is to point out that such a focus has little explanatory power; it tends to reduce politics to a Punch and Judy show, a sort of soap opera. One reason for this is that most of the narratives, including those written by academic writers such as Bongiorno (2022) and Errington and van Onselen (2021) tend to focus on what might be termed the surface of politics, the interactions of individual politicians. They rarely invoke longer term structural issues of the type that might explain why such individuals managed to achieve prominence, and why they acted as they did. It is the longue durée that this chapter employs to explain what went wrong after 2013.

This also means understanding the way in which liberalism has mutated in Australia in response to the changing circumstances of the country. One needs to appreciate those changes if one is to understand why those who claim the title 'liberal' failed so miserably in the period from 2013 to 2022.

Australian liberalism

Governments must act within the constraints placed on them by the circumstances in which they are placed. Menzies cannot be criticised because he did not behave like an idealised purist economic liberal. Inspired by a clear set of liberal principles, clearly enunciated in *The Forgotten People*, and in a political environment that was friendly to increased state control and technocracy, Menzies pursued policies that sought to encourage "lifters" and individual initiative. But there can be no mistake as to what ideals guided Menzies, no confusion as to the type of social and political order for which he stood. Hence, he opposed the extension of government and bureaucratic power in the 1943 and 1946 referenda, contested the attempt by the Chifley Government to nationalise the banks and ended petrol rationing when he came to power in 1949. It is also clear that the Australian people were willing to go down the more liberal path of Menzies as opposed to the more bureaucratic regulatory option offered to them by Labor.

This is important; the course of Australian history, from the granting of responsible government to the twenty first century, indicates that liberalism is the dominant political philosophy informing its political life. When J.S. Mill published *On Liberty* in 1859 newspapers in both Sydney and Melbourne devoted leading articles to this book (Melleuish 2015: 6-12). W.M. Hughes (1970: 6-12) lauded Mill's ideas in *The Case for Labor* while Mill's ideas on freedom of speech are quoted in R.G. Menzies' *The Forgotten People* (2017: 11-16). This liberalism is not static or doctrinaire, except in a few rare cases such as John Hewson, but pragmatic and non-dogmatic, informed by principles of individualism, freedom and a desire for human dignity. In line with liberalism generally it also recognises the right of individuals to be non-political and to cultivate their own gardens, a principle that can be found in Menzies' *Forgotten People*.

A similar case can be made for John Howard. The Coalition had been on track to win the 1993 election but failed because of *Fightback!* a prescriptive and complex plan devised by John Hewson that frightened the Australian electorate at a time when the country was emerging from recession. *Fightback!* was too doctrinaire and, perhaps, too political. Howard won because he was "non-threatening" and promised an age that would be "relaxed and comfortable". Howard understood that liberalism in Australia included the right not to be involved in politics, a point made earlier by Malcolm Fraser when he said that he wished to get politics off the front pages of the newspapers.

Liberalism in Australia has mutated on a number of occasions, owing to changing circumstances. Beginning largely as classical liberalism, it was transformed in the late nineteenth and early twentieth century into a mode of liberalism that embraced the role of the state as a means of enhancing the individual and protecting his or her rights. Then, from 1914 to 1944 it went on life support as a Liberal Party largely disappeared, only to be reborn in the guise of Menzian liberalism.

To understand the problems of the Liberal Party in recent years it is necessary to appreciate the sort of liberalism that Menzies stamped on the new Liberal Party of 1944. Menzies was essentially Burkean in his political outlook. He understood that freedom was embodied in institutions that had been inherited from one's forebears; liberty was not an abstract ideal that existed outside of the actual practices of a given political order. Menzies' Burkean approach is found amongst the Founding Fathers of the Commonwealth Constitution, including Alfred Deakin (Chavura and Melleuish 2015).

Menzian liberalism was the expression of a particular cultural matrix, a culture of 'modest comfort', that characterised Australia during the first half of the twentieth century. It expressed the values of respectable, white collar church going people. This was a society marked by

Sabbatarianism. Australians welcomed a degree of state regulation if it helped to preserve their personal circumstances, such as occurred with newsagents, hoteliers and pharmacists. As W.K. Hancock (1930: Chapter 4) put it, the state was used to protect individual rights.

Menzian liberalism suited this Australia during a golden age of Australian history, especially as it emerged out of war and into the prosperous years of the 1950s and 1960s (Kemp. 2021; McLean, 2013: chapter 8). It was pragmatic, financially responsible and it created the conditions for economic and social growth. It still had a recognisable "forgotten people" in the shape of a large number of clerical workers in industries such as banks and insurance that required manual recording of such things as payroll and invoices.

The cultural matrix that supported those "forgotten people" was, however, dissolving. The decline of religious observance in the 1960s went in tandem with the end of Sabbatarian Australia as Sunday was opened up to both shopping and entertainment. In the 1970s the expansion of ready credit, exemplified by the increasing availability of credit cards, replaced the older principle of 'saving for a rainy day' with an encouragement to spend. Then, in the 1980s, the coming of automation destroyed large sections of the old (male) clerical class. At the same time, Australian manufacturing industry was in decline. The expansion of university education, something that Menzies had hoped would expand the white collar group voting Liberal, produced instead a new educated class, many of whom were professionals and who found Labor more congenial to their interests, especially amongst those employed in the caring and educational industries.

A new cultural matrix was emerging in Australia by the 1980s and 1990s and this questioned the continuing relevance of the old Menzian style of liberalism. The development of post materialism and its accompanying individualistic values in Australia during the 1970s and 1980s also made Menzian liberalism increasingly unstable, not least because of its emphasis on the family

A changing cultural matrix

Two major changes have impacted the environment in which Australian politics functioned by the late twentieth century. The first is that an age of prosperity has replaced that of modest comfort. Tacitus and Seneca are surely correct when they write that prosperity is often more difficult to come to terms with than adversity. The Australian people had responded magnificently to the challenges of the Depression and to World War Two once they understood the nature of the threat at the end of 1941. Prosperity dissolves this sort of social solidarity (Melleuish 2018).

The second has been the growth of Rationalism in Australian politics. Rationalism has been part of the dominant outlook of the Labor Party since its time in office during World War Two when it bought the proposition that the problems of the country could be solved through bureaucratic planning. It was encompassed in H.V. Evatt's grandiose plans for increased Commonwealth power and his depiction of the Commonwealth Constitution as belonging to the horse and buggy age (Post-War Reconstruction, 1942: 117). It has also increasingly come to infect the Liberal Party as can be seen in *Fightback!*

The growth of the university educated class and the bureaucracy has seen rationalism became increasingly prevalent in the Australian cultural matrix. I explored this in 1998 when I argued that Australian political culture was becoming dominated by a number of packaged ideas or packages: the republic, multiculturalism, economic rationalism, the clever country (Melleuish 1998), and since that time we have had the ultimate "package" in the shape of climate change. All of these packages have a distinctive set of features: disgust with the existing arrangements, a belief that a more "rational" set of arrangements is needed that is fuelled by utopian expectations that such actions will usher in a much improved world. They combine abstract rationality with an often high level of emotionalism. Climate change combines utopianism, fear of a threatening outside force and a desire that government should protect its citizens. They are the antithesis of Menzian liberalism founded on reasonableness, and the need to behave in a balanced and dignified way. The other problem was, as

I pointed out at the time, that this abstract rationalism, fuelled by high levels of emotion, generated in opposition to it, what I described as the new populism.

How was Menzian/Burkean liberalism to survive in this new changed environment? It is clear, that by the 1990s the "forgotten people" and the culture in which it was embedded, was largely gone. It is worth pointing out that the Australian Labor Party faced similar problems during these years with the destruction of first the agricultural working class in the 1950s and then the urban manufacturing working class in the 1980s. The Labor Party underwent something of an identity crisis at this time, as it was accused of having betrayed its traditional working class base. It could, however, draw on its tradition of bureaucratic rationalism going back to the "glory days" of Reconstruction and Whitlam, combined with a progressive post materialist agenda designed to appeal to those working in bureaucratic organisations, especially government ones.

Where was liberalism headed? One possible direction was to embrace a hardline economic liberalism such as was embodied in *Fightback!* It failed miserably.

Ultimately the Liberal Party found that its only option was to return to John Howard. It was Howard's great achievement to remake the Menzian tradition of Burkean liberalism. It is difficult to get a proper appreciation of Howard because so much of the commentary on him was both hostile and unfair. One has only to read the nonsense by the likes of Robert Manne, Guy Rundle and Donald Horne. Howard was not an ideologue libertarian, just as Malcolm Fraser was not in this mould. If anything, Howard was really a "social liberal" as can be seen in his approach to welfare. But he also had auctoritas because of his willingness to address difficult issues and to challenge fortuna, as in the case of the GST.

Howard's metaphor of the "Broad Church" is very Menzian, even if Howard meant something more like via media than broad church. After all, Menzies was a Burkean liberal who also honoured Mill.

I commented in 2009 about John Howard as follows (Melleuish 2009: 23-4):

> Howard has been a successful prime minister because he has juggled the various imperatives that now face any democratic leader. These are:
>
> 1. The need to encourage practices that will enhance the productivity of the economy and deliver a reasonable standard of living.
>
> 2. The need to deal with the consequences of a social order that has become more competitive and individualistic as a result of demography and pressure on resources.
>
> 3. The need to allocate scarce resources at a time when every interest group around can provide good reasons why it should get an extra slice of the pie.
>
> 4. The need to provide security in a world that no longer has the same shape that it had fifteen years ago; especially with the growth of terrorism. Howard demonstrated his willingness to protect Australians through such measures as his hardline policies on border protection.
>
> 5. The need to provide leadership that minimises the possible stasis that will result from the inevitable distrust that grows up between the leadership elite and the citizens who placed them in power.
>
> 6. Following on the above, the need to prevent 'bad things' happening to Australians.

Howard had to perform an extraordinary balancing act to reconcile all of these imperatives and his achievement still remains impressive. In the final analysis it comes down to a mixture of judgement, instinct and luck. And Howard in his period as prime minister generally managed to combine these three elements with great success. He had, in his favour, the fact that he is not a particularly cerebral politician and so is not plagued by the need to engage in endless intellectual self-reflection. He was not, in Michael Oakeshott's terms, a "rationalist". Rather, having served a somewhat unlucky and dispiriting apprenticeship in the 1980s, he honed his political skills and became a master craftsman in his chosen profession. His leadership exemplified his skill and his skill enabled him to treat fortune in a somewhat rough fashion.

The Howard years proved that Menzian/Burkean liberalism still worked in Australian politics because, despite the extravagant claims of Labor being the "party of progress", the instincts of the Australian people largely continued to be liberal in a broad and non-dogmatic way. When the Howard Government was voted out of office in 2007 it was because he was too successful in creating an Australia that was "relaxed and comfortable" so that Kevin Rudd won by appearing to be even more "relaxed and comfortable".

One of Howard's achievements was to contain populism, which had surged in the early 1990s in response to the rationalist Keating project (Melleuish 1998: chapter 8). After the 1996 election, One Nation surged, especially in Queensland where it won 11 seats at the 1998 state election. But by the early years of the new millennium One Nation had disappeared from the scene and the Liberals and Nationals largely reabsorbed the populist dissidents of the 1990s. Interestingly, the Democrats also disappeared as a party during the first few years of the new millennium.

Beyond 2007

The end of the Howard years provides an important clue to what came afterwards. WorkChoices was made possible by accident when, against the odds, Howard won control of the Senate at the 2004 election. At one level, WorkChoices was inspired by a traditional liberal vision of an Australia composed of self-employed "lifters" doing things for themselves in a world in which wealth was relatively equally diffused across the wider society. At another level it was a utopian vision of a small business paradise where, as in free selection one hundred and fifty years earlier, individuals and their families could be free and independent. One suspects that, as with free selection, it was a dream that, left to its own devices, would have eventually soured.

The point is that the defeat of 2007 put an end both to Howard and to this traditional aspect of Australian liberalism that had been absorbed into Menzian liberalism. In part WorkChoices failed because, in the new environment of twenty first century Australia, it seemed to indicate that Howard no longer wished to 'protect' the Australian people. These circumstances left open the future of Menzian liberalism.

One possible goal would have been to bring together those who were instinctive Burkean liberals from a range of cultural backgrounds. I have had students from South East Asia argue in class that Confucian values were Australian values and, in many ways, they are correct, in the sense that Confucianism has a high respect for family and tradition. Burke's values were not narrow and parochial; amongst other things he engaged in the prosecution of Warren Hastings for his behaviour in India. Equally Menzies sought to overcome Australian sectarianism. Just as the Liberals were able to welcome Catholics into the fold during the 1980s so it needed to extend its cultural range in the twenty first century.

In both the major political parties the old ideals were largely gone and in their place there emerged a simple desire to gain office and wield power. Burke (1815: 335) legitimised parties in the English-speaking world in the following terms: "Party is a body of men unified for promoting by their joint endeavours the national interest, upon some particular principle in which they are all agreed."

Or as Gilbert and Sullivan put it, one is born either a little liberal or a little conservative.

The post-2007 disease affected both sides of politics. Its primary effect was to shift the focus of politics from principle and national interest, the ultimate foundation of party politics, to power and personality. It is quite clear, for example, that the struggles between Rudd and Gillard were not about matters of principle but about the personality of Rudd and his competency. The sole goal was the gaining of office, which was why the ALP was willing to suffer Rudd as its leader, and the maintaining of office, which is why they dispatched him.

It took all of Howard's considerable political skills to ensure a high level of stability during his prime ministership. He clearly established his authority as leader and possessed the capacity to keep the troops in line. When Howard left it was a generational change. Rudd was the first "baby boomer" prime minister. Rudd clearly set the pattern for what would occur with the Coalition governments after 2013. Rudd was very popular with the wider public as he radiated a calming and protective personality; in 2007 one could feel "relaxed and comfortable" with Rudd. It was one thing to project this populist image, quite another to conduct government in an orderly fashion. Rudd became prime minister with no ministerial experience; he had a considerable ego and a temper to match. He was an outsider in terms of his connections within the Labor Party and the usual fate of such individuals is to be on the margins. Yet, he ended up as prime minister, with somewhat disastrous consequences.

His replacement by Julia Gillard was meant to be a return to normalcy, the only problem being that the deposition of Rudd poisoned the political atmosphere so much that such a return was not possible. Moreover, Rudd set the precedent, that the Liberals would subsequently follow, of working to undermine his successor. Moreover, it should be noted that the differences between Rudd and Gillard were never about ideology and policy; two matters dominated the struggle: the desire to win and maintain power and the issue of a functional government. And, of course, there were matters of personality.

In the void that was created by the end of the old political framework of Australian politics in the 1980s the Labor Party has coped much better than its opponents. There are several reasons for this, including the more authoritarian nature of the party which goes back to its original implementation of the pledge in the 1890s, and hence its capacity to rein in dissidents. This was once a real problem for the Labor Party as it led to splits and fractures, but once power replaced principle in the party greater stability was achieved. The Labor Party was able to solve its leadership issues in 2013 when it changed the way in which it chose leaders.

Whereas Labor was once a party of splitters, the Liberals have increasingly fallen into being a collection of factions. Is this a reversion to the nineteenth century model of liberal politics when factions coalesced around particular leaders? Does this mean that the best way of considering the post Howard Liberals is in terms of personality, power and their capacity to exercise that power? There are ideological divisions within the Liberal Party that are grounded in the "Broad Church" divide, in particular the divide between Burke and Mill. As I have argued, Menzies is best understood as a Burkean liberal who was willing to invoke Mill's principle of liberty. The problem with Mill is that his liberal universalism combined with a progressivism that led to a disparagement of those who had not advanced far enough on the ladder of progress. Hence Mill (1971: 192), an employee of the East India Company, happily opposed political rights for Indians and was wary of giving the franchise to the uneducated. Mill (1971: 192) commented:

> In proportion as success in life is seen or believed to be the fruit of fatality or accident, and not of exertion, in that same ratio does envy develop itself as a point of national character. The most envious of all mankind are the Orientals.

The contemporary idea of the "deplorables" leads back to Mill and it can be argued that a twenty first century Mill would be very woke.

A "Broad Church" based on Burke and Mill was always going to be precarious. The other issue is that under Whitlam, Labor absorbed the Millian heritage as it sought to become progressive. Millian universalism fitted in well with its growing rationalism and faith in bureaucracy. It also became increasingly prevalent in sections of the Liberal party who favoured its progressivist predilections. The problem was, and remains, that Burkean liberals and Millian liberals start from completely different places; one favours universalism while the other understands that rights and liberties are grounded in particularity. One has either to manage these differences or suppress them.

Failures post 2013

Howard, as we have argued, held the Broad Church together through an act of will, despite its contradictions. But he was still essentially a Menzian liberal in the Burkean mould. There was no new synthesis after Howard. Instead, there were conflicting camps, a void of principles and a struggle for power in which matters of personality and competence came to the fore. Commentators rightly focused on matters of personal failings and dysfunctional governments. In considering Coalition performance between 2013 and 2022 what is surprising is that these three men should have failed, often ignominiously. All three had extensive political experience (unlike Kevin Rudd in 2007) and two had been Rhodes Scholars and had proven intellectual capabilities. The third, Morrison, had attended a top rate selective school. In academic terms possibly two of them were the best credentialed leaders that the Liberal Party has had. Why then did they not put their mark on the country? I think that the answer is what I have termed the void, the inability to recraft a form of principled liberalism, based on the established traditions of the Liberal Party for the twenty first century.

The odd thing is their backgrounds: Of the four Liberal leaders from 2007 to 2022, three of them came from a non-Liberal background being individuals who found it expedient to join the Liberal Party in order to pursue a political career. As Cory Bernadi (quoted in Manning 2015: 82) put it:

> It would be great to see someone leading the Liberal Party who hadn't been a member of the Labor Party [Brendon Nelson], hadn't contemplated joining the Labor Party [Turnbull, Hockey, Abbott] or wasn't a DLP supporter [Abbott].

None of the four were Burkean Liberals in the Menzies sense. Under these circumstances it was no wonder that there was no real attempt to reformulate the Menzian liberal tradition.

Under these circumstances, it is no wonder that narrative of Australian politics for the period 2007 to 2022 focused on the personalities of the leaders and their struggle for power. In particular, there was a change in focus from developing good policies to winning elections and ensuring that the government of the day enjoyed a positive image. This is especially true for the years during which the Coalition held office, 2013 to 2022.

The Abbott Government had energised itself in opposition by opposing the Gillard Government on a small number of key policies, including stopping the boats and ending the carbon tax. It did not provide a positive liberal vision of the future, such as John Howard provided in 1996 with his vision of Australia as relaxed and comfortable, which in turn resonated with the desire of Malcolm Fraser after 1975 to take politics off the front page of the newspapers.

Abbott's achievement was not to keep politics off the front page of the newspapers but to cement their place on it. In many ways this was unavoidable because the culture became increasingly politicised with the development of new forms of media, first of all the twenty four hour news cycle and then the variety of social media.

The focus turned very much to public opinion polling and how well the government of the day was doing in the polls. Abbott came to power with an agenda, some of which was achieved quite easily but he was saddled with promises not to reduce funding in a number of areas, including health, education, the ABC and SBS, made just prior to the election (Errington and van Onselen 2015: 15). This was done because Abbott was so desperate to attain power because he had come so close in 2010. This was combined with a desire to cut spending after the excesses of the Labor years. These two desires were contradictory; one cannot claim that there is some sort of "crisis" in public finance while also promising not to cut spending. He also advocated his 'signature' policy of paid parental leave that would be very expensive.

What was absent was a clear vision of the type of country Abbott desired Australia to become or the sort of people that he saw as his people. This is best summed up in many ways by a statement that David Flint made about Abbott many years ago: that he supported the right of Australians to attend the Revesby Workers Club even if he would not go there himself. He did not tap into a populist vein, such as Rudd had. It is difficult to put a finger on why a particular leader is loved. Ben Chifley was clearly loved and yet his speeches are somewhat dry though with a genuineness that is often lacking in the contemporary world. The problem with Abbott's behaviour as Opposition Leader was that it led to him being viewed as a somewhat harsh figure who did not invite love and, as Machiavelli points out is crucial, respect. Eating a raw onion leads lo contempt, not love.

As with Howard, Abbott faced considerable criticism, some of it quite unfair, but unlike Howard he was not given the opportunity to build respect for himself. Whereas Howard had the 1996 gun laws, Abbott had the disaster of the 2014 budget that did nothing to improve his image (Patrick 2016: 35-49). He may have been able to ride out the situation by finding a policy that could provide a vision for his government, as Howard had done with the GST, but such eluded him. He came to be seen as someone who broke his promises and therefore was tricky. Instead, his government found itself caught increasingly in the Credlin problem (Savva 2016). Certainly, the major narratives of the Abbott Government focus very heavily on Abbott and his relationship with Credlin.

Again, as with Rudd, the issue became the way in which the government functioned rather than what it did. Rudd was a frenetic micro-manager; in Abbott's case, it was his chief of staff who played this role.

The first two years set the pattern for the following seven years. Tony Abbott lacked the capacity to develop a new vision of liberalism. The leader failed to win significant public support and to stamp their authority on the party. This was because there continued to be a void of ideas and principles at the centre of the party. The only consolation was that a similar void existed with the Opposition.

Malcolm Turnbull can be seen as representing the rationalist spirit of the age with his support for taking action on climate change. He was extraordinarily ambitious but, like Abbott, did not come out of a liberal "forgotten people" background. Turnbull had supported the very unBurkean project of an Australian republic Turnbull possessed an enormous ego and a 'whatever it takes' attitude to achieve power, as can be seen in the his campaign to be preselected for Wentworth. Turnbull spoke about being agile and presented himself as progressive in his support for same sex marriage, which is sometimes regarded as the high point of his prime ministership. But Turnbull failed to inspire a new liberal vision, and he was certainly no Menzian.

What allowed these shenanigans was the weakness of the Opposition, led by Bill Shorten who was widely regarded as tricky and shifty. Aaron Patrick commented that even with Abbott, Shorten was Abbott and Credlin's best chance of staying in power (Patrick 2016: 123).

In 2019 the unpopularity of Bill Shorten and a set of Labor policies that antagonised key sectors of Australian society allowed Scott Morrison to slip back into power. Labor replaced Shorten with Albanese, someone who was no friend to liberal values. Albanese, however, cleverly underwent an image makeover, making him appear as a kindly uncle, many of my students view Albanese as an 'Uncle figure' (van Onselen and Errington 2022: 51-2). He was as unthreatening as Kevin Rudd was in 2007 and John Howard in 1996. He could not be accused of trickiness dating back to the Rudd-Gillard years when he was an honourable supporter of Rudd.

If the Coalition was to retain power in 2022 it needed to consolidate an image of trustworthiness based on some sort of vision and clear enunciation of liberal principles. This was something that Morrison could not provide. He seemed to be obsessed with winning elections and fell into the trap, as had Abbott before him, of failing to stamp his authority on the government once he had led it to victory. Instead, Morrison became known for his trickery and dubious judgement, more concerned with winning the next election than with achieving something while in government. It was the case that he had to deal with the Covid 11 pandemic from early 2020 but it is worth comparing how he fared compared with the various state premiers. Australians have traditionally wanted both a degree of freedom combined with a desire that the government look after them and protect them. As World War Two indicates, they have been willing to endure considerable government control if they believe that the goal is worth it. In many ways this willingness to endure embodied a sense of civic patriotism, and it would be only temporary. That is why they chafed under continued rationing once World War Two was over and elected the Menzies Government in 1949.

The state premiers understood this reality and were able to use it to their advantage. They played on the desire for protection, even if on some occasions they went too far, just as Labor had on occasions during World War Two. Morrison failed to appreciate the extent that this desire for protection formed part of the liberal tradition in Australia, whereby the state protected the interests of individuals. He had already indicated his misunderstanding when he dealt with the South Coast of NSW bushfires prior to the pandemic. Again, it is interesting that for many of my students, who come from the South Coast, and some of whom are Liberals, it was Morrison's behaviour during the bushfires that rankles the most. He might not have been able to hold a hose, but he could have been more reassuring about the future. Ironically, Morrison's government engaged in a lot of protection, perhaps too much, during the pandemic with such measures as job keeper but failed to communicate that effectively to the Australian public. The public perception was that the heavy lifting was being done by the states and that, if anything, the Commonwealth was impeding those efforts.

Moreover, Morrison inherited the mantle of being "Mr Tricky" from Shorten. He also had to deal with the constant sniping of the man whose office he had usurped, Malcolm Turnbull, in the same way that Gillard had suffered Rudd (Patrick 2022). Not only did Morrison fail but he left the Liberal Party even further down the void than it had ever been.

Moving forward

It is interesting that the Labor Party was elected in 2022 on the tried and proven principle of appearing to be unthreatening and trustworthy. The public did not know Albanese but it did know that Morrison was tricky like Shorten and that was enough to mean the end of the Coalition Government.

One should point out that the Labor government that came to power in 2022 faced similar issues to what the Coalition Government faced during its time in office. While it has focused, perhaps excessively, on progressive issues such as the Voice and climate change it has also given indications in such policy areas as industrial relations and economics that it wishes to go back to more traditional stances that predate the Hawke and Keating years, as if to recover its heritage. These fit in well with the rationalist and somewhat authoritarian nature of the party. Whether they will deliver good government is another matter.

In these circumstances, it would also make good sense for the Liberal party also to go back and reexamine its Menzian heritage as the foundation of twenty first Australian liberalism. I would still argue that liberalism remains the central set of political principles in Australian political life. But it needs to be a mode of liberalism that emerges out of the Australian experience, not one that espouses abstract universal ideals. Menzies provided such a liberalism with the 'forgotten people' but the forgotten people in their 1942 manifestation are no more, and liberal principles need to adapt to the reality of the present.

It can be argued that the 'No 'vote in the recent Voice referendum is a positive development for liberalism in Australia. It indicates that Australia remains a liberal polity that rejects any idea of privilege, especially as manifested in bureaucratic organisations.   Liberals need to understand the significance of what happened in October 2023 and build on it to create a new liberal vision for twenty first century Australia. Any party professing liberalism needs to realise that principle and the national good are its foundation, not just the pursuit of power.

References

Bongiorno, F., *Dreamers and Schemers: A political history of Australia,* Melbourne: LaTrobe University Press, 2022

Burke, E., *Works: Volume 2,* London: Rivington

Chavura S., and Melleuish, G., "Conservative instinct in Australian political thought: The Federation debates, 1890–1898", *Australian Journal of Political Science*, 50(3), 2015, 512-28

Errington W., and van Onselen, P., *Battleground: Why the Liberal Party Shirtfronted Tone Abbott,* Carlton: Melbourne University Press, 2015

Errington W., and Van Onselen, P., *How Good is Scott Morrison?* Sydney: Hachette, 2021

Hancock, W.K., *Australia,* London: Benn, 1930

Hughes, W.M., *The Case for Labor,* Introduction by Sir Robert Menzies, Sydney: Sydney University Press, 1970 [1910]

Kemp, D., *A Liberal State 1926-1966,* Carlton: Melbourne University Press, 2021

Labor in Power Episode 1, 1993. https://youtu.be/qj3yCInCGos?si=3PcLr3pNNl-h2WNvF

Machiavelli, N., *The Prince,* Ed. Quentin Skinner & Russell Price, Cambridge: Cambridge University Press, 1988

Manning, P., *Born to Rule: The unauthorised biography of Malcolm Turnbull,* Carlton: Melbourne University Press, 2015

Mill, J.S., *On Liberty, Representative Government, The Subjection of Women,* London: Oxford University Press, 1971

McLean, I.W., *Why Australia Prospered,* Princeton: Princeton University Press, 2013

Melleuish, G., *The Packaging of Australia,* Sydney, UNSW Press, 1988

Melleuish, G., "Distributivism: The Australian Political Ideal?" *Journal of Australian Studies,* 62, 1999. 20–9

Melleuish, G., *The Power of Ideas,* Melbourne: Australian Scholarly Press, 2000

Melleuish, G., "Introduction: Liberalism and Conservatism", in Melleuish G., (ed), *Liberalism and Conservatism,* Ballarat: Connor Court Publishing, 2015

Melleuish, G., "Democracy, Liberalism and the Challenge of Social Solidarity", *Social Science,* 7, no 7, 1998, 110. https://doi.org/10.3390/socsci7070110

Menzies, R.G., *The Forgotten People and Other Studies in Democracy,* Sydney: Angus and Robertson, 2017 [1943]

Patrick, A., *Credlin & Co: How the Abbott Government Destroyed Itself,* Melbourne: Black Inc, 2016

Patrick, A., *Ego: Malcolm Turnbull and the Liberal Party's Civil War,* Sydney: HarperCollins, 2022

Post-War Reconstruction: A Case for Greater Commonwealth Powers, Canberra: Government Printer, 1942

Savva, N., *The Road to Ruin: How Tony Abbott and Peta Credlin destroyed their own government*, Melbourne: Scribe, 2016

van Onselen P., Errington, W., *Victory: The Inside Story of Labor's return to power*, Sydney: HarperCollins, 2022

3

The Forgotten Menzies Speech
– and what would Menzies think of the Liberal Party and the Coalition 2013-2022

Graeme Starr[1]

Most people with a real interest in Australian political affairs are familiar with Sir Robert Menzies' magnificent 1942 address and radio broadcasts, *The Forgotten People*. Few, however, have given any attention to a much more relevant speech – which we can think of as *The Forgotten Speech of 1944* – in which Menzies subtly outlined the organisational principles that enabled him to determine the course and character of federal politics over the next half of a century and beyond.

This speech was made when Menzies, gave an address to the first meeting he called in Canberra on 13 October 1944 to form the new Liberal Party (Menzies 1944 – see Starr 1980).

The Forgotten Speech gives us the best available clue to answer the

---

[1]   This was written just before Graeme Starr died in March 2021, so was his reflections on the Federal Liberal Party at that time. It has been slightly edited and amended.

inevitable question: What would Sir Robert think of the Liberal Party today?

The real answer, of course, is simply that nobody knows – except perhaps for a few people who actually knew Menzies and shared his thoughts. Fortunately, however, we can make a pretty reasonable educated guess, based on his dissection of his old party – the United Australia Party or the UAP – when it faced critical organisational problems in 1944 following its election debacle in 1943 when it was almost outpolled by the Country Party.

Menzies had led the UAP as prime minister from 1939-41. He was forced to resign in 1941, with Artie Fadden, leader of the Country Party becoming prime minister for 40 days. The Fadden Coalition government fell on the floor of the House of Representatives in September 1941 and was replaced by the John Curtin led Labor Party. The Coalition parties then decided to make Fadden the leader of the opposition although Menzies was still leader of the UAP. He then retired to the backbench and former prime minister and former Labor prime minister, Billie Hughes became leader of the UAP. Following the 1943 election debacle Menzies assumed leadership of the opposition and set about forming a new political party – the Liberal Party (see Martin 1993 for details).

Menzies was a loyal party man, but when he found that his old party was flawed with irreparable organisational defects, he called for its dissolution and its replacement with a new and principled Liberal Party.

Late in 1944, Menzies invited representatives from a number of political groups opposed to "socialism", "bureaucratic administration", and "the restriction of personal freedom" to attend a conference in Canberra with the aim of "securing unity of action and organisation" among those seeking more realistic solutions to Australia's political and economic problems (Starr 1980)

His long-forgotten opening speech to that conference stressed the importance of organisation. Naturally, he alluded to political faith and he suggested a range of policy approaches, but from the outset his concern was with the defects in the UAP and what could be done about them. This is where we get our clues as to what Menzies might think of the Liberal Party today.

The **first defect**, he said, was that there was "no true nexus between the Federal Parliamentary Party and those who are to do the political work in the field". UAP councils, when they held them, were little more than media events or fund-raisers, rather than hard policy debates where MPs could be held answerable to their supporters.

Second, apart from occasional election policy statements, there was "no comprehensive statement of our political objectives". Thus, some members, even parliamentary, had no real idea about the basic principles of their party. The new Liberals overcame this defect by making a clear distinction between "policy" (the day-to-day fighting program determined by the parliamentary party) and "platform" (the party organisation's statement of principles on which members could confidently expect policy to be based).

Third, there was "no process of consultation between those *in* and those *out* of Parliament" to bring about appropriate revisions of policy. The UAP had nothing like the Liberal Party's joint policy committees which for many years were effective in ensuring that organisational views had the attention of parliamentary policy-makers.

Fourth, the party was known by too many names. The name "United Australia Party" had lost its intrinsic significance. The party had become corrupted by organised factions to which many members gave their prior loyalty, and often even by coalitions of factions conspiring against the remaining unaligned members.

Fifth, there was no properly organised arrangement for conveying the party's views to the public. Branches, for example, were often mere phantoms, existing only on paper, irrelevant to their communities and without the vital capacity to act as two-way conduits between the government and the public.

Sixth, there was no constant political organisation in the electorates. Membership numbers had fallen to insignificance. Nationally, the party had fewer than 100,000 members in an Australian population of more than seven million. Lacking a popular base, professional field staff and other essential resources, the UAP was not capable of real political campaigning but was forced to waste its money on crude public relations and expensive advertising campaigns.

Seventh, the party had lost the interest or support of young people who looked elsewhere for their political future.

The last but possibly the most important defect identified by Menzies was that "we lean too heavily upon individual donations and have no adequate rank and file finance". The UAP had no effective finance code, which meant that parliamentarians, candidates and other policy-makers were sometimes involved in raising funds and even in deciding how funds should be spent. Menzies insisted that policy-making must be insulated from the fund-raising process. All responsible leaders have agreed – but every former party director could write a book about that.

Menzies identified the structural flaws in the UAP and set about correcting them with a new party based on sound political and organisational principles. Some reflection on the relevance of those principles might still be a useful exercise – especially as the "new" party reaches its 75th anniversary next year.

And added comment is what would Menzies think of the leadership turmoil that has overtaken both the Liberal and National parties in opposition and government. In opposition between 2007-2013 the Liberals had three leaders – the Nationals were more stable at that time. In government under the period under review there were three Liberal leaders while the Nationals also went through gyrations with four leaders. While leadership changes are not unknown in non-Labor politics especially when in opposition, and increasingly across all parties (Tiffen 2017) and Menzies himself was a victim, he might nevertheless be surprised that the party of stability became so unstable.

So, what would Menzies think of today's Liberal Party? If he used the same criteria that he applied to his assessment of the UAP in 1944, his opinion might not be altogether favourable.

References

Martin, A.W., *Robert Menzies A Life Volume 1 1894-1943*, Carlton: Melbourne University Press, 1993

Menzies, R.G., "Menzies Opens the Canberra Conference 13 October 1944", in Starr, G., (ed), *The Liberal Party of Australia: A Documentary History*, Melbourne: Drummond/Heinemann, 1980, 73-6

Tiffen, R., *Disposable Leaders: Media and Leadership Coups from Menzies to Abbott*, Sydney: NewSouth, 2017

Part 2:
The Coalition and Institutions

4

The Coalition and the Institutions of Government (2013-2022)

John Halligan

Introduction

Coalition governments in the 2010s inherited the Howard Government model covering relationships within the executive branch, public service reform, and a template for public governance that would reflect the conventions of Westminster such as responsible government. However, leadership instability in office became normal for governments post-Howard, which meant variations in prime minister styles, approaches to institutions and interpretations of the model.

Over time, the questions of accountable and responsible government were disregarded, sometimes recklessly, opportunities to address questions of integrity were ignored and accountability issues were amassed. The capability of the public service was neglected because of the sustained emphasis on salary caps, outsourcing and reliance on alternative advisory sources. In this period, the long-term trend for depreciating parliament became more pronounced and a range of accountability deficits emerged in the public sector. There was an attrition in public governance, an increase in perceived corruption and core institutions were in a worse condition by the 2022 election.

This chapter first examines Australian traditions and broader trends in government and the dynamics of politics and modernising of government, and considers the Coalition inheritance. The bulk of the chapter addresses core institutions of government: parliament, the public service, and the political executive and its machinery.

Coalition models of governance

The Howard Government provided a model for the Coalition governments in the 2010s covering relationships within the executive branch, public service reform including a small state, and a template for stable, competent government that allowed for pragmatism where appropriate. John Howard learnt from mistakes (eg compulsory outsourcing of IT infrastructure) and was capable of U-turns (eg the shift from a contracting public service to a more reflective and balanced approach and integrated governance: Halligan 2005, 2008). With the advantage of four terms Howard was able to draw on experience to make sound appointments for both the public service and the prime minister's office. Howard successfully managed relationships with ministers, the parliamentary party and the public service. This was due in large part to Howard's effectiveness in handling cabinet government (Kelly 2005; Strangio et al 2017: 216).

Leadership instability in office became the new normal for governments post-Howard and was reflected by two prime ministers being dispatched by Coalition parliamentary parties. Tony Abbott and Malcolm Turnbull had different styles and approaches to public governance. Abbott exemplified a dysfunctional prime minister who could not learn and change his behaviour despite a caucus revolt. Abbott abdicated his role as leader in favour of his chief of staff who sought to direct cabinet ministers, made political appointments of forgettable outsiders as heads of two key central agencies and whose limitation was "a tendency toward cognitive closure in the face of complex problems that require flexibility" (Strangio et al 2017: 305). In contrast, Turnbull sought to follow Westminster traditions in employing a career professional as head of his department and the public service and initiated both a review of the public service and the forerunner of the Digital Transformation Authority, both of which had durable institutional impacts.

The Morrison Government inherited mind sets from previous Coalition governments and a governing model from the previous Howard Government but departed from the latter in highly distinctive ways. Using two elements of "statecraft" (see Evans and McCaffrie

2016), the primary governance objective was winning elections, and the governing code (ie principles, practices and methods) accorded primacy to the evasion of working within the rules and conventions of responsible and democratic government.

This was based on a mode of leadership and the reliance on partisan governance as a means of achieving objectives. Elements of Scott Morrison's leadership style have been characterised by a number of epithets: imperious, megalomaniacal, secretive, blame shifting, duplicitous, a propensity to lie, weakly focused on policy and an aversion to accountability, responsibility and transparency (Errington and van Onselen 2021; Keane 2021; Savva 2022; Taflaga 2023; Tiernan 2021). The self-proclaimed "bulldozer" (Savva 2022) marshalled the machinery of government through the cultivation of partisan governance. Politicisation of the public service and partisanship had long been a feature of Australian governments and was reflected in the evolving role of ministers and use of partisans in the public sector (e.g., the influence of the prime minister's office) (Halligan 2020). Partisan governance is of a different order. In addition to politicisation dimensions, it entails prioritising party and ministers' interests over the public interest, heightened politicisation of public service, and extending partisanship to an unrivalled extent throughout the public sector including greater use of patronage.

Political executive

The political executive consists of the prime minister, ministers, cabinet and the accoutrements of partisan advisory offices. How it operates depends substantially on the leadership style of the prime minister. The concentration of power under Morrison consisted of five components: the Department of Prime Minister and Cabinet (DPMC) headed by a political appointee and fixer[1]; a highly influential and interventionist prime minister's office; and control of cabinet processes through chairing cabinet committees and running the cabinet office. There were also two unique components: the addition of the National Cabinet that could operate unfettered for many purposes; and the expansion of the prime minister's portfolio responsibilities.

The Prime Minister's Office (PMO) is expected to exercise influence, but this needs to be tempered by respect for roles and relationships, a balance that had been realised by earlier governments, including those of Howard and Turnbull. Under Morrison the PMO displaced the DPMC to an even greater extent than in the past, which was facilitated by a politically compliant head of DPMC, and by being more interventionist than its predecessors in the workings of government in general. More than its predecessors, the government "assiduously bred the culture of secrecy that permeates from the Prime Minister's Office (PMO) down" (Tiernan 2021).

Prime Minister Morrison chaired eight cabinet committees (notably Expenditure Review, Governance and National Security). In addition, a Cabinet Office Policy committee (COP) was established with the prime minister being the only member. This was a highly active cabinet committee that considered "major policy issues on an as needs basis, including early-stage consideration of strategic issues, specialist advice on nationally significant issues and rapidly evolving situations". COP also covered preliminary discussion of policy prior to the formal cabinet process.[2] As a cabinet committee, it was not subject to FOI requests, and records are not available until 2039. There was also the creation of an executive body composed of external appointments and located in the Department of the Prime Minister and Cabinet, the National COVID-19 Coordination Commission. It subsequently became an advisory body, although without a legislative basis and transparency (Hicks 2020).

During Covid-19, the Council of Australian Governments forum was replaced by a National Cabinet comprising essentially the same government leaders. Their deliberations were not publicly accessible because cabinet confidentiality was invoked, even though the standing of the entity was deemed to be different to a conventional cabinet (Toomey 2022a).

The ultimate and unprecedented aggrandisement of prime ministerial power occurred when Morrison appointed himself to the portfolios of five of his ministers without advising parliament, relevant departments, the public, or even the minister in most cases. According to the Solicitor-

General (2022: secs 44, 48) "an unpublicised appointment to administer a department ... fundamentally undermines ... the relationship between the Ministry and the public service". Further, the ability of parliament and the public to determine "which Ministers have been appointed to administer which departments is critical to the proper functioning of responsible government, because it is those appointments ... that determine the matters for which a Minister is legally and politically responsible".[3] The Bell Report (2022) investigated the issues also.

Parliament and accountability

Executive-legislative relations can be fraught with tensions as the power imbalance changes over time. Legislation passed by compliant parliaments during the last two decades facilitated "a creeping expansion of executive powers and non-compellable and non-reviewable discretions of Ministers" (Triggs 2018).[4] Much depends on the extent to which the political executive seeks to exploit its position by either constraining or ignoring routine processes. Under the Morrison Government the magnitude and range of tactics used, and the resolute pursuit of executive advantage, surpassed previous governments.

The Morrison Government was responsible for "implementing measures and introducing practices that limited government transparency and accountability, both to parliament and to the Australian public" (Middleton 2023: 21). It was said to have downgraded the parliamentary role by not giving it much work following an election in which little policy was promised, and with a few notable exceptions policy initiatives were not apparent in its legislation program (Middleton 2023: 24). The volume of bills presented to the House of Representatives in non-election years for the 46th parliament was well down compared to previous parliaments (Parliament of Australia 2022). Westminster conventions were disregarded but not when they enabled secrecy or political advantage. Budget dates were changed before the 2019 and 2022 elections to provide a springboard for the Coalition's "campaign embedded with billions of dollars in grants, particularly for coalition target seats" (Middleton 2023: 32).

Observers have noted that the Commonwealth parliament sat during previous emergencies without the restrictions imposed by the Morrison Government during the Covid-19 pandemic (e.g., Hobbs and Williams 2023; Mills 2020). Australian governments evaded accountability by suspending parliament. Several in state jurisdictions particularly affected by the Covid-19 rarely met while the "Commonwealth Parliament failed to meet regularly at a critical time when many Australians were suffering considerable alarm and anxiety" (Hobbs and Williams 2023: 10-11). The emergency response "either eliminated or .... substantially compromised Parliament's capacity to perform" its multiple roles, which meant its "only role during the pandemic was to provide the Government with supply and appropriation" (Mills 2020: 16,18).

Three indicators show the impact on parliament under Morrison: closing off (gagging) debate, evading parliamentary control by using delegated legislation and proscribing scrutiny, and disregard of parliamentary committee reports. Gagging debate in parliament through the use of closure motions has been long established. However, the Morrison Government moved more successful closure motions than any other government since the Commonwealth was established. There were 332 successful closure motions years from 2019 to 2022 (RMIT ABC Fact Check 2022).

Delegated legislation is a valuable tool for ministers to be able to act swiftly as required for adjustments to law. When used for major policy, it becomes more problematic. Ministers' use of delegated legislation has increased greatly over time (doubled over thirty years: CPI 2020). A Senate standing committee (SSCSDL 2021: 8-9) observed that the "trend towards an increase in delegated legislation is accompanied by a trend over time for increasing amounts of delegated legislation to be exempt from disallowance". In 2019, the percentage for exemptions approached 20 per cent.[5] The Senate committees for Scrutiny of Delegated Legislation and the Scrutiny of Bills have regularly expressed concerns about the increasing activities excluded from examination, and "challenged the governance arrangements involving both the use of non-disallowable regulations and the loose definitions that allowed certain expenditure to escape scrutiny" (Middleton 2023: 28).[6] The

Scrutiny of Bills Committee reported that "it had written to the finance minister repeatedly since 2014, complaining that parliament was not able to properly examine government spending" (Middleton 2023: 29).

One of the strengths of the Australian Parliament has been the investigative and review work of its committees, particularly those in the Senate (Halligan et al 2007). The Senate President produces six-monthly reports on the status of government responses to recommendations made in committee reports. In recent years, these have indicated that the government had not responded to many reports and ignored deadlines (e.g. Senate 2022). Also, public servants taking questions on notice in Senate estimates had increased substantially but many remained unanswered, particularly on sensitive matters, and not within deadlines (Senate Hansard 2023; Mazengarb 2022).

Overall, in the two terms of Morrison Government, Parliament was treated "more as something between a political weapon and an inconvenience" (Middleton 2023: 21). At the same time, deficiencies in Parliament's functioning that arose during the pandemic also reflected "deeper, longer-term problems of parliamentary control by the executive" (Hobbs and Williams 2023: 3).

Accountability deficits with oversight and review agencies

The disregard for the work of oversight, review, access to information and appeals agencies became prevalent. Three cases are discussed here.

Official documents recognise that accountability (and transparency) are fundamental features of the Australian National Audit Office (ANAO). The demand for its services has increased with the addition of extra entities, yet fewer performance audits could be undertaken because of the resource squeeze (Auditor-General 2020b), which amounted to a significant reduction in the ANAO's capacity to hold the executive branch to account. Seeking to minimise open scrutiny, cutting resources and constraining the AG's activities can be interpreted as symptomatic of a governmental system that undervalues accountability. The Auditor-General's office, the ANAO, has been part of the executive branch of government and the DPMC has had responsibility for the administration of the Auditor-General's appointment, a long-standing anomaly in the Australian system compared to other anglophone counterparts. Much depends on how governments use this prerogative.

A further example of limiting oversight capacity existed with the Australian Human Rights Commission (AHRC), an independent national institution for promoting human rights through programs and inquiries into issues, which handles thousands of complaints annually (Human Rights Law Centre 2022). The Morrison Government relied on appointment of commissioners without the use of a public process based on merit. There was also a major shortfall in funding, particularly as the level of complaints soared. One consequence of the appointment process was that AHRC was not reaccredited in 2022 by the Global Alliance of National Human Rights Institutions as an A-status national human rights institution (SCA 2022).

Australia has had a *Freedom of Information Act* for forty years. The FOI regime has been "undermined in practice by inordinate delay, under resourcing and the abuse of statutory exceptions" (CPI 2022: 1). There have been lengthy delays in responding to FOI requests with the statutory time limit being ignored, a large increase in the proportion of requests refused in whole, and a marked decline in those granted. Questions have also been asked about how the appeals system earned the appellation of a "culture of secrecy" while internal (and external) reviews were rising substantially (CPI 2022: 9-10).

Australian Public Service

The issues and problems that had to be resolved through Coalition programs for the Australian public service varied with the prime minister as did the means of addressing them. The smaller government agenda (including economy and efficiency objectives) ran in some form throughout the three governments. It could be both an end in itself and/ or a means to attaining a budget surplus. Less clear was a concern with effectiveness although the reliance on blunt instruments had impacts. Political control was also central although the level of intervention varied between governments and often took the form of informal directives. Two quite different reform programs were initiated. Abbott launched the National Commission of Audit following his predecessors at federal and state levels while Turnbull instigated a major review of the public service. Morrison's approach was reactive to reform and ad hoc.

Smaller government, contestability and efficiency 2014-17

The rolling back the state agenda (under the Coalition government 1996-2007) had a great impact on the shape of the central state with extensive outsourcing and privatisation. A new Coalition Government in 2013 employed a National Commission of Audit (2014) to identify and articulate many of the main themes. Such an audit had been used by a succession of newly elected usually conservative governments, state and national, to critique the parlous condition of the jurisdiction's finances and to prescribe major changes (Jones and Prasser 2014). Most of the key recommendations accepted by the Coalition Government in this case were funnelled through the Department of Finance to form the basis of the several components of the "transformation agenda" (Halton 2015: 12). The main elements were smaller government, efficiency through contestability, functional and efficiency reviews and staffing efficiencies (i.e. caps and cutbacks).

First was the smaller government initiative (Cormann 2014), which was depicted as "about clarifying lines of accountability and cutting waste and duplication, while improving the efficiency and focus of the public service" (Halton 2015: 14). Several major agencies had previously been brought under ministerial departments, notably Centrelink which had been created under the Howard Government with a board but was subsequently stripped of it and independence in 2004 (Halligan and Wills 2008).

Under the smaller government program, several principal agencies were abolished (2014-2015), totalling 38 across five phases with several making a substantial contribution to saving costs. The majority were consolidated or merged, consolidation normally meaning incorporation in a ministerial department. Following the initial phases, the termination of principal agencies dwindled as the supply of options petered out. Attention turned to secondary agencies, a multitude of often modest and specialised committees, councils, boards, consultative bodies and working groups were discontinued. There were significant savings from phase 1, and to a lesser extent in phase 2, but a handful of terminations accounted for most of the economising. Most terminations produced no cost savings as 87 per cent came from secondary bodies, usually advisory committees. Much of the savings came from back-office mergers as a shared services program came into play in the second phase.[7] At the symbolic level, secondary bodies sometimes of a marginal nature were pursued (Halligan 2016).

The second component was centred on the Australian Public Service and associate agencies. an "Efficiency through Contestability Programme" for examining government activities and services with reference to contestability. A phased program between 2015-2017 entailed stocktakes of portfolios (ministerial departments and associated agencies); contestability reviews of departmental functions; and functional and efficiency reviews which evaluated the alignment of functions with government priorities, and whether an activity or service could be delivered by alternative means at a higher quality and lower cost (Halton 2015).

Under the Abbott Government, APS staff were reduced, and staffing ceilings were introduced, along with a commitment to holding average staffing at the 2006-07 level. Spending on labour contractors more than doubled over four years to 2016-17, while expenditure on consultants increased by more than 40 per cent. Over the same period, spending on APS wages and salaries was flat (IRAPS 2019: 186).

How much did the margins of the state change? The secondary bodies that experienced a demise generally did not carry much weight beyond a relatively narrow sphere, but they did provide access points for external contributions to government processes. The case for economy was expressed through expenditure cuts designed to reduce the budget deficit. The focus on achieving a surplus continued to be the mantra of Coalition governments until displaced by the exigencies of Covid-19 which forced a conversion to deficit budgets.

The influence of specific aspects continued with shared services, the ceilings on employing APS staff, and the externalisation of public service work (the value of consultancy services increased from under $400 million to over $1.1 billion in the decade up to 2018-19: ANAO 2020: 45). The value of management services procured from the big four consulting companies increased by 1276% between 2012-13 and 2021-22 (CPI 2023).

APS reform 2019-22

The second reform program, the 2019 Independent Review of the Australian Public Service (the APS Review) was established "to examine the capability, culture and operating model of the APS". The public sector "needs to drive policy [and] to engage with the key policy, service delivery and regulatory issues" (Turnbull and O'Dwyer 2018). The APS Review was claimed to be the most comprehensive since the Coombs Royal Commission (RCAGA 1976), and its 40 recommendations covered a range of dimensions starting with delivering improved outcomes. The others included defining the elements of a "successful transformation" (e.g. progress targets and "deep cultural change"); a united APS; external partnerships; embracing new technology; investing in people and capability; and improved leadership and governance (IRAPS 2019).

The Review was initiated in 2018 by the Turnbull Government but was completed in 2019 under another prime minister (Morrison) who held strong views about the role of the APS that differed from his predecessor. The Morrison Government ran its own "reform" agenda with a set of guidelines produced to pre-empt the publication of the Review's report (Morrison 2019), and with recommendations that conflicted with the APS Review (Australian Government 2019; IRAPS 2019). The unhappy co-existence of a major reform program and a separate government reform agenda meant the review process was constrained, its independence questioned, and core recommendations overridden. The review was also oblivious of the concurrent subterranean behaviour of Robotdebt ministers and senior public servants and Michael Pezzullo's machinations that subsequently surfaced (see below).

There were multiple strands to reform implementation. The Secretaries Board was redefined as a corporate leader of the "enterprise", which was to "operate as an APS enterprise management board" with three priorities. The first was support of the Covid-19 response and recovery and leading cross-cutting government priorities; accelerate digital transformation; and strengthen APS workforce planning and capabilities and professional streams for developing specific capabilities (Gaetjens and Woolcott 2020). There was some strengthening of the central agency level. The head of DPMC and the APS Commissioner became partners in oversighting the reform agenda through the Secretaries Board. The Commissioner's role was enhanced by becoming the pivot for the emerging professional streams that were intended to increase employees' capabilities in critical disciplines or functional areas and to address capability gaps. Three streams were created: data, digital and human resources. Apart from the focus on professionalisation and collaboration and use of cross-APS networks, the themes were standards, career pathways and long-term capability. There were meant to be results for the APS (e.g. overall effectiveness and performance).[8] It was recognised that the Commission should play a stronger role in standards and capability and craft development (Halligan 2023a). [Academy]

Meanwhile other central agencies continued to upgrade their services. A report on ensuring institutional integrity in the public service was a response to an APS Review recommendation that identified capability gaps and accountability as a missing link (Sedgwick 2020). The APS Review (IRAPS 2019: 223) recommended enhancing evaluation capability across the service to ensure that programs and policies were evaluated systematically. This capability was to occur at three levels: cabinet requirements, agency evaluation and plans, and the Department of Finance's role. Finance had been developing a central evaluation function by building expertise and practices, including guidelines to ensure program evaluation reflected the Enhanced Performance Reporting Framework (under the *Public Governance, Performance and Accountability Act 2013*) to provide public and parliamentary understanding about resource use. This was meant to be achieved through the information provided under the reporting regime of corporate plans, portfolio budget statements and annual performance statements (Morton and Cook 2018)[9] As the lead central agency in the small government reform phase, Finance maintained ongoing initiatives, notably support for shared services operations and provider hubs (e.g., the Shared Services Transformation Initiative for reducing duplication).

Undermining the institution

Changes to the standing of the traditional public service over time have reduced its significance and impaired its functioning (Halligan 2020; Prasser 2023) Under Morrison, seven factors undermined the institution. Firstly, there was the continuation of cutbacks and salary caps, which disincentivised the public service. Secondly, there was the large-scale externalisation of public service work to the private sector. Thirdly, public servants interactions with ministers and their advisers too often involved being pressured to be highly responsive or being bypassed or their roles displaced by partisan operatives.[10]

A fourth factor was the denial of a fundamental role of the public service, the provision of policy advice. The condition of policy capability had been highly problematic in Australia and comparable countries for over a decade (Craft and Halligan 2020), yet the Morrison Government's diagnosis and solutions ignored the evidence about the weaknesses. Enhancing policy capability was recommended in the 2010 Blueprint but an agenda was not formalised until a decade later under the leadership of a secretaries' group and dedicated staff in a policy hub (DPMC 2019). The environment was not however propitious as the newly elected prime minister deprecated the policy development role and declared that the public service was to focus on implementing and delivering services. The Morrison Government assumed responsibility for the policy role (although it had offered scant policy objectives in the March 2019 election), and the public service was left with the residual role of advising on challenges to its implementation (Podger and Halligan 2023; Grattan 2019b).

A fifth dimension was the sacking of departmental secretaries, for which there were precedents (e.g., Abbott's dispatching of three on becoming prime minister). The modern practice of the prime minister's choice for the head of Department of the Prime Minister and Cabinet was continued, but only Turnbull's choice was a conventional career professional. In turn Morrison replaced him with a political fixer. Morrison undertook a radical reduction in the number of departments that enabled the "sacking" of five departmental secretaries (Whyte and Rollins 2019), most of whom were associated with developing policy capability.[11]

The other contributors to the malaise of the public service and the operation of government were first the behaviour associated with Robotdebt, which implicated ministers and senior public servants, and provided one of the worst failures of modern government. The further addition, which may be symptomatic of institutional degeneration, was Michael Pezzullo's behaviour while departmental secretary of the Home Affairs Department. Ministers and intermediaries were apparently recipients of his private advice and posturing. While the initial machinations pre-dated the Morrison Government, they were given a fillip by the opportunities it provided. Pezzullo's actions in seeking to expand his domain, reshape organisational restructuring, influence policy beyond his role, non-observance of the code of conduct, and undermining leadership was unparalleled for a senior departmental secretary in modern government. He was asked to stand aside from his position pending an investigation of media revelations (see McKenzie et al 2023) and then removed for breaching the government code of conduct. Home Affairs has had a history of internal issues (Keane 2023), and chronic problems prompted reviews that reported major issues with priorities, systems, capability and performance (Nixon 2023; Parkinson et al 2023). Concern has been expressed about "whether Pezzullo's behaviour represented a more systemic problem of APS leaders failing to meet their responsibilities" (Podger 2023b).

In addition, there were other indicators of departmental malfunctioning, such as weaknesses in the handling of performance management, which came to head under the Albanese Government (Hehir 2023).

Robodebt

The issues were epitomised by a program involving automated

debt matching (known as Robodebt) that calculated debts based on income averages and resulted in traumatised citizens and severely compromised public servants. The government knowingly acted unlawfully, negligently and secretly and refused to take responsibility for the scheme's failure. After four years of citizen protestations, public inquiries and expert advice on the issues it agreed to refund 470,000 invalid debts (SCARC 2021). The Royal Commission on the scheme (RC 2023) produced 57 recommendations, and a summation from the Royal Commissioner:

> It is remarkable how little interest there seems to have been in ensuring the Scheme's legality, how rushed its implementation was, how little thought was given to how it would affect welfare recipients and the lengths to which public servants were prepared to go to oblige ministers on a quest for savings. Truly dismaying was the revelation of dishonesty and collusion to prevent the Scheme's lack of legal foundation coming to light. Equally disheartening was the ineffectiveness of ... institutional checks and balances ... in presenting any hinderance to the Scheme's continuance (RC 2023: iii).

The ramifications of the Royal Commission's report (RC 2023) have continued to reverberate because of the impact on the standing of the public service and the integrity of public governance. Podger's (2023a) report to the Royal Commission indicated the systemic issues and the ways in which practice in agencies had departed from both the principle of and legislation for the public service.

Partisanship, private interests and patronage and democratic system

Partisan governance

Patronage and politicisation exceeded that of the Howard Government by a large margin. Practices under the Morrison Government (2018-22) converted questionable precedents into a distinctive style of partisan governance. Analysis of the breadth and range of malfeasance indicates the need to differentiate a distinctive type of partisan governance to encapsulate the extensions to and maintenance of control. Of interest is the extent to which decisions are shaped and constrained by institutional factors or by the drive of political actors to implement partisan agendas. Politicisation had already become of paramount importance as a driver of change. Previous discussion of stages of politicisation in anglophone countries (Halligan 2020) do not account for recent cases. A hyper-politicisation form is more complex particularly where partisan governance is being cultivated to secure more complete control over the apparatus of government and to ensure longevity in office.

Politicians asserting their role over bureaucrats is commonplace, but it is the intensity of control that matters. The breadth and depth of politicisation is important where there is greater pressure for political control across and within public agencies. The Morrison Government's conception of the public service was of a malleable tool with more limited roles which was subservient to political masters and secondary to the private sector. The dominance of the minister's authority and influence allowed them to override rules, processes and guidelines. Political advisers were pivotal with ministerial staff operating in parallel to, or instead of, the public service, and the prime minister's office steering from the centre. The public service was now not simply promiscuous in serving the government of the day but was owned by it.

Politicisation in decision making is normalised in specific fields for partisan advantage. The aggregation of these elements when scaled up provides a system that accords the political executive the plenitude of power, and when applied consistently across government forms the basis for partisan governance. This mobilisation of partisan personnel and ministerial power enables the political executive to serve private rather than public interests. Governments that pursue comprehensive and systemic politicisation of the executive branch with such partisan intentions have a propensity to employ corrupt practices and to rely on accountability evasion.[12]

Pork barrelling for party/partisan interests

Pork barrelling is "the exercise of public powers, such as the making of grants or commitments to build infrastructure, in a biased or 'partial' manner that favours the interests of a political party, rather than the public interest" (Twomey 2022b: 141). Governments have long exploited various means for advantaging areas or groups, including the famous case of pork barrelling, the "whiteboard" affair.[13] That the Morrison Government pattern was on a much larger scale is indicated by a sample of cases examined by the Auditor-General (2020a, 2021, 2022). They indicate that there were marked failings with process, the roles of ministers and political advisers, and the distribution of grants. There was usually a marked partisan bias in the decisions (favouring government seats and marginal electorates), heavy reliance on ministerial discretion and ministerial panels in selecting recipients of grants, and the use of ministerial staff to produce lists of awardees in parallel with those from public servants. There was a failure to conform to rules and guidelines laid down in legislation or developed with respect to specific grant programs, and the replacement of merit-based recommendations produced by departments and agencies with ministers' recommendations. Reasons were not provided for decisions. They remained secret because they departed from guidelines about following merit as the core principle or because politicians' rationalised that they or grant recipients knew best. Finally, shameless displays of pork were sanctified by the notion that this was the "way things were done" despite the extent to which this was occurring reaching new levels.

Ministers acted with the belief that they were beyond the law because it was not criminal behaviour and therefore fair game. In the most egregious case, the Community Sport Infrastructure Program, the Minister was judged to have provided "a clear case of corrupt conduct by any reasonable standard: the wilful and deliberate abuse of money and power for political gain". It was argued that serious cases of corruption can be investigated where they do not meet the criminal threshold (Whealy 2020). The Grattan Institute concluded that ministers' level of discretion was the key enabler and that a higher risk of politicisation existed where the process was neither open nor competitive (Wood et al 2022a: 15, 18).

In addition to pork barrelling, there were other types of cases involving funding that failed due process and transparency tests. Political advertising had been a long-standing practice of various governments (SFPARC 2005) but became a public issue as symptomatic of what a think tank termed 'new politics' prompting a review because of its scale and use with prior to elections (Wood et al 2022c). A legal specialist argued that "government advertising to reinforce positive impressions of the incumbent party is a form of institutional corruption – it is the use of public funds for the illegitimate purpose of electioneering" (Tham 2019).[14]

Patronage and partisan control

The other major issue was the use of appointments to public bodies for implementation control and patronage. The question of the political backgrounds of board appointees had received attention before. A corporate governance study reported issues with the appointment processes based on interviews with senior officials from boards and the public service (Edwards et al 2012). In the subsequent decade, issues with the nature of appointments reached much higher levels.

The Administrative Appeals Tribunal (AAT) plays a major role in reviewing administrative decisions made by government covering inter alia child support, family assistance, visas and veterans' entitlements. A range of decisions in other fields, such as freedom of information, may also be reviewed. The Senate Legal and Constitutional Affairs References Committee (SLCARC 2022) reported on the performance and integrity of the administrative review system, observing that a change to the selection process in 2019 had raised concerns. The Attorney-General introduced a revised protocol for appointments that allowed the government to decide on the appointments rather than adhere to those recommended by the AAT (SLCARC 2022: 40-44). The committee reported a lack of transparency with AAT appointments, concerns about the risk of patronage because of the process, disquiet about the trend in appointments, and the numerous appointments and reappointments made immediately before the 2019 election.[15]

A well-documented pattern for political appointments to become more prominent emerged during the 2010s. Political appointees were defined as "people who ... had worked for a federal political party in either a paid or voluntary capacity" (Wilkinson & Morison 2022: 1). The proportion of AAT political appointees was low under the Howard (6 per cent, the average for four terms, 1996-2007) and Rudd/Gillard/Rudd (5 per cent) governments. Political appointments subsequently rose to 23 per cent for the Abbott/Turnbull Government (2013–2016), 35 per cent for the Turnbull/Morrison Government (2016–2019) and 40 per cent under the Morrison Government (2019–2022) (Wilkinson and Morison 2022: 1,19-20). Other recent trends were the increase in appointing senior members without legal qualifications; and that political appointees were more likely to be appointed full-time and as senior AAT members than non-political appointments (Wilkinson & Morison 2022: 2-4; Wood et al 2022b: 18).

The pattern of politicised appointments for the AAT was also apparent with other tribunals. The range of diplomatic positions awarded to politicians also increased. The stacking of public boards with political appointments was rife, with prestigious positions being said to be rewards for party loyalists (Wood et al 2022b: 12, 16, 20).

Para-public service

The implosion of the consultancy industry in 2023 following public disclosures of corrupt practices added a new dimension. The big four consultancy companies had long presided over much of the Canberra public sector as an integral part of the operations of government, although beyond normal accountability and oversight mechanisms. This condition had been an issue, but while ministers who had been consultants and/or advocates of relying on external expertise were influential, the value of consultancy services increased, and use was normalised at a higher level of dependence. Once subject to careful scrutiny by a new government, the main issues, including corrupt practices, were more clearly exposed: details on the scale of their para government realm, questions about the costs of relying on consultants at the expense of public service capability development, and particularly issues about conflicts of interest and major breaches of trust (SFPARC 2023). The latter question led to the downfall of one company, PricewaterhouseCoopers (PwC), which had used privileged access to confidential tax information to benefit their multinational clients. This case had ramifications for the roles of the consultancy industry discussed below.

Corruption, and trust in government, politics and democracy

A revealing source of the Australian condition was Transparency International data for perceived corruption because it allowed comparisons over time and with other countries. Australia has not been among the most highly ranked countries for low corruption, a status normally reserved for small countries such as Denmark and New Zealand. It nevertheless was in the top ten until its score dropped across a decade from 85 to 73. This was the biggest drop of any OECD country (with the exception of Hungary), while its rank slumped from 7th in the world in 2012 to 18th in 2021 (Transparency International Australia 2022).

Australia experienced a consistent decline in trust in politics since 2007, in contrast to other democracies where fluctuations were more normal. While multiple factors appear to have been relevant, poor government performance (eg managing the economy) and detachment from politics (particularly disengagement from major parties) were the main reasons (Dassonneville & McAllister 2021: 291). In addition, by 2019 voters' trust in government had declined to the lowest figure in 50 years: 75 per cent believed "people in government looked after themselves" whereas only 25 per cent thought they could be trusted. Finally, satisfaction with democracy has plummeted from 86 per cent in 2007 to 59 per cent in 2019 (Cameron and McAllister 2019: 98; Cameron and McAllister 2020: 15-16).

Institutional redux?

A turbulent decade and departures from fundamental principles of public governance culminated in a pendulum swing and review by a new Labor government of how the Australian system had been operating at the federal level. The public service had been traumatised by the integrity issues raised by the Robodebt Royal Commission, the apparent contempt for the code of conduct displayed by the suspended head of the Home Affairs Department, and revelations about corrupt practices and accountability deficits under the Morrison Government (Halligan 2023b). Too many ministers of the crown were associated with a range of questionable practices. The need to rebuild institutions and refine the foundational elements of the Australian system of government had finally come to the fore.

The Albanese Government elected mid-2022, has had an unrivalled opportunity and circumstances to drive one of the most comprehensive reform programs of modern Australia. Core governance institutions had to be reinstitutionalised, the core principles reaffirmed, the political penchant for corrupt practices minimised, and the public service reformed.

Its public service agenda was partly an extension of the APS Review (IRAPS 2019) because of the acceptance of the recommendations and the continuity of key participants who were now in central agency leadership positions. Principles, values and revised frameworks were now a priority, and the craft of public administration (Shearer 2022) came to the fore. The overdue rebalancing of the system (Halligan 2020) was now apparent in official statements about rebuilding capability through "increasing the number of direct, permanent public sector jobs, reducing the use of consultants and outsourcing, abolishing the average staffing level cap, and restoring the independence of vital public sector institutions" (APSC 2022). A plethora of audits, reviews, and taskforces have been investigating accumulated issues as well as means for moving forward. The government's APS priorities have covered integrity, capability, model employer and the centrality of people and businesses to policy and services (Gallagher 2022). It subsequently focused on stewardship as a panacea in proposed amendments to the *Public Service Act*,[16] which also included reviving mandatory capability reviews and constraints on ministers directing secretaries on staff employment. This was before the Pezzullo episode cast doubt on the reliance on and integrity of senior leadership.

Under the second stage of reform (Gallagher 2023; de Brouwer 2023), a centrepiece is a merit and integrity-based framework for appointing and performance managing senior public servants, including secretaries. Development of the APS culture through top-down leadership has become an imperative. The APS Commissioner acquired augmented responsibilities for initiating inquiries into breaches of the Code of Conduct. A centrepiece is the reduction in the reliance on external consultants and contractors by strengthening internal capability and introducing an in-housing consulting capacity, Australian Government Consulting, and an APS Strategic Commissioning Framework (Australian Government 2023) that precludes the outsourcing of core functions. Much of the Minister's statement otherwise reports on ongoing activity across several areas (e.g., digital; evaluation, pay fragmentation). There is the promise of further reform, but question remain about the pace of change and the insufficient attention to embedding reform permanently. The ultimate goal is "to rebuild the culture of frank and fearless advice, integrity and stewardship" (Gallagher 2023), except an institutional vision has only been emerging piecemeal, a roadmap has not been provided and significant reviews have not been acted upon (e.g., the review of board appointments).[17]

Conclusion

The dilemma for democratic systems has been how to entrench principles and practices that strengthen the integrity and effectiveness of the governmental system in the public interest while recognising that public governance in anglophone systems is malleable and susceptible to governments that exploit the rules and opportunities provided by democratic government. Comparable Anglophone countries, such as Canada and the United Kingdom, have also experienced chronic issues with the functioning and performance of their institutions.[18]

The public service is meant to serve the government of the day and executive dominance of parliament will remain, errant political executives are likely to remain an issue. The Australian political environment has continued to display tendencies that do not contribute to and could counter good public governance and public trust, including polarisation that promotes divisiveness and misinformation and affects the quality of public policy.

References

ANAO/Australian National Audit Office, (2023), *Annual Report 2022-23*, Commonwealth of Australia.

APSC/Australian Public Service Commission, (2022), *State of the Service Report 2021-22*, Canberra: Commonwealth of Australia. https://www.apsc.gov.au/working-aps/state-of-service/2022/report/commitment/state-service-report-chapter-7-future-work/75-rebalancing-aps

APSC/Australian Public Service Commission, (2023), *Annual Report 2022-23*, Canberra: Commonwealth of Australia.

Auditor-General, (2020a), *Award of funding under the community sport infrastructure program*, Australian National Audit Office Report No.23, 2019–20, Commonwealth of Australia.

Auditor-General, (2020b), *Australian Government Procurement Contract Reporting Update*, Australian National Audit Office, Report No.27, 2019–20, Information Report, Commonwealth of Australia.

Auditor-General, (2021), *Administration of commuter car park Projects within the urban congestion fund*, Australian National Audit Office Report No. 47, 2020–21, Commonwealth of Australia.

Auditor-General, (2022), *Award of funding under the safer communities fund*, Australian National Audit Office Audit Report No16, 2021–22, Information Report, Australian National Audit Office.

Australian Government, (2019), *Delivering for Australians: A world-class Australian Public Service: The Government's APS Reform Agenda*, Canberra: Commonwealth of Australia.

Australian Government, (2023), *APS Strategic Commissioning Framework*, Canberra: Commonwealth of Australia.

Bell, V., (2022) *Report of the Inquiry into the Appointment of the Former Prime Ministers to Administer Multiple Departments*, Canberra: Commonwealth of Australia, 25 November.

Cameron, S., and McAllister, I., (2019), *The 2019 Australian federal election: Results from the Australian election study*, School of Politics & International Relations, ANU.

Cameron, S., and McAllister, I., (2020), *Trends in Australian political opinion: Results from the Australian election study 1987–2019*, School of Politics and International Relations, ANU.

Carney, T., (2018), "The new digital future for Welfare: Debts without Legal proofs or moral authority", *UNSW Law Journal*, 41(1), 1-16.

Charles, S., and Williams, C., (2022), *Keeping them Honest*, Melbourne: Scribe.

Cormann, M. (Minister for Finance), (2014), *Smaller and More Rational Government 2014-15*, Ministerial Paper, Canberra: Commonwealth of Australia.

CPI/Centre for Public Integrity, (2020), *Executive law-making doubles while accountability decreases*, Briefing paper, https://publicintegrity.org.au/projects/executive-power/.

CPI/Centre for Public Integrity, (2022), *Delay and decay: Australia's freedom of information crisis*, Briefing paper, August, https://publicintegrity.org.au/wp-content/uploads/2022/09/FOI-Delay-and-Decay-Final.pdf.

CPI/Centre for Public Integrity, (2023), *Opaque big four contracts increase 1276%*, Briefing paper, July. https://publicintegrity.org.au/research_papers/big-four-contracts-increase-1276/.

Craft, J., and Halligan, J., (2020), *Advising Governments in the Westminster Tradition: Policy Advisory Systems in Australia, Britain, Canada and New Zealand*, Cambridge: Cambridge University Press, 2020.

Dassonneville, R., and McAllister, I., (2021), Explaining the decline of political trust in Australia, *Australian Journal of Political Science*, 56(3), 2021, 280-297.

Davis, G., (2021), "The first task is to find the right answer... Public service and the decline of capability", Jim Carlton Annual Integrity Lecture, Melbourne Law School, Melbourne University, 11 May. https:// www.accountabilityrt. org/the-first-task-is-to-find-the-right-answer-public-service-and-the-decline-of-capability/.

de Brouwer, G., Keynote Address, Institute of Public Administration Secretary Series, National Press Club, Canberra, 27 June 2023.

DPMC/Department of the Prime Minister and Cabinet, *APS policy capability roadmap: A practical plan to lift policy capability across the APS*, Canberra: Australian Government, 2019

Edwards, M., Halligan, J., Horrigan, B., and Nicoll, G., *Public Sector Governance in Australia*, Canberra: ANU Press, 2012.

Errington, W., and van Onselen, P. (2021), *How good is Scott Morrison?* Sydney: Hachette Australia.

Evans, H., (2007), "The Senate", in Hamilton", C., and Maddison, S. (2007), *Silencing dissent: How the Australia government is controlling public opinion and stifling debate*, Allen and Unwin, 199-21.

Evans, M., and McCaffrie, B., (2016), "From austerity to the new economy – prime ministerial leadership in a time of mistrust", in C., Aulich (ed.), *From Abbott to Turnbull: A New Direction?* West Geelong: Echo Books, 345-366.

Gaetjens, P., and Woolcott, P., (2020), *Open Letter to the APS*, 4 September.

Gallagher, K., (2022), Albanese Government's APS Reform agenda. Speech to the Institute of Public Administration Australia, 13 October.

Gallagher, K., (2023), Annual Statement on APS Reform, Speech, 2 November. https://ministers.pmc.gov.au/gallagher/2023/annual-statement-aps-reform

Gourley, P., (2023), "What happened to reform 'on steroids'?" *Inside Story*, 14 June. https://insidestory.org.au/what-happened-to-reform-on-steroids/.

Grattan, M., (2019a), "Morrison brings his own man in to head the Prime Minister's department", *The Conversation*, 25 July, https://theconversation.com/morrison-brings-his-own-man-in-to-head-the-prime-ministers-department-120973.

Grattan, M., (2019b), "View from The Hill: Morrison won't have a bar of public service intrusions on government's power", *The Canberra Times*, 13 December, https://theconversation.com/view-from-the-hill-morrison-wont-have-a-bar-of-public-service-intrusions-on-governments-power-128880.

Halligan, J., (2005), "Public Sector Reform", in Aulich, C., and Wettenhall, R. (eds.), *Howard's Second and Third Governments*, Sydney: UNSW Press, 21-41.

Halligan, J., (2008), "The Search for balance and effectiveness in the Australian Public Service" in Aulich, C., and Wettenhall, R., (eds), *Howard's Fourth Government*, Sydney: UNSW Press, 13-30.

Halligan, J., (2016), Mapping the Central State in Australia, Paper for Panel 13 Mapping the State: Old and New Explanatory Perspectives, Research Committee 27, IPSA 2016 World Congress, Poznan, 23-28 July.

Halligan, J., (2020), *Reforming Public Management: Impact and Lessons from Anglophone countries*, Cheltenham: Edward Elgar.

Halligan, J., (2023a), "Public administrative reform" in Australia in S. Goldfinch (ed), *International Handbook of Public Administration Reform*, Cheltenham: Edward Elgar.

Halligan, J., (2023b), "Corruption, Accountability Deficits and Government Failure in Australia", in Farazmand, A., and Atkinson, C., (eds), *Corruption and Accountability Problems in Modern Government: A Comparative Analysis*, Routledge, forthcoming.

Halligan, J., Miller, R., and Power, J., (2007), *Parliament in the 21st century: Institutional reform and emerging roles*, Melbourne University Press, 2007.

Halligan, J., and Wills, J., *The Centrelink Experiment: Innovation in Service Delivery*, ANU Press, 2008.

Halton, J., (Secretary, Department of Finance), (2015), Public Governance, Performance and Accountability Reforms, Speech for 2015 Senate Occasional Lecture Series, Parliament House, Canberra.

Hehir, G., (2023), Keynote, Institute of Public Administration Secretary Series, National Gallery of Australia, Canberra, 12 September.

Hicks, E., (2020), *Private actors and crisis: Scrutinising the National Covid-19 Commission Advisory Board*, Policy Brief No.4, Melbourne School of Government, University of Melbourne. https://government.unimelb.edu.au/__data/assets/ pdf_file/0006/3457725/ GDC-Policy-Brief-4_Private-Actors-and-Crisis_final. pdf.

Hobbs, H. and Williams, G., (2023), "Australian Parliaments and the Pandemic", *University of New South Wales Law Journal*, 46(4), forthcoming.

Human Rights Law Centre, (2022), Morrison government must ensure the independence and effectiveness of the Australian Human Rights Commission, 7 April, https://www.hrlc.org.au/news/2022/4/7/morrison-government-must-ensure-the-independence-and-effectiveness-of-the-australian-human-rights-commission.

IRAPS/Independent Review of the Australian Public Service, (2019), *Our Public Service Our Future: Independent Review of the Australian Public Service*, Canberra: Commonwealth of Australia.

Jones, K., and Prasser, S., (2014), *Audit Commissions: Reviewing the Reviewers*, Connor Court Publishing, Ballarat.

Keane, B., (2021), *Lies and Falsehoods: The Morrison Government and the new culture of deceit*, Richmond: Hardie Grant Books.

Keane, B., (2023), "Mike Pezzullo and the trashing of the Australian Public Service", *The Mandarin*, 26 September.

Kelly, P., (2005), Re-thinking Australian Governance – The Howard Legacy, Cunningham Lecture 2005, *Occasional Paper Series 4/2005*, Canberra: Academy of the Social Sciences in Australia.

McKenzie, N., Bachelard, M., and Ballinger, A., (2023) "Five years. A thousand messages. How a top public servant tried to influence governments", *Sydney Morning Herald*, 24 September, https://www.smh.com.au/national/ five-years-a-thousand-messages-how-a-top-public-servant-tried-to-influence-governments-20230919-p5e5ss.html.

Marsh, I., and Miller, R., (2012), *Democratic Decline and Democratic Renewal: Political Change in Britain, Australia and New Zealand*, Cambridge: Cambridge University Press.

Mazengarb, M., (2022)., Dozens of questions on climate and energy policies go unanswered by Morrison, *Renew Economy*, 24 January.

Middleton, K., (2023), "Delegating Democracy: Parliament in the Morrison Era", in McCaffrie, B., Grattan, M., and Wallace, C., (eds), *The Morrison Government: Governing through crisis, 2019-2022*, UNSW Press, 21-34.

Mills, S., (2020), "Parliament in a Time of Virus: Representative Democracy as a "Non-Essential Service"", *Australasian Parliamentary Review*, 34(2), 7-26.

Morrison, S., (2019), Speech, Institute of Public Administration, 19 August, Canberra: Parliament House.

Morton, D., and Cook, B., (2018), "Evaluators and the enhanced Commonwealth performance framework", *Evaluation Journal of Australasia*, 18(3), pp.141-64.

National Commission of Audit, (2014), *Towards Responsible Government: The Report of the National Commission of Audit Phase One*, Canberra: Commonwealth of Australia.

Nixon, C., (2023), Rapid Review into the Exploitation of Australia's Visa System, 31 March, https://www.homeaffairs.gov.au/reports-and-pubs/files/nixon-review/nixon-review-exploitation-australia-visa-system.pdf.

Parkinson, M., Howe, A., and Azarias, J., (2023), *Review of the Migration System: Final Report*, Australian Government, Department of Home Affairs, Commonwealth of Australia.

Parliament of Australia, (2022), House of Representatives Legislation Statistics, https://www.aph.gov.au//media/02_Parliamentary_Business/22_Chamber_Documents/224_Statistics/House_of_Representatives/Statistics_Historical/legislation_statistics.

Podger, A., (2019), "Report on public service overhaul a good start, but a parliamentary inquiry is needed", *The Conversation*, 19 December, https://theconversation.com/report-on-public-service-overhaul-a-good-start-but-parliamentary-inquiry-is-needed-127602.

Podger, A., (2023a), *Report to the Royal Commission into the Robodebt Scheme*, Royal Commission into the Robodebt Scheme, https://robodebt.royalcommission.gov.au/publications/andrew-podger-ao-report-robodebt-royal-commission.

Podger, A., (2023b), "The Pezzullo Affair shows it's time to clarify the APS values and responsibilities", *The Mandarin*, 6 October.

Podger, A., and Halligan, J., (2023), "Australian Public Service Capability", in Podger, A., Hon Chan, H., Su, T-t and Wanna, J., (eds.), *Dilemmas in Public Management in Greater China and Australia: Rising Tensions but Common Challenges*, Canberra: ANU Press, 375-400.

Prasser, S., (2023), *Politicisation: The attack on merit and our way of life*, The Centre for Independent Studies, Analysis Paper, 52.

RC/Royal Commission into the Robodebt Scheme, (2023), (Royal Commissioner: Catherine Holmes), *Report*, Canberra: Commonwealth of Australia.

RCAGA/Royal Commission on Australian Government Administration (Chairman: H. C. Coombs), (1976), *Report*, Canberra: Australian Government Publishing Service.

RMIT ABC Fact Check (2022), "Haines says the current government has gagged debate in parliament more than any government in history. Is that correct?", https://www.abc.net.au/news/2022-05-11/fact-check-helen-haines-gag-motion-parliament-history/101052778.

Sargeant, J., Coulter, S., Pannell, J., McKee, R. and Hynes, M., (2023), Review of the UK Constitution: *Final Report,* London: Institute for Government and Cambridge: Bennett Institute for Public Policy.

Savva, N., (2022), *Bulldozed: Scott Morrison's fall and Anthony Albanese's rise,* Melbourne: Scribe.

SCA/Sub-Committee on Accreditation, Global Alliance of National Human Rights Institutions, (2022), *Report and recommendations of the virtual session of the sub-committee on accreditation* (SCA), 14-25 March.

SCARC/Senate Community Affairs References Committee (2021), *Centrelink's compliance program – Fifth interim report,* Commonwealth of Australia.

Sedgwick, S., (2020), *Report into consultations regarding APS approaches to ensure institutional integrity,* Canberra: Australian Public Service Commission.

Senate (2022), *President's Report to the Senate on the Status of Government Responses to Parliamentary Committee Reports* as at 30 June.

Senate Hansard (2023)., *Budget – Consideration by Estimates Committees,* Canberra: Commonwealth of Australia, 11 September, 47-8.

SFPARC/Senate Finance and Public Administration References Committee (2005), *Government advertising and accountability,* Australian Government.

Shearer, C., (2022), *Constructing the craft of public administration: Perspectives from Australia,* Cham: Palgrave Macmillan.

SLCARC/Senate Legal and Constitutional Affairs References Committee, (2022), *The Performance and integrity of Australia's administrative review system,* Canberra: Commonwealth of Australia.

Solicitor-General, (2022), In the matter of the validity of the appointment of Mr Morrison to administer the Department of Industry, Science, Energy and Resources.

SSCSDL/Senate Standing Committee for the Scrutiny of De legated Legislation (2021), *Inquiry into the exemption of delegated legislation from parliamentary oversight, Final Report,* Commonwealth of Australia.

Strangio, P., 't Hart, P., and Walter, J., (2017), *The Pivot of Power: Australian prime ministers and political leadership, 1949-2016,* Carlton: Melbourne University Publishing.

Taflaga, M., (2023), "The Liberal Party of Australia", Gauja, A., Sawer, M. and Sheppard, J., (eds.), *Watershed: The 2022 Australian Federal Election,* Canberra: ANU Press.

Tham, J. C., (2019), "Government advertising may be legal, but it's corrupting our electoral process", *The Conversation*, 10 April, https://theconversation.com/government-advertising-may-be-legal-but-its-corrupting-our-electoral-process-115061.

Tiernan, A., (2021), "Accountability is under threat. Parliament must urgently reset the balance", *The Conversation*, 28 October.

Triggs, G., (2018)., Jim Carlton memorial lecture – The decline of democracy in a post truth era, 24 March. https://www.accountabilityrt.org/gillian-triggs-jim-carlton-memorial-lecture-the-decline-of-democracy-in-a-post-truth-era/

Transparency International (2022), Australia's worst-ever corruption score points to urgent need for national integrity commission, 25 January. https://transparency.org.au/worst-ever-corruption-score/

Turnbull, M., and O'Dwyer, K., (2018), Joint Media Release: Review of the Australian Public Service, 4 May.

Twomey, A., (2022a), "Cabinet Conventions and National Cabinet", *Public Law Review*, 33(2), 112-126.

Twomey, A., (2022b), "When is pork barrelling corruption and what can be done to avert it?" In Independent Commission Against Corruption, *Report on investigation into pork barrelling in NSW*, New South Wales Government.

Whealy, A., (2020)., Sports rorts expose coalition's tame corruption watchdog plan, *Australian Financial Review*, 21 January.

Whyte, S., and Rollins, A. (2019) 'Public service overhaul: 18 departments down to 14, five secretaries sacked', *The Canberra Times*, 5 December.

Wilkinson, D., and Morison, E., (2022), Cronyism in Appointments to the AAT: An empirical analysis, Discussion paper, Australia Institute.

Wood, D., Griffiths, K., and Stobart, A., (2022a), *New politics: Preventing pork-barrelling*, Grattan Institute.

Wood, D., Griffiths, K., Stobart, A., and Emslie, O., (2022b), *New politics: A better process for public appointments.* Grattan Institute.

Wood, D., Stobart, A., and Griffiths, K., (2022c), *New politics: Depoliticising taxpayer-funded advertising*, Grattan Institute.

Young, A.L., (2023), *Unchecked Power? How Recent Constitutional Reforms are Threatening UK Democracy*, Bristol University Press.

Young, S., and Tham, J., (2006), *Political Finance in Australia: A Skewed and Secret System, Report No. 7*, Democratic Audit of Australia, Canberra: Australian National University.

Endnotes

1   Phil Gaetjens was critiqued inter alia for his report on the sports rort (Charles and Williams 2022). and for his failure on act on Morrison's secret ministerial appointments (Bell 2022).

2   https://web.archive.org/web/20210320181323/https://www.directory.gov.au/commonwealth-parliament/cabinet/cabinet-committees/cabinet-office-policy-committee

3   See also the Bell (2022) report on the question of multiple portfolios.

4   Examples include the powers for detaining asylum seekers and terror suspects (Triggs 2018).

5   Changes to the Biosecurity Act extended the powers of the minister for health when an emergency existed, but the disallowance option was not available to parliament.

6   According to Middleton (2023, 28), "these concerns predated the pandemic and, in the latter case, dated back to the labour governments of Kevin Rudd and Julia Gillard".

7   A shared services program was implemented to lever economies of scale following recommendations of the National Committee of Audit (NCA 2014; Halton 2015).

8   https://www.apsc.gov.au/initiatives-and-programs/aps-professional-streams

9   However, as the Auditor-General observed (Hehir 2023) departments were not reflecting the expectations in their reporting,

10 For example, the reliance on ministerial advisers in grant allocation processes.

11 Note Podger's (2019) judgement: "The prime minister's claim that his restructuring will ensure "congestion busting" and a much improved "line of sight" is contrived and almost certainly illusory."

12 For a discussion of corruption in the Australian context see Halligan 2023b.

13 Ros Kelly, Minister in the Keating Government, allocated funds that heavily favoured Labor seats (Young and Tham 2006). Unlike the recent cases, the minister resigned.

14 Politicised messaging can also arise in other forms. An egregious example was the health minister's inclusion of his party's logo on a message about the government's purchase of further vaccines (Wood, et al 2022c: 19).

15 Dissenters such as Terry Carney (2018) were not renewed.

16   Public service experts were dismissive of this apparent centrepiece of public service reform for the government's first term (Gourley 2023; Podger 2023b).

17   The Review of Public Sector Board Appointments Processes led by Lynelle Briggs was announced in early 2023. A report was received and public release expected late 2023, but it is still with the government in 2024. https://www.apsc.gov.au/initiatives-and-programs/workforce-information/research-analysis-and-publications/state-service/state-service-report-2023/integrity/review-public-sector-board-appointments-processes.

18   See the debates about the UK constitution (Sargeant et al 2023; Young 2023), and the issues raised in *Policy Options* in Canada during the last year.

5

The Coalition and Public Inquiries 2013-2022

Scott Prasser and Andrea Wallace

Introduction

This chapter analyses the Coalition Government's deployment of public inquiries during its nine years in office. It does not attempt to provide a detailed account of every public inquiry appointed as other studies have done, but rather assesses whether there were any distinguishing features and controversies of the Coalition's use of public inquiries compared to previous governments especially in relation to the most recent Coalition administration, the Howard Government (1996-2007).

Defining public inquiries

Just to be clear, public inquiries in this chapter are defined as those temporary, ad hoc bodies, appointed by executive government with their members drawn from outside government usually having public hearings or some form of public consultations and which release their reports. Public inquiries are not those appointed or run by existing bodies like the Productivity Commissions or by parliamentary committees. Public inquiries may be non-statutory without any powers of investigation which now constitute the majority appointed, or statutorily based inquiries such as royal commissions with coercive powers of investigation. These are fewer in number but the most prestigious and the most expensive form of public inquiry.

Public inquiries have a long history in Westminster democracies like Australia being appointed by the states prior to federation and then by the new Commonwealth Government. Their reports have often been a precursor to major reforms and policy changes and have also exposed corruption and maladministration and reported on calamitous events like natural disaster or accidents. Federally, there was an upsurge in their use with the Whitlam Labor Government (1972-75) which has continued unabated since under subsequent Coalition and Labor administrations (Prasser 2021: 66-72). Analysing a government's use of inquiries can help identify a government's policy priorities, its decision-making style in terms of its willingness to consult, use evidence, rely on expert advice, and to promote open debate.

Issues concerning public inquiries

One of the key issues concerning public inquiries is why they are appointed. Are they are appointed for legitimate reasons to provide expert independent advice, to promote consultation, to clarify the facts about an issue or in some cases to expose corruption? Alternatively are they established for more politically expedient reasons like to delay decision-making, show an illusion of concern, attack opponents, blame avoidance or to find roles for partisans? Another concern has been about the quality of their reports and whether some forms of inquiries like royal commissions are really capable of providing advice on complex policy issues (Phillimore and Wilkins 2023). Lastly, the lack of implementation of their recommendations is another complaint while more recently there has been growing concerns about the powers, costs and duration of some royal commissions.

What the Coalition did

Appendix 1 provides a list of major public inquiries appointed by the Coalition between 2013-2022. It is not comprehensive because of the lack of centralised data records, but it highlights the major inquiries appointed by the Coalition during this period.

Opposition promises

Governments rarely come to office with a clear plan concerning the appointment of public inquiries and their overall role. It is very much an ad hoc affair. They do, however, make promises in opposition concerning the intention to appoint certain inquiries. These inquiries might be on areas where under the previous government policy and administrative flaws have been exposed and there is need for serious review. Some of these might involve a scandal or allegations of corruption which an opposition may want to expose by an inquiry. In other cases, inquiries are promised to appease some group that have a complaint on a particular issue. Making such promises is good politics and easy to do. Inquiries may also be where an opposition has a new policy idea but want it developed further by an expert public inquiry and to test public reaction. Incoming governments usually have some focus on programs and institutions they believe need reviewing partly because of their age and partly to make room for their own initiatives.

Prior to coming to office in 2013 the Coalition had been promising numerous reviews and inquiries – over 50 at one stage, which some thought "could tax its management and political capability" (Uren 2013). Not all were appointed. Some took some other form of more internal reviews or by consultancies, but there several key ones which included:

- *National Commission of Audit* (NCOA) (appointed October 2013)
- *Review of Indigenous Training and Employment* (appointed October 2013)
- *Financial System Inquiry* (appointed November 2013)
- *Review of the National Curriculum* (appointed January 2014)
- *Teacher Education Ministerial Advisory Group* (TEMAG) (appointed February 2014)
- *Royal Commission into the Home Insulation Scheme* (appointed December 2013);
- *Royal Commission into Trade Union Governance and Corruption* (appointed March 2014).

Some of these reflected inquiries of partisan revenge while others had a more ideological orientation.

Inquiries of partisan revenge

The Abbott led Coalition came to office with a reputation of unrelenting attacks on the Rudd and Gillard governments with Abbott being seen as an ideological warrior if a somewhat contradictory one, with a strong chief of staff under Peta Credlin. This combination translated into a government with a strong centralised politically dominated administration under close supervision by the Prime Minister's Office (Grattan 2016; Patrick 2016 – see Chapter 4). Consequently, several of the inquiries promised by the Coalition were seen to be framed very much from this perspective driven primarily by the politics of revenge – to highlight the previous administration's flaws so as to further undermine its credibility. Two royal commissions stood out in this regard – the *Royal Commission into the Home Insulation Scheme* and *Royal Commission into Trade Union Governance and Corruption*.

What made *Royal Commission into the Home Insulation Scheme* appear to be an inquiry seeking revenge was because the home insulation program had long been wound up and been reviewed by a parliamentary committee, the Australian National Audit Office (ANAO) and a external public inquiry and thus a further review, especially a royal commission, was not needed and seemed to some, excessive – a political "witch-hunt" instigated by a very political government.

The other inquiry, the *Royal Commission into Trade Union Governance* while investigating trade union corruption, a legitimate concern, was seen to be more about seeking to embarrass the Labor Party given how trade unions were intricately related to the ALP and that its new leader, Bill Shorten, was a former union leader. Further, argued one senior union official, it was just a continuation of the Coalition's long antipathy against the trade union movement and "getting new ammunition to fight old battles"[1] (Lyons 2014). Moreover, Abbott when a minister in the Howard Government had been instrumental in appointing a royal commission that was seen as an attack on the trade union movement (Marr 2003)[2] so this latest royal commissions was just a continuation of the same approach. Although the Commission's chair,

Dyson Heydon, was a former High Court judge, allegations during the inquiry that he had Liberal Party links, and that only one conviction from the commission's final report was ever successful, added to the perception that this royal commission was politically motivated.

There was a counter to these assessments. *The Royal Commission into the Home Insulation Scheme* for instance, was assessed as revealing flaws in Commonwealth government decision making and administration not previously exposed and thus deserved attention (Sedgwick 2015). Similalrly, the *Royal Commission into Trade Union Governance* despite its political motivation highlighted serious regulatory gaps in relation to trade unions that were subsequently addressed by the Coalition (Forsyth 2017).

Of course, to place these inquiries into context it should be appreciated that other governments have appointed inquiries, including royal commissions, as acts of political revenge (see Prasser 2021: 174-8). The most recent example being the Albanese Government's *Royal Commission into the Robodebt Program* (Holmes Royal Commissiom) which some saw as being very much in the same vein. After all, the program had been wound up, compensation paid and some administrative processes changed. What had not been achieved was the full exposure of the Coalition's responsibility for the mismanagement of the scheme which is what the Holmes Royal Commission achieved. The more telling issue though, for the Coalition, was whether their royal commissions were not so much needed but whether they were worth it politically in terms of the damage they inflicted on the previous administrations? Or did they tarnish more the Coalition allowing it, and especially Prime Minister Abbott, to be easily painted as an ideological, fixated and revengeful government and prime minister acting more like they are still in opposition scoring points than seeking to govern the country? The issue should rest with former Liberal Prime Minister, John Howard assessment. He believed these two royal commissions had been formed for "narrow targeted political purposes" that was "an abuse of power" and smacked of being a "political vendetta" and therefore were ill-advised (Howard 2014).

Ideological and partisan inquiries

Related to inquiries of revenge are those inquiries that seem to pursue purely ideological and partisan goals under the guise of an "independent" public inquiry. Such inquiries produce contrived reports giving the government predetermined findings. Many governments have appointed such inquiries although some do it better than others by careful selection of members, cleverly worded terms of reference and processes that can withstand criticism. As a result, their reports are gauged as being legitimate and there is greater success in their recommendations being actually implemented with limited resistance (Prasser 2021: 170-3).

Certainly, several early Coalition inquiries were seen as being just fronts for the new government's perceived ideological agenda. Foremost of these was the *National Commission of Audit* (NCOA), promised, as noted, by the Coalition whilst in opposition, to "examine the scope and efficiency of the Commonwealth Government" (NCOA 2014: i). The NCOA was seen as a vehicle to implement the Coalition's supposed "neoliberal" agenda of expenditure and programs cuts. Similar bodies had been appointed by incoming Howard Government and several State Coalition governments (Jones and Prasser 2013). The NCOA's impact, however, like the similar body established by the incoming Howard Government, was minimal. It reported too late for the 2014-15 Budget and thus predictions that it would herald major cuts were unfounded and so instead it should be seen "mostly as theatre" (Wettenhall and Gourley 2016: 79). Again, the NCOA was another example of further misjudgement by the Abbott Government. Was it created primarily to satisfy the party faithful or was it really designed to provide a blueprint to the new government? In the end it was largely ignored thus dashing the hopes of supporters, but in the meantime, it had created unnecessary adverse publicity and speculation as to where "cuts" might occur.

The *Review of the Australian Curriculum* was another inquiry initially perceived on its appointment to be ideological. This was primarily because one of its two members, Dr Kevin Donnelly, was regarded as a "ideological warrior" since he had been a member of the right of centre Institute of Public Affairs and had worked in previous Liberal administrations. In addition, its second member, Professor Ken Wiltshire was described as a "business academic" lacking in educational expertise[3] (Taylor 2018: 260-1). Regardless, this inquiry's final report was moderate, largely endorsed the National Curriculum, and its major recommendations were accepted by the Education Council. Early critics of the inquiry came to see the review as making worthwhile findings (Louden 2014). It also received a good response from key education professional groups. This is another inquiry where there were legitimate public concerns and which could have avoided adverse reactions had more care been made about its membership.

Criticisms of a different kind were levelled at the *Teacher Education Ministerial Advisory Group* (TEMAG). The criticism was largely not that it was ideological or that the review was not needed, but rather that it was chaired by Greg Craven, Vice-Chancellor of the Australian Catholic University, Australia's largest provider of teacher courses that had often been criticised for its low entry requirements. Consequently, some saw Craven as being inappropriate to head an inquiry to improve the quality of initial teacher education courses (McTiernan 2015). This criticism ignored that the Review had seven other members from a wide cross-section of the teaching profession, other universities and recognised education experts. The final report's recommendations were well received, endorsed by Education Council, and largely implemented over the succeeding terms of the Coalition.

There were other inquiries that while having members who appeared to be partisan did not produce partisan or ideological reports. For instance, the *Review of the Demand Driven Funding System* concerning universities with David Kemp, a former Liberal education minister and Andrew Norton his one-time adviser, endorsed the demand driven system of the previous government contrary to the government's expectations while some of its warnings were ignored (Bell and Probert 2016: 230-01).

The lessons from these inquiries is that sensitive and important inquiries require subtle handling by a government in terms of their announcements, terms of reference and memberships to avoid them being unnecessarily attacked. These inquiries and royal commissions demonstrated how the Coalition exercised considerable political misjudgement in the selection of their memberships and how they framed and presented these inquiries. As a result, the Coalition in several major policy areas failed to shift the focus of the debate and thus policy direction, from where it had long been, to where they had long advocated.

Inquiries appointed for policy renewal and evaluation

Governments often appoint inquiries to evaluate a policy, program or institution to promote policy renewal. Sometimes it is one inherited from its predecessor. It may also be where there was already strong bipartisan support, success and where they have had some major role in the past. Appointing such inquiries reminds the electorate of a government's earlier leadership in the area. Several inquiries stand out in this regard.

The most significant was the Murray *Inquiry into the Financial System* (2013). The Coalition in 1979 had appointed the first review into this area – the *Committee of Inquiry into the Australian Financial System* (Campbell Inquiry) that began the move to financial deregulation. It was followed by Labor's *Inquiry into Australia's Financial System Inquiry* (Martin Inquiry 1983) that allowed the Hawke-Keating Government to progress the implementation of the Campbell Report. The momentum was maintained and refreshed by Howard Government's 1996 *Inquiry into the Financial System* (Wallis Inquiry) which reinvigorated the policy. Given that it had been seventeen years since the Wallis Review, then the appointment of the Murray Review was overdue. It reflected the Coalition's continuing stake in this policy area. Its membership was expert, like Murray himself, its processes exemplary and its recommendations accepted and implemented over several subsequent years. It was complemented by the Harper-led *Competition Policy Review* which "undertook a stocktake of the competition policy framework across the Australian economy". Nor was Murray Review compromised by the later more regulatory oriented *Royal Commission into Misconduct in the Banking, Superannuation and Financial Services Industry* as Murray himself later confirmed (Murray 2020).

Yet, important as these inquiries were, and although in line with previous Coalition policy directions, they did not seem to have the same public profile, interest and impact as their predecessors. Nor it seemed did they attract the same level of interest by the Coalition as had been the case previously. Perhaps it was because they were not as groundbreaking as they were originally. There were also the distractions of the ongoing turmoil within the government concerning the negative fallout from the Coalition's first 2014-15 budget, disquiet about the performance of Joe Hockey as Treasurer, and then Abbott's replacement by Turnbull.

The *Reference Group on Welfare* under Patrick McClure was another inquiry about policy renewal. It was a follow up to the Howard Government's 1999 *Welfare Reference Group* also chaired by McClure, and regarded as being successful in terms of impact and implementation (McClure 2021). McClure believed welfare reform was an ongoing process and thus he saw this second inquiry as an extension of the first. As is examined in more detail in this volume (see Chapter 10) this second review did not have the same impact as the first, becoming a victim, as is the theme of this volume, of the Coalition's internal turmoil, the change of leadership and responsible minister[4] and the lack of clear strategic policy direction.

Another inquiry that was an overdue review of an important and changing area was the *Independent Review of Nursing Education* appointed in December 2018 by the National Party Minister for Regional Health, Senator McKenzie. The previous nursing review had reported in 2002 under the Howard Government. Chaired by Professor Steven Schwartz, it reported in September 2019 and made important recommendations about the quality of nursing education. Oddly, it took the Health Minister Hunt (McKenzie had changed portfolios) two years (September 2021) to respond to the Review's 26 recommendations (Hunt 2021), which at best can be described as perfunctory. It seems odd that a government appoints an inquiry and then takes so long to respond to its recommendations. This delay, combined with the poor response to the recommendations, suggests the Nursing Review, established as it was before the 2019 election, was very much just one of showing symbolic concern (Bolton 2020). It was another missed opportunity.

Another major inquiry of review was the non-statutory *Independent Review of the Public Service* (Thodey Review) and is discussed in Chapter 4. Appointed by Turnbull but reporting to the Morrison Government and with different ministers overseeing the process, it has had mixed reviews with some arguing its motivation was unclear, its terms of reference imprecise, its membership lopsided, its methodology fumbling, its research base thin and its impact uncertain (see Gourley 2023). Every government it seems likes to have a major review of the Australian Public Service, but since Whitlam's 1974 *Royal Commission into Australian Government Administration* (Coombs Commission), none have come up to the same mark and the Thodey Review confirmed that trend.

For a political party supposedly not strongly interested in education it is worth noting that the Coalition appointed 16 inquiries into school, university and vocation education issues during this period[5] (see **Appendix 1**). This is highest number appointed among the last five federal governments (Whitlam, Fraser, Hawke-Keating, Howard, Rudd-Gillard).[6] Eight inquiries were into universities, one into vocational education, and the remainder into schools related matters (as mentioned). Perhaps, this number reflected the Coalition's desire to raise their profile in this area, to resolve some of their own policy dilemmas and those made in response to emerging challenges confronting the sector. Of interest is that Education Minister Senator Birmingham had his Department of Education and Training (DE&T) review of just the university funding reviews conducted since 1988. There had been eight in all (DE&T 2015). The report noted the similarity of many of the different reports including those dating back to the Howard Government's 1997 West *Review of Higher Education* to which it inexplicably never responded.

The cult of the royal commission?

The most distinctive feature of the Coalition's use of inquiries during this period was its quick and frequent resort to royal commissions, appointing eight in nine years (see **Appendix 1** and **Table 1**). While fewer in number compared to some previous federal governments,[7] it was nevertheless a significant number, an increase over its immediate

Labor predecessor (that had appointed only one royal commission) and more than the four appointed by the Howard Government.

As discussed, the first two appointed by the Abbott Government were seen to have been highly politically motivated. Two more were appointed by the Turnbull Government (see **Table 1**) in response to erupting scandals and media coverage. The first of these, the *Royal Commission into the Protection and Detention of Children in the Northern Territory* (2016) was a joint Federal-Northern Territory inquiry that was established quickly once the issue had aired on national television. By contrast, the second, *Royal Commission into Misconduct in the Banking, Superannuation and Financial Services Industry* (Hayne Royal Commission) had been resisted by the Turnbull Government for some twelve months arguing that existing regulatory arrangements were able to deal with the complaints of banks' wrongdoing. Eventually, given media pressure and that from the National Party, never an admirer of banks, the Turnbull Government relented. Its announcement was seen as an embarrassing backdown by the government. The Hayne Royal Commission was to have major reverberations across the banking sector. Some commentators saw it have negative impacts on the economy (Mohl 2019). Others thought it had been too soft on the banks (Economist 2019). The opposition complained that the Coalition was not fully implementing its recommendations (see Coorey 2019).

The remaining four royal commissions were appointed by the Morrison Government. It is these that have attracted particular attention because of the number appointed, their timing of appointment, the nature of several of their topics and the way they set the policy agenda in different areas. The first of these was appointed only a month after Morrison became prime minister in August 2018 (*Royal Commission into Aged Care Quality and Safety*) and just six months out from the impending federal election. The second, the *Royal Commission into Violence, Abuse, Neglect and Exploitation of People with Disability* was appointed in April 2019 later on the very eve of the May election. Both these royal commissions had the hallmarks of being part of an election strategy of clearing the decks of any possible issues that could undermine the Coalition's immediate electoral prospects. Such inquiries are labelled as governments using inquiries for "kicking an issue into the long grass" or blame avoidance. What better way to do so, it has been argued, than to appoint a royal commission which does not to report till way after an election (Sulitzeanu-Kenan 2006). The *Royal Commission into National Natural Disaster Arrangements* was the third appointed and established in 2020 was a typical response to a calamitous bushfires that ravaged New South Wales and Victoria during 2019-20 (Eburn and Dover 2015). It was also an area where Morrison had received considerable criticism for being absent on an overseas holiday at this time so this royal commission could be seen as having wider political motivations than many other disaster reviews (Schirmer and Dare 2023: 233).

The last one, the *Royal Commission into Defence and Veteran Suicide,* was interesting given that the Morrison Government had already formed a permanent commission to investigate these issues with equivalent royal commissions powers of investigation.[8] This did not satisfy, however, those groups and individuals personally affected by such tragic events (O'Sullivan 2021). They were desirous of elevating the issue further and having a dedicated royal commission was, in their eyes, the best way to achieve that goal. The increasingly politically vulnerable Morrison Government thus gave in to such public pressure and established in July 2021 a stand-alone royal commission.

This demand for royal commissions and the Coalition Government's too easy willingness to comply, has provoked some commentators to argue that this represents a dangerous trend of the "cult of the royal commission" (Kelly 2020) – the belief that because of a loss of trust in existing government institutions and the inability of the increasingly fractious political system to forge consensus, only a royal commission can deliver solutions to complex policy and political issues. It is argued that this resort to royal commissions is not some passing fad but reflects as Kenenth Hayne observed, who chaired the *Royal Commission into Banking,* that such continued demand for royal commissions indicates that something is amiss "about the state of our democratic institutions". They are no longer trusted to perform their basic policy development, adjudicatory and investigatory functions (Hayne 2019: 8).

Consequently, in these circumstances royal commissions receive a status so elevated that it makes it difficult for any government to reject or even to moderate their recommendations, regardless of how inappropriate or costly they may be. Such criticisms are not new. They have been made in the past concerning narrowly focussed disaster inquiries (Eburn and Dover 2015), but is becoming increasingly applied to recent royal commissions. Indeed, a major criticism of the *Royal Commission on Aged Care* was that it proposed massive increases in spending that was not only outside its terms of reference, but ignored already large expenditure increases in this and related areas (Carling 2023).

The other problem with some inquiries with multiple members is their failure to produce a unanimous report. This undermines any inquiry's credibility, impact and thus its value in tackling major issues. *The Royal Commission on Aged Care* two royal commissioners disagreed on 43 of the 148 recommendation (Burton 2021). Similalrly, the final report of the *Royal Commission into Disability* was characterised by disagreements among its seven members on several key issues and thus was seen to have been a major failure (see Chambers 2023).

Table 1: Royal commission appointed 2013-2022

Royal Commission	Date of appointment	Prime Minister	Members	Chair
Royal Commission into Institutional Responses into Child Sexual Abuse	2013	Gillard (ALP)	6	Former Supreme Court Judge
Royal Commission into the Home Insulation Scheme	2013	Abbott	1	Former Supreme Court Judge
Royal Commission into Trade Union Governance and Corruption	2014	Abbott	1	Former High Court judge
Royal Commission into the Protection and Detention of Children in the Northern Territory	2016	Turnbull	2	Former Supreme Court Judge
Royal Commission into Misconduct in the Banking, Superannuation and Financial Services Industry	2017	Turnbull	1	Former High Court judge

Royal Commission into Aged Care Quality and Safety	2018	Morrison	2	Former Public Service Commissioner and former Federal Court judge
Royal Commission into Violence, Abuse, Neglect and Exploitation of People with Disability	2019	Morrison	7	Former State Supreme Court judge
Royal Commission into National Natural Disaster Arrangements	2020	Morrison	3	Ex-military office holder
Royal Commission into Defence and Veteran Suicide	2021	Morrison	3	Former deputy commissioner NSW Police

One other issue is the costs of royal commissions. There has long been concerns about royal commissions costs which are more expensive than non-statutory inquiries because of their formal and quasi-legal procedures. Prior to the Coalition the most expensive Australian public inquiry to date was the 2013 *Royal Commission into Institutional Responses to Child Sexual Abuse* which cost $342 million. This has been surpassed by the *Royal Commission into Disability* estimated to cost $527 million when it was established but has now reportedly to cost $600 million.

Conclusion

Overall, the Coalition Government appointed a moderate number of public inquiries, mostly of the policy advisory non-statutory type, but at a slower rate than many of its predecessors. Some had been promised in opposition reflecting the Coalition's particular preferred policy directions. Others were appointed in response to unexpected crises and events or when some policy problem emerged. Most served legitimate public policy purposes of consultation, gathering of evidence and review by expert members. Like with inquiries appointed by previous governments those appointed by the Coalition had varying impacts. Some had their recommendations quickly accepted but their implementation was slow. Others which had their implementation closely monitored and supported by ministers and departments had more success. And some, like the Nursing Review were almost ignored and the government responses perfunctory. In several cases the Coalition appointed inquiries into issues that although highly sensitive and political in nature, nevertheless had real issues to be reviewed like the two royal commissions into the home insulation scheme and trade union governance, and the *National Curriculum Inquiry* but were handled in a ham-fisted way in terms of their membership and general establishment. These inquiries were not perceived to be completely independent, that most valuable asset that a public inquiry brings to government, and thus were devalued despite their potentially important findings.

Under Morrison the Coalition came under more strident criticism concerning its over-willingness to appoint royal commissions to get itself out of a difficult political situation rather than to confront the problems in the areas under review and attack. This may be because of Coalition's political vulnerability after the 2016 election when it only had a one seat majority. Such vulnerability was heightened by Coalition's internal instability with the turnover of prime ministers and ministers (and leaders of the National Party). Increasingly, the Coalition looked more and more like what frustrated its supporters and attracted wider criticisms – a government totally politically driven for immediate survival, unable to steer to any true course, to maintain any consistency, so as to arrive at any desired policy destination.

Despite being in office for nine years the Coalition never saw the public inquiry as anything more than an instrument for executive government manipulation. Suggestions by former Labor Treasurer John Dawkins (1984) to better integrate public inquiries into the policy development process like in Scandinavian countries (Pronin 2023) was beyond its scope, but it in that the Coalition was not alone. Oddly, although appointing eight royal commissions, the Coalition never showed any awareness of the 2009 Australia Law Reform Commission's (ALRC 2009) review of the *Royal Commission Act 1902* (Cth) that had been appointed by the Rudd Government. To date, no government, Labor or Coalition has ever responded to its 80 of more recommendations that may have improved the public inquiry instrument.

What was distinctive about the Coalition and its employment of public inquiries? The answer is that it wasn't – distinct that is, just more of the same "ad hocery", appointing inquiries for a mixture of reasons, and as Patrick McClure says in Chapter 10 concerning his inquiry – it was a missed opportunity all round.

References

Australian Law Reform Commission, (ALRC), *Making Inquiries: A New Statutory Framework*, Report 111, Canberra: Commonwealth Government, 2009

Bolton R., "Government in no hurry on nursing", *Australian Financial Review*, 9 November 2020

Burton, T., "Why we need a royal commission into royal commissions", *Australian Financial Review*, 6 March 2021

Carling, R., "The fiscal implications of public inquiries", in Prasser, S., (ed), *New directions in royal commissions and public inquiries: Do we need them?* Redland Bay: Connor Court Publishing, 2023, 243-56

Chambers, G., "Disability royal commission: Dithering fuels discord and an uncertain future for many of our most vulnerable", *The Australian*, 29 September 2023

Coorey, P., "Labor says PM squibbed on Hayne", *Australian Financial Review*, 6 February 2019

Dawkins, J., "Reforms in the Canberra System of Public Administration", Sir Robert Garran Oration, 15 November 1984, in *Commonwealth Record*, 12-18 November, 1984, 2315-21

Department of Education and Training, *Higher Education in Australia: A review of reviews from Dawkins to today,* Canberra; Department Education and Training, 2015

Eburn, M., and Dover, S., "Learning Lessons from Disasters: Alternatives to Royal Commissions and Other Quasi-Judicial Inquiries", *Australian Journal of Public Administration,* 74(4), 2015, 495-508

Economist The, "Australian banks: Profit and Loss", 9 February 2019, 60

Forsyth, A., "Law, Politics and Ideology: The Regulatory Response to Trade Union Corruption in Australia", *University of New South Wales Law Journal,* 40(4), 2017, 1-30

Gourley, P., "The 2018-19 Thodey Review into the Australian Public Service", in Prasser, *New directions for royal commissions and public inquiries,* Redland Bay", 149-170

Grattan, M., "There's never been a better time to change Prime Minister" in Aulich, C., (ed), *From Abbott to Turnbull: A New Direction?* West Geelong: Echo Books, 2016, 1-22

Grattan, M., "The Morrison Government, 2019-2022: A Story of Crisis and Character", in McCaffrie et al, *The Morrison Government*, 1-20

Hayne, K.M., "On Royal Commission", Address, Centre for Comparative Constitutional Studies Conference, Melbourne Law School, 26 July 2019

Howard, J.W., *John Howard: Lazarus Rising - A Personal and Political Autobiography,* Sydney: HarperCollins, 2010

Howard, J.W., "John Howard questions Coalition's two royal commission", *The Guardian,* 15 September 2014

Hunt, G., *Australian Government Response to the Independent Review of Nursing Education,* Canberra: Commonwealth of Australia, September 2021

Jones, K., and Prasser, S., *Audit Commissions: Reviewing the Reviewers,* Melbourne: Connor Court, 2013

Kelly, P., "The cult that won false hopes in 2020", *The Australian,* 23 December 2020

Louden, W., "National Curriculum Review", *The Conversation,* 12 October 2014

Lyons, T., "Crippling Unions: Abbott's Anti-Worker Agenda", Speech at Chifley Research Centre, Melbourne, 29 October 2014

Marr, J., *First the Verdict: The Real Story of the Building Industry Royal Commission,* Annandale: Pluto Press, 2003

McCaffrie, B., Grattan, M., and Wallace, C., (eds), *The Morrison Government: Governing through Crisis, 2019-2022- Australian Commonwealth Administration Series,* Sydney: UNSW Press, 2023, 1-20

McClure, P., "Hearts and heads" The Challenge of welfare reform", in Frame, T., (ed), *The Desire for Change, 2004-2007 The Howard Government Volume IV,* Sydney: UNSW Press, 177-93

McTiernan, A., MP, *Commonwealth Parliamentary Debates,* House of Representatives, 11 August 2015, 89

Mohl, A., "Hayne's $65b shock" *Australian Financial Review,* 13 December 2019

Murray, D., "David Murray's verdict on the Hayne Commission", *Australian Financial Review,* 2 February 2020

O'Sullivan, K., "Defence families put long-tested faith in suicide inquiry", *The Australian,* 26 April 2021

Patrick, A., *Credlin & Company: How the Abbott Government Destroyed Itself,* Carlton: Black Inc Publishing, 2016

Phillimore, J., and Wilkins, P., "Can – and should – royal commissions provide policy advice? in Prasser, *New directions in royal commissions and public inquiries,* 277-292

Pronin, K., "Commissions of inquiry in the Nordic countries", in Prasser, *New directions in royal commissions and public inquiries,* 367-86

Prasser, S., *Royal Commissions and Public Inquiries in Australia,* Sydney: LexisNexis, 2021

Regan, S., *Australia's Welfare System: A Review of Reviews: 1941-2013,* Canberra: ANU Press

Schirmer, J., and Dare, L., "Navigating Cumulative Disaster: Drought, Bushfire, Flood and Pandemic," in McCaffrie et al, *The Morrison Government,* 227-39

Sedgwick, S., "Still more to learn from 'pink batts", *Canberra Times,* 4 August 2014

Sulitzeanu-Kenan, R., "Scything the grass: agenda setting consequences of appointing public inquiries in the UK: A longitudinal study", *Policy and Politics,* 35(4), 2006, 629-50

Tylor, T., *Class Wars: Money, Schools and Power in Modern Australia,* Clayton: Monash University Press, 2018.

Uren, D., "Too many inquiries could prove taxing for the Coalition", *The Australian,* 6 June 2013

Wettenhall, R., and Gourley, P., "The public sector", in Aulich, *From Abbott to Turnbull,* 69-91

APPENDIX 1:

INQUIRIES APPOINTED BY THE COALITION 2013-2022

(Each entry includes inquiry chair and the number of members)

2013

National Commission of Audit
    Shepherd [3]
Review of Demand Driven Funding System
    Kemp-Norton [2]
Financial System Inquiry
    Murray [5]
Review of Indigenous Training and Employment
    Forrest [1]
Inquiry into Online Health Record System
    Royle [3]
Aviation Safety Regulation review
    Forsyth [3]
Reference Group on Welfare Reform
    McClure [3]
Royal Commission into the Home Insulation Scheme
    Hanger [1]
Review of the Australian Curriculum
    Donnelly-Wiltshire [2]

2014

Independent Review into Port of Gladstone
    Johnson [3]
Expert Panel into renewable Energy Target Scheme
    Warburton [4]
Teacher Education Ministerial Advisory Group
    Craven [8]
Royal Commission into Trade Union Governance and Corruption
    Heydon [1]
First Principles review of Defence
    Peever [1]
National Opera Review
    Nugent [4]
Review of Medicines and Medical Services Regulation
    Sanson [3]
Competition Policy Review
    Harper [4]

2015
Defence Abuse Taskforce
    Cornall [1]
Review of research Policy and Funding Arrangements
        Watt [3]

2016
Royal Commission into the Protection and Detention of Children in the Northern Territory[9]
        White and Gooda [2]
Independent Intelligence Review
        L'Estrange [2]

2017
Expert Advisory Panel on National Year 1 Literacy and Numeracy Check
        Buckingham [6]
Inquiry into National Freight and Supply Chain Priorities
        Calfas [4]
Independent Review into Rural, Regional and Remote Education
        Halsey [1]
Indian Economic Strategy
        Varghese [1]
Review to Achieve Educational Excellence in Schools
        Gonski [8]
Review of Australian Sports Integrity Arrangements
        Wood [3]
Royal Commission into Misconduct in the Banking, Superannuation and Financial Services Industry
        Hayne [1]
Review of the Australian Charities and Not for Profits Commission Legislation
        McClure [4]

2018
Review of the regulatory Capability and Culture of the Department of Agriculture and Water Resources in the Regulation of Live Animal exports
        Moss [1]
Comprehensive Review of the Legal Framework of the National Intelligence Community
        Richardson [1]
Independent Review of the Australian Public Service
        Thodey [6]
Review of the Australian Qualifications Framework
        Noonan [7]

Review of the Higher Education Provider Category Standards
    Coaldrake [1]
Royal Commission into Aged Care Quality and Safety
    Briggs and Pagone [2]
Independent Review of Freedom of Speech in Australian Higher Education Providers
    Franch [1]
Expert review of Australian Vocational and tTaining System
    Joyce [1]
Review into Integration, Employment and Settlement Outcomes
    Shergold [1]

2019
Independent Panel Report on Fish Deaths
    Vertessy [1]
Independent Review of Nursing Education
    Schwartz [1]
Review of Australia's Science and Research Priorities
    Thomas [9]
Royal Commission into Violence, Abuse, Neglect and Exploitation of People with Disability
    Sackville [7]
Review of Senior Secondary Pathways into Work, Further Education and Training
    Shergold [7]
Independent Review of the Retirement Income System
    Callaghan [3]
Review of Foreign Aid Priorities
    Richardson [1]

2020
Royal Commission into National Natural Disaster Arrangements
    Binskin [3]
National Review of Hotel Quarantine (First Review)
    Hilton [1]

2021
Quality Initial Teacher Education Review
    Paul [4]
Regional Telecommunications Review
    Hartsuyker [5]

Royal Commission into Defence and Veteran Suicide
Kaldas [3]
National Review of Quarantine (second review)
Halton [1]
National Mental Health Workforce Strategy Independent Taskforce
Taylor and Brideson [21]
Defence Innovation Review
Peever [1]
Review of the Australian Payments Systems
Farrell [1]

2023
Quality of Advice Review
Levy [1]

Endnotes

1   This refers to the Fraser Coalition Government's *Royal Commission into the Federated Ship Painters' and Dockers' Union* (Costigan Royal Commission) which was seen as a vehicle to attack the then Labor opposition, though it actually backfired on the Fraser Government.

2   This refers to the Howard Government's 2001 *Royal Commission into the Building and Construction Industry* and the Howard Government's waterfront reforms.

3   Professor Ken Wiltshire was the JD Story Professor of Public Administration at the University of Queensland and so was not a "business academic" and had conducted several reviews for federal and state Labor administrations on curriculum and education related issues.

4   Kevin Andrews had been the sponsoring minister of the second McClure Review but he lost his ministerial position when Turnbull became prime minister in September 2015.

5   This excludes the NCOA which had several chapters of school funding and universities.

6   The Rudd-Gillard governments appointed, 5; Howard Government, 6; Hawke-Keating, 24; Fraser, 8, and Whitlam 20, though the different lengths of office of each government needs to be appreciated.

7   Whitlam 13, Fraser, 8, Hawke-Keating 12, Howard 4, Rudd-Gillard 1.

8   National Commissioner for Defence and Veteran Suicide Prevention.

9   A joint Commonwealth and Northern Territory royal commission.

Part 3: Managing the Policies

6

Economic Policy

Robert Carling

Introduction

This chapter aims to evaluate the economic policy record of the Coalition governments in office from September 2013 to May 2022. Although the Liberal and National parties were in office in coalition throughout this period there were in fact three governments led by Tony Abbott, Malcolm Turnbull and Scott Morrison, each with its own distinctive policy emphases and each dealing with a different set of background conditions.

In evaluating the economic policies of these governments, we first examine the results of macroeconomic stabilisation polices and distinguish between the period before the coronavirus pandemic and the period of the pandemic, which produced unique challenges. This part focuses on fiscal and monetary policies and results in terms of the volatility of economic growth, employment, unemployment and inflation.

The second part looks at the underlying performance of the economy as measured by average growth rates and trends in productivity and living standards. We examine where the policies that could have made improvements in these areas were adopted or were lacking, and the extent to which the Coalition adhered to its stated core values.

Framework for assessment

The framework for assessment of the Coalition Governments' economic policies used here is in two parts.

The first element is basic macro-economic management that any government regardless of political colour should be expected to handle responsibly. These are matters such as budget deficits and debt, inflation and the policy responses to exogenous shocks such as the Global Financial Crisis and the coronavirus pandemic.

But economic policy isn't only a matter of responsible macro-economic management. The second set of criteria consists of the core values, guiding beliefs and ideological leaning that political parties bring to the task of economic policy in government. Parties do not commit in detail to any particular ideology, but they do place their policies loosely under the umbrella of a set of principles drawn from their favoured ideology or branch of economic thought.

The Liberal Party, for example, has never been wholly committed to free market or classical liberalism, but has espoused some of the principles drawn from these doctrines or some approximation of them.

Parties' statements of principles reveal how they believe they can best achieve economic advancement to the benefit of the citizenry at large. In government they can be assessed according to the quality of these principles, their consistency in adhering to them and the results in the form of economic and employment growth, productivity growth, unemployment and the trend in living standards.

Basic macroeconomic management

Such was the magnitude of the coronavirus pandemic shock and its economic impact that in assessing the macro-economic management performance of the Abbott, Turnbull and Morrison Coalition Governments of 2013 to 2022 it is best to examine two separate timespans: the years before the coronavirus pandemic, approximated in financial year terms as 2013-14 to 2018-19; and the years of the pandemic, approximated as 2019-20 to 2021-22.

This is the approach taken in **Table 1**, which also displays averages for previous ten-year periods for comparison.

The Liberals' 2013 election platform was summarised in Tony Abbott's oft-repeated pledge to "end the waste, repay the debt, stop the new taxes and stop the boats" (Abbott 2010). This related in part to macro-economic management. The Coalition Government also declared a "budget emergency" (Abbott 2013) – the rhetorical equivalent of budget "black holes" discovered by previous new governments.

Table 1: Fiscal and inflation indicators, period averages

	9 years to 2021-22	3 years pandemic	6 years pre-pandemic	10 years to 2012-13	10 years to 2002-03
Percent of GDP					
Underlying budget cash balance	-2.5	-4.1	-1.7	-0.6	-0.6
Budget payments	26.3	28.7	25.1	24.3	24.8
Tax receipts	22.3	22.7	22.1	22.4	22.4
General government debt (end-period):					
Gross – at face value	39.0	39.0	27.8	16.8	7.2
Net – at market value	22.5	22.5	19.2	10.4	4.2
Percent Growth					
Real per capita budget payments	2.5	5.4	0.7	1.9	1.7
Consumer Price Index	2.3	3.2	1.9	2.7	2.6

Sources: Commonwealth Budget Papers, Oct. 2022, BP1, Statement 11
Consumer Price Index, March Quarter 2023, Australian Bureau of Statistics

Emergency or not, the budget had been in persistent and sizeable deficit since the Rudd government's large fiscal stimulus in 2008 and 2009 in response to the Global Financial Crisis (GFC). As a result,

Commonwealth public debt had increased substantially from the very low levels left by the Howard government in 2007.

To call this an "emergency" was an overstatement that Abbott probably came to regret when the deficits proved difficult to reverse in government, but the label served a political purpose.

Meanwhile Joe Hockey, as Treasurer-to-be, had declared that what he termed "the age of entitlement" (Hockey 2012) had ended, attempting to prepare the ground for restraint in social security and welfare spending, which was rightly seen as the key to enduring reductions in the budget deficit. As Hockey was to find in the public and media response to his first budget in 2014, the sense of entitlement in the community was in fact still very much alive.

One of the new government's first acts – following in the Howard Government's footsteps – was to appoint a National Commission of Audit (NCA) of government expenditure (Griffiths 2014). The Commission was headed by prominent businessman Tony Shepherd, assisted by former Secretaries to the Departments of Treasury and Finance among others. The Commission was asked to make recommendations that would produce a sustainable budget surplus of 1 per cent of GDP within ten years. It duly produced a report with many recommendations, including controversial measures such as a lift in the age pension eligibility age to 70 and the introduction of a patient co-payment with Medicare benefits (NCA 2014).

Some of the Commission's recommendations were included in the Abbott Government's first budget in May 2014. With the benefit of hindsight, the media and public hostility to that budget made it one of the defining moments of the Abbott Government and on some accounts marked the beginning of the end of Abbott's leadership.

The budget also included a temporary (three year) increase in the top marginal rate of personal income tax (the budget repair levy) – as much to demonstrate that the burden of fiscal consolidation was being shared as for the amount of extra revenue it would raise. While the levy was one of the few measures actually implemented – making a mockery of the government's claim to adhere to the principle of low taxation – it did nothing to appease those portraying the budget as an assault on the welfare state.

Despite a firestorm of criticism, the 2014 budget's expenditure restraint measures were in aggregate modest by the standards of earlier fiscal consolidation episodes such as those of the Hawke Government in the late 1980s and the Howard Government in the late 1990s. Policy measures were expected to clip $44 billion from aggregated deficits in the four years to 2017-18[1] – a figure that includes the revenue benefit of the budget repair levy – and a little more than 1 per cent of GDP in the fourth year itself. These are not huge sums.

The fate of the 2014 budget was not helped by the political composition of the Senate, where the government lacked the numbers to implement expenditure restraint measures, but other contributing factors included: unwise commitments made in the 2013 election campaign which came back to haunt the government; the political failure after the election to prepare public opinion for a tough budget; and the cumulative impact of a long-term shift in the electorate towards dependence on government.

In the event, deficits in the four years from 2014-15 exceeded the estimates in that year's budget by a total of $60 billion. Curiously, however, expenditure actually undershot the estimates despite the failure of many of the restraint measures to be implemented. Rather, it was a revenue shortfall of $80 billion that more than accounted for the deficit over-run as commodity export prices and wage growth were both weak, eroding company tax and personal income tax revenue respectively.

As this drag on revenue eased, the deficit shrank rapidly in 2017-18 and 2018-19 – when for practical purposes it disappeared – although the Treasury's estimate of the structural position (after stripping out favourable but temporary factors) was still a small deficit.[2]

The government therefore had some claim to success – albeit delayed – in closing the deficit it had inherited. While the pick-up in revenue contributed, so too did success in slowing the growth of expenditure – not primarily through the curbs to social benefits attempted in the 2014 budget but through restraint in functions that either had a lower political profile or did not require specific legislation to be implemented, such as basic departmental running costs.

As a result, the real growth of per capita payments slowed from an annual average of 1.9 per cent in the ten years to 2012-13 to 0.7 per cent in the next six years to 2018-19. Payments as a percentage of GDP had eased back by about one percentage point. The Minister for Finance, Senator Matthias Cormann, played an important part in these outcomes before he resigned from the Senate in 2020.

Nevertheless, an increase in gross Commonwealth debt to 28 per cent of GDP in June 2019 (from 17 per cent in June 2013) stood as a legacy of the large deficits earlier in the Coalition Governments' terms.

In the 2019 pre-election budget the Treasurer Josh Frydenberg tabled estimates of modest budget surpluses in the four years ahead, although as usual with forward estimates there was no guarantee they would actually be achieved. Leaving aside such standard caveats, Frydenberg's budget estimates were soon to be upended by the economic consequences of the coronavirus pandemic.

On the inflation front, despite the Reserve Bank of Australia's independence in pursuing an inflation target, the outcome is ultimately the responsibility of the government of the day. Inflation as measured by the Consumer Price Index, after remaining within the Reserve Bank's target range of 2-3 per cent for many years, dropped below it at the end of 2014 and remained there for most of the next five years, getting as low as 1.0 per cent at one point.

Although the deviation from target was small most of the time, the Reserve Bank drew criticism from some economists for not loosening monetary policy enough and for keeping unemployment higher than it needed to be and the growth of wages too low. With the benefit of hindsight this looks like a minor blemish on an otherwise very long and successful inflation targeting experience, but the criticism stuck and also reflected on the Morrison Government.

Some economists also argue that fiscal policy was too tight during this period, reflecting a deficit "fetish" which had prevailed for many years in Australia under different governments (Holden 2023). However, if average economic growth was sluggish, it had more to do with structural policy and low productivity growth than with a lack of macroeconomic stimulus. Fiscal policy must also be mindful of the government's balance sheet, and debt had increased substantially over ten years of deficits – a much longer period than in earlier cycles. The return to budget balance or surplus in 2018-19 seemed appropriate for the macroeconomic conditions of the time.

One test of macroeconomic management is the volatility of economic growth and unemployment. In the first six years of the Coalition Governments the external environment was relatively benign apart from weakness in commodity export prices up to 2017 followed by a resurgence. These movements in the terms of trade imparted significant volatility to nominal GDP, which was reflected in tax revenue, but annual growth of real GDP remained in the narrow band of 2-3 per cent and unemployment in the 5-6 per cent range. Volatility of these real economy variables was therefore low.

However, while the macro economy exhibited stability the *average* growth of real GDP and incomes was lacklustre – a topic to which we return later.

As with fiscal management, any disappointment with macro-economic performance up to the end of 2019 was about to be put into perspective by the shock of the pandemic.

Management of economic shocks

Economic management rarely goes according to plan, and one of the tests of success is how the economic managers respond to the unexpected. This was demonstrated starkly with the onset of the coronavirus pandemic in early 2020.

It must be said at the outset that the public health policy response to the pandemic and the economic policy response were so intertwined that it is difficult to assess one without assessing the other. However, it is not the purpose of this paper to evaluate the public health policy response. It has been both strongly praised for its public health benefits and strongly criticised for its social distancing excesses. But for the purposes of this chapter, we must take it as a given.

With that starting point, the best that can be said is that against the odds Australia achieved the pronounced 'V' shape recovery that few envisaged in the depths of the record economic contraction in the first half of 2020. Real GDP and employment have returned to their pre-pandemic trend growth paths and unemployment has plumbed 50-year lows.

However, there is strong evidence that the combined fiscal and monetary policy support measures of 2020-2022 went well beyond what the social-distancing measures called for. Just as lockdowns were doing enduring harm to the supply side of the economy, particularly labour supply, fiscal and monetary policy were injecting massive stimulus to aggregate demand. The initial burst of stimulus packages could perhaps be forgiven in the midst of the great uncertainty in early 2020 about the course and severity of the pandemic. It should soon have become clear, however, that too much stimulus was being poured into the economy.

This was the work of both the government running the budget and the Reserve Bank running monetary policy, and it is not as if each didn't know what the other was doing. The Governor of the Reserve Bank has stated publicly that the combined stimulus was excessive (Lowe 2022).

On the fiscal side alone, the International Monetary Fund kept a tally of all countries' economic policy responses and in 2021 revealed that among advanced countries Australia's budget measures (increased spending and tax relief) were exceeded (as a percentage of GDP) by only three countries: the US, the UK and New Zealand (IMF 2021). As reported in the 2022-23 Commonwealth budget, Australia's total support was $343 billion ($314 billion in economic measures and $29 billion in health measures), or 16.6 per cent of GDP, with 93.5 per cent of it being spent in the four years to 2022-23.

These fiscal measures were made more potent than they would

normally be as a result of the Reserve Bank's 'quantitative easing' actions. In other words, as the government was issuing huge sums of bonds to finance its deficit, the Bank was scooping up similar sums in the secondary market through money creation, in effect delivering monetary financing of the very large deficit.

For some time in 2020 and 2021 inflation remained quiescent as social distancing denied households and business the normal opportunities to consume and invest. However, when the clamps came off in late 2021 and more so in 2022 the results were seen in an upsurge in inflation, reinforced by the effects of the February 2022 Russian invasion of Ukraine on certain key commodity prices. As is now well known, inflation reached a peak of almost 8 per cent in 2022.

One highly respected economic modeller, Chris Murphy, has estimated that excessive fiscal and monetary stimulus added 3 percentage points to the inflation rate in 2022, which would otherwise have peaked below 5 per cent (Murphy 2023). The excessive stimulus resulted in destabilisation of the economy, with consequences that will be felt for years.

Murphy estimates that the pandemic-related fiscal stimulus provided $2 of compensation for every $1 of income lost by the private sector because of Covid-19. The largest contribution came from the *JobKeeper* scheme, which was kept in place for twice as long as originally intended and, according to many assessments, was poorly designed in a great hurry. For example, businesses were able to lodge claims for *JobKeeper* compensation solely on the basis of predicted sales revenue shortfalls, with no requirement for checking of outcomes against predictions.

While it is true that the Morrison Government was operating in a climate of great uncertainty and was pressured by the Opposition and State governments to do even more, it must be held responsible for its part in an unwarranted loosening of the Commonwealth purse-strings, driving up inflation and destabilising the economy more than was unavoidable as a result of the public health policy measures.

Inflation will eventually be tamed, but the enduring legacy of the fiscal responses to the pandemic will be a Commonwealth gross debt burden that surged by another 11 percentage points of GDP from 2019 to 39 per cent in 2022 (having been 5 per cent in 2007). One does not need to have a "debt and deficit fetish" to be concerned about this increase in debt and the consequent increase in the debt service burden.

In 2021 the Morrison Government stepped back from the well-established fiscal strategy anchor of achieving a balanced or surplus budget on average over the course of the economic cycle. The Treasury was projecting sizeable deficits as far as the eye could see, cycle or no cycle. Treasurer Josh Frydenberg retreated to the much more modest guidepost of steering debt as a proportion of GDP onto a downward trajectory.

As was not foreseen then but is now a matter of record, however, the economy became so over-heated and commodity export prices remained so strong that the budget deficit – thanks to surging revenue - shrank rapidly and was transformed into a significant surplus of more than $20 billion in 2022-23. Although this happened on the Albanese Labor Government's watch, it was not due to any measures of fiscal restraint of that government and would almost certainly also have happened had the Coalition remained in government. The stunning budget turnaround was, however, due at least in part to temporary favourable conditions and a structural deficit was expected to reassert itself.

Economic performance, 2013 to 2022

Given that economic performance in the term of any government continues to be influenced by the policies of the previous government, albeit to a diminishing extent as time goes by, it is not straightforward to set a period over which to fairly assess one government's economic policy results. As the Coalition came to office in September 2013 and left it in May 2022, for simplification we use the financial years 2013-14 to 2021-22, but in the knowledge that the policies of the Labor Government before September 2013 and of the Coalition Government up to May 2022 continued to influence outcomes under the new governments that succeeded them.

Table 2 contains the key data on real GDP and incomes, real wages and living standards, productivity and employment for the nine years to 2021-22 and the preceding two ten-year periods, both of which contained a mix of Coalition and Labor governments.

Table 2: Economic performance indicators

	9 years to 2021-22	10 years to 2012-13	10 years to 2002-03
Average annual percentage changes			
Real GDP	2.3	3.0	3.8
Real GDP per capita	1.0	1.4	2.7
Real net national disposable income per capita	1.3	2.3	2.8
Real household disposable income	0.5 (to 2020)	2.5	n.a
Real wage price index (year to June)	-0.1	1.0	n.a
Real AWOTE (year to June)	0.2	1.7	1.8
Labour productivity	1.4	1.7	2.7
Multi-factor productivity	0.9	0.1	1.6
Employment	1.9	2.0	2.1

Sources: Australian National Accounts: National Income, Expenditure and Product, Dec 2022, Australian Bureau of Statistics

Melbourne Institute of Applied Economic and Social Research: Household, Income and Labour Dynamics in Australia Survey, 2022
Wage Price Index, Australia, Dec 2022, Australian Bureau of Statistics
Average Weekly Earnings, Australia, Nov 2022, Australian Bureau of Statistics
Labour Force, Australia, Mar 2023, Australia Bureau of Statistics

Real GDP growth averaged 2.3 per cent in the nine years to 2021-22, significantly lower than the prior ten-year averages. This partly reflected lower population growth, but even in per capita terms annual real GDP growth shrank to only 1.0% in the nine years. Removing the pandemic years does not make much difference, as they included both a decline and a sharp rebound. Average real GDP growth in those years was 1.9 per cent.

After allowing for the increase in the terms of trade, real net national disposable income per capita averaged 1.3 per cent growth in the nine years, well down on the 2.3 per cent average for the previous ten years (when the terms of trade improved more rapidly) and the 2.8 per cent in the ten years before that, when real GDP per capita grew much more rapidly and the terms of trade increased moderately.

Focusing more on the household sector, median real household disposable income – for which data are more limited – rose by 2.5 per cent a year in the ten years to 2012 but only 0.5 per cent in the seven years to 2020 and actually fell in absolute terms from 2013 to 2018. The wage price index in real terms slowed from growth of 1.0 per cent a year in the ten years to June 2013 to minus 0.1 per cent in the nine years to June 2022. Real average weekly ordinary time earnings slowed from average growth of 1.8 per cent in the ten years to 2002 to 1.7 per cent in the next ten years and 0.2 per cent in the nine years to 2022.

The pattern of lacklustre growth in real GDP in the last nine years and flat or only slightly improving average real living standards is clear and paints an unflattering picture of economic performance under the Coalition Governments. Underpinning it has been weak productivity growth. Real wages and real per capita incomes cannot sustain solid growth without faster productivity growth than we have seen in recent times.

However, with labour productivity growth having slowed commensurately with real GDP growth, employment growth has held up and has been remarkably stable at an average of close to 2 per cent a year over the nine years to June 2022 and each of the preceding ten-year periods. The jobs have been generated, but the productivity of jobs as well as of capital has sagged.

To what extent can Coalition Government policy be blamed for weak growth of productivity and real incomes? This trend was well under way before the election of the Abbott Government, but the Coalition at least failed to turn it around and presided over a further trend deterioration before the coronavirus shock.

The engines of productivity growth are complex and economic policy is but one influence on them. Much has been written about the waves of productivity enhancing reform in the 1980s and 1990s and its part in driving a long advance in Australian prosperity.[3] The reform era is generally believed to have ended soon after the turn of the century, although the continuing benefits of earlier reforms underpinned further progress for some years, reinforced by an upsurge in commodity export prices and the terms of trade from 2003 onwards. Productivity growth eventually ran out of puff, though it should be noted that Australia was not alone in that regard (Dieppe 2020).

The Coalition governments from 2013 onwards had reform ideas but were unable to carry them forward either because of poor political management, Senate obstruction of government legislation, leadership instability in the Liberal Party, or the (related) distraction of disagreements over climate change policy. As a result, those governments have been strongly criticised for the lack of reform – though this does beg the question as to what kind of reform they should have pursued. They should have been driven by their core values but too often were not.

Core Coalition values

The Liberal and National Parties have been a Coalition in both opposition and in government, but the Coalition has always been dominated by the Liberal Party. To the extent the Coalition has adhered to a set of core values, they have been the values articulated by the Liberal Party, with the National Party sometimes in accord but at other times driven by pragmatism.

However, the Liberal Party has been better at articulating core values in opposition than at governing consistently in accordance with those values. Thus, Liberal Opposition leaders such as Menzies in the 1940s, Fraser in the 1970s, Hewson in the 1990s, Howard in both the 1980s and the 1990s and Abbott in the 2010s were effective in articulating core values tailored to the circumstances of the times and – with the exception of Hewson – were very successful at the ballot box.

The extent to which they adhered to core values in government varied, and in general diminished the longer they remained in government as the vagaries and political scars of office led pragmatism to replace principle when there was a need to choose.

Fundamentally, this is the economic policy story of the Coalition governments from 2013 to 2022.

The current Liberal leader, Peter Dutton, in April 2023 nominated five Liberal core values (Dutton 2023):

- small government which promotes freedom;
- policy, especially on energy, that is grounded in pragmatism;
- lower taxes and incentivising aspiration;
- government which governs for the many rather than that which shows favouritism to the few; and
- responsible government, especially regarding economic management.

This list would have sat comfortably with previous Liberal Opposition leaders, but at times in the past some have also emphasised a commitment to:

- free markets and open trade and investment;
- robust federalism or 'states rights' to prevent over-centralisation in Canberra;
- light regulation;
- property rights and the rule of law;
- personal responsibility and self-reliance; and
- policy predictability and consistency.

Although the Coalition Governments from 2013 to 2022 never committed to these exact principles at the one time, it is not unreasonable to use them as a basis for evaluation of their economic policies.

There was a lot of pro-free market rhetoric and some glimmers of action, but by and large the Coalition did not govern in conformity with these principles.

Economic freedom

The Heritage Foundation of the US (Heritage Foundation 2023) and Canada's Fraser Institute (Fraser Institute 2023) construct indexes of economic freedom for a large number of countries. While much depends on the indicators chosen and the weights assigned to them in constructing the indexes, Australia's rankings in these annual surveys provide a rough indication of our absolute and relative performance towards more or less economic freedom. An improvement in our rankings might have been expected had the Coalition governed in accordance with its stated principles.

However, while there was considerable volatility in Australia's rankings over the period from 2013 to 2022, there was no discernible trend towards improvement. The Heritage Foundation analysis points to a flat absolute score and ranking from 2013 to 2021 followed by a sharp deterioration since then. The Fraser Institute points to a flat absolute score with a slight improvement in the ranking up to 2020 (latest available). In interpreting these results, it is important to observe that Australia's ranking was and remains quite high and is in competition with such champions of economic freedom as the US, Switzerland and Singapore to move higher – a challenging task for any government even if they are fully motivated.

Size of government

Larger government, other things being equal, leads to higher tax burdens and/or public debt, greater diversion of resources from potentially more productive uses in the private sector to the public sector, and slower trend economic growth (Booth 2016). The federal government does not control the total size of government in Australia but it has by far the largest influence both through its own-purpose expenditure and grants to the States and local government.

As discussed above, the Coalition aimed to reduce Commonwealth spending as a proportion of GDP but had limited success before the pandemic and then presided over an even larger increase in two years (seven percentage points) than achieved by the Whitlam Government in the 1970s (six percentage points). The difference in the latest episode was that the pandemic-induced upsurge was almost completely reversed in the subsequent two years to 2022-23.

However, the Coalition cannot claim victory. The surge in nominal GDP in 2021-22 and 2022-23 made it easy to reduce government spending relative to GDP. On another measure, real per capita budget payments in 2022-23 were still 9 per cent higher than their 2018-19 pre-pandemic level.[4] The lavish government spending during the pandemic helped deepen the public's faith in government as the saviour in times of adversity, whether at the level of the individual, the firm or the community as a whole. Moreover, while pandemic spending was soaring and then receding, the long-term upward trend in social spending remained intact for the victor in the 2022 election – whether Coalition or Labor – to face in government. The Coalition governments of 2013 to 2022 had done little to curb the rapid structural growth of spending entrenched by the previous government in programs such as the NDIS, school education, child care, aged care and health. Total social spending advanced from 13.5 per cent of GDP in 2012-13 to 14 per cent ten years later.

The Coalition government's last budget in March 2022 showed post-pandemic Commonwealth payments settling at a level around two percentage points of GDP higher than before the pandemic and the new government's 2023-24 budget confirms that for the years 2023-24 and beyond.

Taxation

The Abbott Government's immediate tax policy priority in 2013 was to deliver on its election pledge to repeal the carbon tax and the mining tax implemented by the previous government.

Otherwise, the Coalition's first five years in office featured tax increases driven predominantly by the objective of reducing the budget deficit in the absence of the social spending restraints it was unable to achieve. These tax increases included:

- the temporary budget repair levy, a two percentage point increase in the top marginal rate of personal income tax to 47 per cent (plus Medicare levy) for three years beginning in 2014-15;
- resumption of indexation of fuel excise, which had been frozen by the Howard Government in 2001;
- the major bank levy (on liabilities of the big four banks and Macquarie);
- further increases in tobacco excise;
- increasing superannuation taxation by limiting tax-free fund earnings on retirement balances to the first $1.6 million (the Transfer Balance Cap) and lowering the threshold for the surcharge tax on contributions to $250,000;
- a proposed increase in the Medicare levy to 2.5 per cent linked to the funding of the NDIS, which the government withdrew when revenue improved.

None of this amounted to 'reform'. It was a collection of piecemeal measures aimed at raising revenue when the deficit was proving to be difficult to reduce. It did not reduce the tax burden or enhance productivity.

Hopes of genuine tax reform were raised when the Abbott Government set in train a white paper on taxation in 2014, leading as a first step to the 'Rethink' tax discussion green paper in 2015 (Treasury 2015). However, this project was cancelled with the change of leadership later in the year.

The new Prime Minister, Malcolm Turnbull, made much of cultivating a culture of enterprise and innovation in an 'agile' private sector – a theme that ultimately led to an enterprise tax reform package in the 2016-17 Budget. This included as its cornerstone a cut in the company tax rate from 30 to 25 per cent to be phased in over ten years and a commensurate tax reduction for unincorporated enterprises.

However, the Turnbull Government was unable to pass the enabling legislation in the Senate and all that was salvaged was a cut for small companies and unincorporated businesses, resulting in a two-tier company tax that arguably added a new distortion in the tax system. Had the enterprise tax plan been implemented in full it would have been an important reform in support of stronger business investment and productivity growth. Business investment, apart from periodic flourishes in mining investment, has continued to languish.

The Turnbull Government turned its attention to the more electorally rewarding field of personal income tax relief when revenue strengthened and announced a package of tax cuts in the 2018-19 Budget – the personal income tax plan – to be implemented over the extraordinarily long period of six years. The Morrison Government enlarged these tax cuts in the pre-election 2019-20 Budget.

Although initially taking the form of a low and middle income tax offset and then increases in some marginal rate thresholds, what has become well-known as Stage 3 – slated for July 2024 – also includes the first significant cuts in marginal rates for many years. For this reason it is a meaningful reform, but at the time of writing, although the changes are set in legislation passed under the Coalition government, its fate under the current Albanese Labor Government remains uncertain.

While there are many critics of Stage 3 on the grounds of the alleged large revenue cost and the distribution in favour of higher income earners, it has been demonstrated that in aggregate these tax cuts do no more than return the proceeds of bracket creep since 2017 (Tilley 2023).

Fiscal federalism

The coronavirus pandemic was a major event in Australian federalism in that it demonstrated the strong powers and autonomy of the States after decades of steady erosion under the overwhelming financial dominance of the Federal government. Whatever one thinks of the way the States acted, the mere fact that such power existed came as a revelation to many people.

However, the underlying financial imbalance between the federal and state governments remains and the conduct of federalism is returning to business as usual after the pandemic. The Coalition governments did nothing in the way of fundamental reform of fiscal federalism and the familiar issues of vertical fiscal imbalance, duplication and overlap, lack of accountability, blame-shifting and cost-shifting all remain.

The Abbott Government set in train a white paper on reform of federalism, but like the white paper on taxation it was shelved by the Turnbull Government.

The Coalition in government made the practice of federalism worse in some respects. One was the restructure of horizontal fiscal equalisation to place a floor under Western Australia's GST share and protect it from the downward pressure that would otherwise have come from equalisation of that state's bountiful mining royalties. Apart from distorting the horizontal equalisation system, this arrangement has come at a huge and enduring cost to the federal budget.

Federalism has also been white-anted by federal government intervention in functions that are clearly the responsibility of state and local government. The Abbott, Turnbull and Morrison governments cannot be blamed for a process that has been steadily under way for decades, but they did nothing to stop it and at the margins made it worse through their enthusiasm for local and community grants for public goods ranging from security cameras to sport facilities and car parks which are not the business of a central government. The Coalition, like other governments before it, brought opprobrium upon itself by distributing these grants for electoral advantage.

Federalism remains a fertile field for reforms that could improve the allocation of resources in the economy and the cost-effectiveness of government programs.

Structural policies

There is a host of other economic policies that come under the broad heading of 'structural' or 'microeconomic' policies which, if well-chosen and designed, can boost productivity growth, labour force participation and the economy's dynamism and flexibility. They include policies in areas such as industrial relations, trade and foreign investment, competition, the financial system, research and development, regulation and red tape, skill training and infrastructure. Some of these require cooperation with State and Territory governments.

The Abbott Government initiated a financial system inquiryand a review of competition policy[5,6] early in its term. The former led to some significant reforms but the latter less so. The Turnbull Government sought to develop priorities by tasking the Productivity Commission every five years to review productivity performance and make policy recommendations to improve that performance. The Commission duly produced a long list of recommendations in its first report in 2017 (Productivity Commission 2017), but it is fair to say that by the 2022 election there had been little policy follow-up and the second review was due.

In the key area of industrial relations, there was much to be done to improve on the policies of the previous Labor government, but the Coalition remained inert in fear of the electoral consequences of deregulation following the fate of its WorkChoices reforms under the Howard Government.

In infrastructure the Coalition substantially increased Commonwealth funding of projects mainly through grants and loans to the states and funding of off-budget Commonwealth entities. While this may have productivity benefits it must also be noted that the government paid little attention to the recommendations of Infrastructure Australia, the independent statutory body established in 2008 to advise governments on infrastructure priorities. Projects favoured for Commonwealth funding were generally not those with the highest benefit/cost ratios.

We could go on with examples, but the broad picture is of some positive 'structural' policy changes being made but in a patchy effort that failed to act on the full range of opportunities available for government policy to address the productivity challenge. Thus, economic reform efforts – which had languished under the previous government – continued to do so after 2013.

Conclusion

Although economists have generally given the Coalition governments' economic policies during this period low marks, they have some achievements to their credit – for example, bringing the budget to balance before the pandemic hit and putting in place the three-stage personal income tax cuts (but leaving the last and most important stage at the mercy of the current government).

Economic growth was modest before the pandemic but there was stability, with low inflation and no clear business cycle. However, the Coalition's stabilisation policy record was then marred by the destabilisation resulting from excessive fiscal support and stimulus during the pandemic, which exacerbated the upsurge in inflation during 2022 and added greatly to public debt and interest expense.

The Coalition set out to strengthen the structural budget position by reining in social spending but made little headway in this endeavour. The growth of social spending remains the key risk to fiscal sustainability and the Coalition has passed the baton to a government whose inclination is only to add more.

Productivity growth, which is the key to greater prosperity, was weak before the Coalition took office and became weaker while it was in office. Although productivity growth is not as readily amenable to government policy as is often believed, a purposeful economic reform effort through coherent, across-the-board microeconomic policy reform certainly helps. While the Coalition achieved some worthwhile reforms, its overall effort was patchy and sometimes inconsistent with its stated values.

It should be said in fairness that the Coalition faced strong opposition from an unsympathetic Senate – where it often lacked the numbers to pass contentious legislation – and from some state governments. However, the Coalition governments also appeared to lack the political skills to overcome opposition – for example, by effectively arguing the benefits of smaller government and free markets.

Finally, the critical assessment presented here is against fixed criteria and is not intended as a comparative assessment. In terms of economic policy performance there have been better and worse governments than those of 2013 – 2022 and there are likely to be both better and (regrettably) worse in the future.

References

Abbott, A., MP, speaking at a Coalition campaign in Brisbane, 8 August 2010 https://electionspeeches.moadoph.gov.au/speeches/2010-tony-abbott

Abbott, A., MP, *Commonwealth Parliamentary Debates*, House of Representatives, No. 5, 2013, 3573

Booth, P., *Taxation Government Spending and Economic Growth*, London: The Institute of Economic Affairs, 2016

Dieppe, A., "The broad-based productivity slowdown, in seven charts," *World Bank Blogs*, 14 July 2020 https://blogs.worldbank.org/developmenttalk/broad-based-productivity-slowdown-seven-charts#:~:text=The%20productivity%20slowdown%20is%20due%20to%20multiple%20factors&text=Working%2Dage%20population%20growth%20has,global%20value%20chains%20has%20stalled.

Dutton, P., MP, *Sir John Downer Oration*, Adelaide, 18 April 2023 https://www.peterdutton.com.au/leader-of-the-opposition-transcript-sir-john-downer-oration-adelaide/

Fraser Institute, *Economic Freedom of the World: 2023 Annual Report*, Fraser Institute, 26 January 2023

Griffiths, E., "Commission of Audit recommends cradle-to-grave cuts in report released by Federal Government," *ABC News*, 1 May 2014

Heritage Foundation, *2023 Index of Economic Freedom*, Heritage Foundation, 2023 https://www.heritage.org/index/ranking

Hockey, J., speaking at The Institute of Economic Affairs in London, 17 April 2012.https://www.smh.com.au/national/the-end-of-the-age-of-entitlement-20120419-1x8vj.html

Holden, R., "Economic Policy in the 46th Parliament," in Grattan, M., McCaffrie, B. and Wallace, C., (eds), *The Morrison Government: Governing Through Crisis, 2019-2022*, Sydney: UNSW Press, 2023, 102-114

IMF (International Monetary Fund), IMF Fiscal Affairs Department, "Fiscal Monitor Database of Country Fiscal Measures in Response to the COVID-19 Pandemic," *International Monetary Fund*, October 2021

Lowe, P., Senate Official Hansard, Economics Legislation Committee, 28 November 2022

Murphy, C., "Fiscal Policy in the COVID-19 Era," *Economic Papers*, 42(2), June 2023, 107-52

National Commission of Audit (NCA), Towards Responsible Government, *Report*, Canberra: Commonwealth Government, February 2014

Productivity Commission, *Shifting the Dial: 5 Year Productivity Review*, Inquiry No 84, Canberra: Commonwealth Government, August 2017

Tilley, P., "3-stage tax cuts versus bracket creep", *Tax and Transfer Policy Institute*, March 2023.

Treasury, *Re:think Tax Discussion Paper*, March 2015.

Endnotes

1   Australian Government, 2014-15 Budget Paper No. 1, Statement 3, 55

2   Australian Government, 2023-24 Budget Paper No. 1, Statement 3, Chart 3.19, 131

3   Australian Government, Australia's Experience with Economic Reform, Treasury Working Paper, October 2018

4   Australian Government, 2023-24 Budget Paper No. 1, Statement 11, Table 11.11, 430-31.

5   This was the *Financial Systems Inquiry* chaired by David Murray, former CEO of the Commonwealth Bank established in 2013.

6   The *Competition Policy Review* was appointed in early 2014 and chaired by Professor Ian Harper who had also been a member of the Howard Government's 1996 *Inquiry into the Financial System* (Wallis Inquiry).

7

Climate and Energy Policy

Aynsley Kellow

Introduction

The period 2013-22 saw climate and energy policy begin with the triumph of Tony Abbott's strong victory in 2013, when the Coalition swept to power thanks to strong opposition to the policies of the Gillard and Rudd governments – especially Gillard's broken promise not to introduce a carbon tax. It ended with defeat, substantially undermined by Teal independents supported and funded by those whose beliefs and interests coincided, who rode a wave of confected claims of 'climate emergency' made possible because the Liberal Party abandoned liberal principles of scientific knowledge and policy, and dragged the Nationals with them in the Coalition.

The Nationals remained more resistant to the enthusiasms of climate change, but ultimately went along with the Liberals rather than stress the Coalition. This chapter develops this theme in greater detail, beginning by looking at how liberalism might have regarded climate science and noting the role of actors like Malcolm Turnbull, Michael Photios and Simon Holmes à Court in climate politics in leading the Coalition to defeat in 2022.

Liberal science

Philosopher of science Karl Popper insisted that the soundness of scientific propositions rested upon the robustness of their predictions –

their ability to withstand repeated attempts at falsification. Even then, we should accept their validity only tentatively, fully expecting future evidence might falsify them. A key to scientific advancement was open debate and contestation; as Popper put it, science advances by disagreement. *The Logic of Scientific Discovery*, to use the titles of two of his notable works, involves *Conjectures and Refutations.*

Much science today is better described by Thomas Kuhn's notion of dominant paradigms defended by their adherents, circling the intellectual wagons to defend the paradigm until forced to abandon it. Thus we frequently see an emphasis on consensus and official representations of "The Science". Such an approach might describe how science operates and possibly advances, but it is essentially a political process, and a poor test of the veracity of propositions. Indeed, as Paul Feyerabend characterised it, scientists are prone to use all sorts of deceptive tricks to defend their preferred beliefs, so an anarchical contest of propositions is to be preferred to "official science". The use of the term 'denier' to attack any dissenter (deliberately invoking 'Holocaust denier') is an example of this in climate science.

Given Popper's fallibilism, it is no surprise that his political philosophy was one of liberalism, captured in his two great works of political philosophy, *The Poverty of Historicism* and *The Open Society and its Enemies.* Political liberalism might be expected to embrace a Popperian scepticism on issues like catastrophic anthropogenic climate change, yet while the Liberal Party in Australia embraced such a tradition under the leadership of Prime Minister Tony Abbott, it drifted into an embrace of "Net Zero" under Prime Minister Scott Morrison – who as Treasurer once brandished a lump of coal in Parliament, taunting the Opposition that it was nothing to be afraid of.

This essay seeks to throw some light on how this abandonment of liberal principles occurred, ultimately removing a key point of difference with the Australian Labor Party that had been electorally propitious in 2013 and the 2019 'Climate Change Election' but the abandonment of which in 2016 almost cost it government. Clearly the leadership of Malcolm Turnbull was a key factor in this trajectory, but I shall argue here there were other factors at work. I begin with a brief account of some key developments during the period.

Abbott had a somewhat pragmatic approach to climate policy, having supported Howard in the adoption of the Mandatory Renewable Energy Target in a vain attempt to stave off Kevin Rudd with his claims of the issue being the 'greatest moral challenge', but then adopting a more critical stance. In December 2009, for example, it was reported that Abbott had dismissed climate science as "crap" (Rintoul 2009). He was then able to reap political capital from Julia Gillard's broken promise that there would be no carbon tax under a government she led, winning the 2013 election comfortably and repealing Gillard's legislation the following year.

It should be noted that Abbott's criticism of the quality of climate science is not without foundation. For all the billions spent on climate science, there has been little change in our understanding of the relationship between atmospheric carbon dioxide levels and global temperatures since the work of Svante Arrhenius in 1896 (Arrhenius 1896). The warming we have witnessed since is very much in line with Arrhenius' prediction, with an increase in carbon dioxide 'in geometric progression, the augmentation of the temperature will increase nearly in arithmetic progression' (Arrhenius 1896: 267). Arrhenius understood that forcing by carbon dioxide became saturated, so the effect was logarithmic, with each successive molecule having less impact.

Modern climate science was initially also consistent with the modest increase in global temperature that has been observed. This was the finding even of a notable activist climate scientist, Stephen Schneider (Rasool and Schneider 1971). Climate alarmism depends entirely upon computer models fed with an assumed positive feedback mechanism, whereby carbon dioxide forcing increases the concentration of water vapour – responsible for about 97% of the greenhouse effect. Interestingly, Australian scientists reported a lack of empirical evidence to support such an assumption (Paltridge, Arking, and Pook 2009).

Predictions projections from climate models have constantly run hotter than observations, as John Christy showed in a submission to the US Congress in 2017 and again in a peer reviewed paper in 2020 (McKitrick and Christy 2020). In 2020 McKitrick and Christy examined the outputs of the 38 newest climate models and compared their global tropospheric warming rates between 1979 and 2014 with observations from satellites and weather balloons. All produced too much warming, with most of the differences statistically significant, and they argued this suggested a structural error in climate models. This finding has recently been confirmed by a team at the US government's National Oceanic and Atmospheric Administration (Zou, Xu, Hao and Liu, 2023). Christy and Richard McNider (2017) previously showed that the warming rate in the satellite record suggested the climate to be only be half as sensitive to greenhouse gases as the average model used by the IPCC for projecting future warming, a finding consistent with an analyses of actual radiation from the atmosphere, rather than model results (van Wijngaarden and Happer,2020; see also Coe et al 2021).

In short, there is adequate *observational* evidence to support a "lukewarmer" position, rather than the catastrophic climate future suggested by the computer models with their warming bias. An important question is therefore why a party with a supposed commitment to political liberalism did not follow Popper's liberal approach to the science surrounding the earth's climate, and instead signed up with the position of the ALP and the Greens, whose acceptance of 'official science' is reminiscent of the Lysenkoism that set Soviet science back decades.

Cliff Ollier (2009: 200) showed the parallels between Lysenkoism and modern climate science: both worked through political organisations (such as the IPCC); both claimed that the science is settled (there is nothing to debate); both disregarded the accumulating evidence that the predictions are wrong; both demonised the opposition (labelling dissenters as "deniers"); both victimised the opposition (loss of jobs or research funds); both related to a current ideology (Environmentalism); both were supported by a vast propaganda machine; a huge bureaucracy where many people have careers dependent upon "the ruling concept".

Those who doubt the existence of a propaganda machine would do well to examine the donations by hedge fund operators through their "philanthropic" foundations, often using 'pass through' funds to mask their role. Recipients include the *Associated Press* and Covering Climate Now, which coordinates coverage of climate change by agencies such as *Agence France Presse* and outlets such as the *Guardian* and *The Conversation* (the latter funded by Australian universities with a policy of refusing to publish 'denier' perspectives). Covering Climate Now also lists the prestigious scientific journals *Nature* and *Scientific American* among the recipients of its coordinated news.

There was in 2007 a brief rebellion in Liberal ranks against "official" climate science. Led by Dr Dennis Jensen, one of the few members to sit in the Commonwealth Parliament with a PhD in science, some Liberal members issued a dissenting report to the House of Representatives Standing Committee on Science and Innovation on carbon capture and storage in August 2007. They staked out a perfectly Popperian criticism of the majority report, stating that: they did not believe the evidence unequivocally supported the hypothesis of Anthropogenic Global Warming (AGW); that the case for AGW was based on theoretical models and unproven economic assumptions; that many eminent scientists had stated that AGW was far from proven; that global warming had been observed on other planets; that science relies on testing hypotheses, not on consensus; and that the Committee had not applied the scientific method. The dissenting report was as good a critique of the state of climate science as one might expect at the time.

But for Abbott's criticism of the quality of the science, the Liberal Party has not since contested the questionable science of catastrophic climate change, and the Teals most recently have been able to exploit this to rob them of votes and seats, claiming there is a "climate emergency". The Liberal Party has not contested the claims of a "climate emergency", and one wonders why not. The "climate emergency" has not been driven by science but was initiated by Greens members of the Darebin City Council in metropolitan Melbourne in December 2016, and subsequently spread globally through green networks. It was then picked up by the Club of Rome, who presented their 'Climate Emergency Plan' in December 2018. Only on 5 November 2019, did scientists get in on the act, when the biology (not climate science) journal *BioScience* published an article that was essentially a petition, endorsed by 11,000 scientists from 153 nations, declaring that Planet Earth was facing a climate emergency. Pushed by Extinction Rebellion and Greta's Fridays for the Future, it was picked up by some national governments and then by the UN Secretary-General Antonio Guterres in December 2020.

All this despite data such as that presented by Bjorn Lomborg that shows clearly that the risk of death from extreme weather events in 2020 is a mere 2 per cent of what it was in 1920 and that from Roger Pielke Jr that the incidence of extreme weather events such as tornados and cyclones has not increased with the modest warming observed. Pielke has also been instrumental in exposing the use of extreme and highly improbable emissions scenarios to produce an extreme and highly improbable future climate what he termed "climate porn" (Pielke Jr 2019; Pielke Jr and Ritchie 2021). Moreover, he also highlighted the role of hedge fund operators Tom Steyer and Michael Bloomberg, with investments benefited by decarbonisation policies, in pushing the extreme and improbable emissions scenario RCP8.5 into US policy and ultimately the IPCC as "business as usual". This was too much even mainstream climate scientists (Hausfather and Peters 2020).

There are, in short, many reasons why Popperian liberalism should have led to more Liberals than Abbott and Jensen and his cohort to question the existence of a 'climate crisis'. The climate models have run hot when compared with observations and are fed with totally unrealistic emissions scenarios as 'business as usual'. The models are validated against the same data from which they are constructed, and as Babyak observed, "If you use a sample to construct a model, or to choose a hypothesis to test, you cannot make a rigorous scientific test of the model or the hypothesis using that same sample data'"(Babyak 2004: 414). The test is the quality of predictions, and comparisons between model runs and observations call further predictions based on those models into serious question.

The failure of the Liberals to contest this climate science left them in 2022 at the mercy of the Teals who were able to harvest votes among the affluent urban voters who believed "The Science"; but the Liberals policy responses also drifted away from liberal principles and were influenced by rent seekers within the party in New South Wales and Simon Holmes à Court.

Liberal policy

If the approach of the Liberal Party strayed from the Popperian scepticism one might have expected from adherents to a liberal philosophy, allowing the Teals to exploit the widespread perception of there being a "climate crisis", its policies aimed at regulating the emission of greenhouse gases adhered no closer to liberalism.

The individual most responsible for this would appear to be Malcolm Turnbull. Turnbull, of course, was responsible as Environment Minister in the Howard government for the decision to phase out incandescent light bulbs. Having seized the leadership from Brendan Nelson, he then supported Rudd's Carbon Pollution Reduction scheme, and lost support and the leadership because of it.

The Howard government declined to ratify the Kyoto Protocol, but was not totally inactive on climate change, introducing the Mandatory Renewable Energy Target and Malcolm Turnbull (as Environment Minister) introduced a particularly illiberal policy to phase out incandescent light bulbs, for dubious environmental benefit, but to the benefit of manufacturers whose sales of compact fluorescent bulbs enjoyed higher margins and were given a boost while LED lighting, which would eventually displace CFLs, was still prohibitively expensive,

Kevin Rudd, of course, made considerable political capital from what he considered the great moral challenge, and flew to Bali to ratify Kyoto. Incoming Opposition Leader Brendan Nelson in mid-2008 sought to develop a new approach to climate change, but was rolled by Turnbull before making any progress.

Abbott: A Conservative with Liberal tendencies

Abbott rode to power in large part on his promise to repeal Gillard's carbon tax, on which she was vulnerable because she had campaigned promising not to introduce such a measure, and adopted his "Direct Action" policy to reduce emissions. But his leadership was constantly being undermined by Turnbull, who eventually prevailed and took the Coalition to the brink of defeat, winning the 2016 election by a single seat.

Turnbull had decided in November 2009 to support the Rudd government's Carbon Pollution Reduction Scheme, in the face of significant disagreement in the joint party room. Liberal MPs Wilson Tuckey and Dennis Jensen attempted an unsuccessful leadership spill and several MPs and Senators criticised Turnbull's position. Several, including Tony Abbott, resigned from the Shadow Cabinet. A week later, Abbott successfully challenged Turnbull for the leadership, winning by a single vote. Abbott then campaigned strongly on climate change, with Julia Gillard having to strike a deal with the Greens and independents to govern after the 2010 election, leading her to promise that there would be no carbon tax under a government she led. Abbott made considerable political capital from what became a broken promise in February 2011 when she announced the introduction of such a policy.

Abbott promised to repeal the tax and adopt a "Direct Action Plan" to secure reductions in emissions of greenhouse gases, and quickly overtook Gillard in polls as preferred prime minister. Abbott quickly repealed the carbon tax after his landslide victory in 2013, and abolished the Climate Commission that Gillard had established, chaired by Tim Flannery. The incoming government also decided in November 2013 not to send a ministerial delegate to the Conference of the Parties to the Framework Convention on Climate Change (COP-19) in Warsaw and then abandoned the Coalition policy to cut emissions by between 5% and 25% on 2000 levels by 2020, committing only to a 5% target.

The Direct Action Plan therefore sought to reduce Australia's emissions to 5% below 2000 levels by the year 2020. A White Paper on the plan was released in April 2014, revealing the centrepiece of the plan was a $2bn Emissions Reduction Fund (ERF) to provide financial incentives to carbon dioxide emitters to reduce their emissions. The ERF was to support a range of abatement programs, including vegetation management, energy efficiency and transport. It was proposed to abolish the Australian Renewable Energy Agency, but this failed, lacking support in the Senate. The Clean Energy Finance Corporation had its scope limited and the MRET was reduced.

The Abbott government also sought to minimise the Lysenkoist nature of the scientific discourse. It offered a $4m grant to the University of

Western Australia to have Bjorn Lomborg establish an offshoot of his Copenhagen Consensus Centre, but this was declined after a revolt UWA staff, who thus demonstrated the extent Groupthink had taken hold in institutions on the issue.

The Department of Prime Minister and Cabinet also proposed an investigation into claims that the Bureau of Meteorology was exaggerating the extent of global warming by, *inter alia*, homogenising past temperature readings, which usually resulted in the past being cooled. Environment Minister Greg Hunt resisted the establishment of a formal investigation and instead established a 'review forum' which found the data were accurate (Sturmer 2016).

Abbott's hardnosed approach to climate change earned him something of a reputation among the environment movement, but his government did not fail to act. It committed at the Conference of the Parties to the Framework Convention on Climate Change at Lima in December 2014 to provide $200m over four years to the Green Climate Fund. Moreover, and more significantly, it committed to the Australian position in the negotiation of the Paris Agreement in December 2015, adopting an economy-wide target to reduce greenhouse gas emissions by 26 to 28 per cent below 2005 levels by 2030. (Ratification occurred under Turnbull).

Turnbull, Bootleggers and Baptists

The fate of the Liberal Party rested very much on the factional politics of NSW. Turnbull belonged to the Moderates, who are really to the Left of the party. Factional leader and lobbyist Michael Photios boasted that "members of the left faction had . . . secured the jobs of Prime Minister [Turnbull] and NSW Premier [Berejiklian]" (Nicholls, 2017). And as Sean Nicholls noted, they also helped secure the next prime minister, because Scott Morrison was a creature of the Alex Hawke led 'soft left' faction, as opposed to the Michael Photios led 'hard left' faction.

His rise and fall saw what in regulatory policy Bruce Yandle (1989) has called 'Bootlegger and Baptist' coalitions between those with interests advanced by regulation and those whose moralising empowers their campaigning. Such coalitions are becoming increasingly apparent around efforts to regulate greenhouse gases.

Turnbull engineered an unsuccessful spill motion in February 2015, then resigned from Cabinet in September, after Newspoll continued to show the government well behind the ALP, and then challenged successfully for the leadership.

Initially, Turnbull largely adhered to previous Coalition policy, and after the system blackout in September 2016 in renewables dependent South Australia, he committed to the construction of the $2 billion 2000MW Snowy Hydro 2.0 (Coorey 2017) – prior to the preparation of any feasibility study. This was widely reported as a 50% increase in capacity for the Snowy scheme and "enough to power 500,000 homes" (Karp 2017). This statement reflected poorly on the standard of journalism on this issue, because this was a pumped hydro *storage* scheme that would actually *consume* energy in order to provide storage to compensate for the unreliability of renewables.

Then, in April 2017, in another move contrary to liberal principles, Turnbull placed export restrictions on LNG exports in response to the high wholesale gas prices resulting from a shortage of gas in the domestic gas market, thanks to restrictions on the development of new gas resources.

The Photios Faction was significant in climate politics because his Premier State Consulting had clients with interests in the area of climate and energy. Among these clients was AGL, owner of the Liddell Power Station which it closed in April 2023 as it moved to grow its renewables portfolio, which benefited from generous government subsidies. Closing Liddell meant less competition, and so AGL did not seek to sell the station, but demolished it. Energy was the centre of a policy fight in the NSW factions around the May 2019 election over the political futures of Abbott and Craig Kelly. Ironically, Abbott had tried, unsuccessfully, to reduce the power of lobbyists in the Liberal Party – in particular to reduce the connections between party office holding and day-job lobbying.

Photios's wife, Kristina, was also listed in the Federal lobbyist register as a director of the firm Clean Energy Strategies, while as the Shooters, Fishers and Farmers Party pointed out (2017), ASIC listed Mr Photios himself, not his wife, as a director. Kristina Photios quit the Party to speak out against a 'vocal minority' of conservatives she claimed were preventing progress on climate policy by the Turnbull government. She claimed the Liberal Party had to move 'back to the centre' and called on 'progressive members' to stand and ensure Prime Minister Malcolm Turnbull was not held hostage to the hard right of the Party (Heath 2016). Both Michael and Kristina Photios advanced the argument that the Liberals were the party that would tackle climate change. Michael Photios addressed meetings of the North Shore Environmental Stewards and encouraged attendees to join the Party – according to one in attendance – in order to try to block the preselection of Abbott in Warringah (Glasgow and Lacy 2017).

The ascension of Turnbull proved beneficial not just for renewables interests generally, but for his son, Alex, whose Singapore based hedge fund Keshik Capital was an investor in the Australian listed renewables company Infigen Energy – along with 32% held by the Children's Investment Fund Management, the hedge fund of Sir Christopher Hohn, who (partly through his philanthropic vehicle) funded Extinction Rebellion to the tune of £200,000. Infigen stock had quadrupled in price when acquired by Spanish utility Iberdrola in October 2020. The young Turnbull learned the trade of regulatory arbitrage trading the debt and assets of energy companies affected by pricing carbon working for his father's old firm, Goldman Sachs between 2010 and 2014 (Macdonald-Smith 2016).

Remarkably, Alex Turnbull was granted extraordinary access to policy-making on climate change – participation in a WhatsApp discussion group where senior policy advisers, press secretaries and department officials discussed energy policy, shortly after the 2016 election. Turnbull Jr reportedly showed no reluctance to express his opinions, with one participant saying "Surely there is enough experts, department advisers, political advisers and ministers involved . . ." (Smethurst 2018).

The relationship between the business affairs of Turnbull Jr and Turnbull Sr are somewhat obscure. We do know, thanks to a (failed) case brought by their family company against a former business partner (Maurtray Pty Ltd v Pillemer Pty Ltd & Ors [2022] NSWSC. 1181), that upon becoming prime minister, Malcolm (alleged the respondent) arranged his affairs to mask the family interests in businesses affected by government policy to avoid declaring these interests on the parliamentary register of interests.

In 2017 Turnbull yielded to pressure to dump the Clean Energy Target that the Chief Scientist Alan Finkel had proposed, instead adopting a National Energy Guarantee (NEG). The NEG was an attempt to assuage those on the right of the party by guaranteeing dispatchable power while cutting emissions. Staff who worked for both the PM and then-energy minister Josh Frydenberg reported that Alex Turnbull's involvement increased when the NEG was being prepared (Smethurst 2018). The NEG failed to do the trick for Turnbull and in August 2018 Peter Dutton challenged unsuccessfully Turnbull for the leadership of the Liberal Party, but the challenge led to another ballot shortly after, in which Turnbull declined to stand, and in which Scott Morrison won as a compromise candidate.

Turnbull was clearly convinced that catastrophic climate change was wreaking havoc on features such as the Great Barrier Reef, now known to be in rude good health. In International Year of the Reef in 2018 he made a grant (after no competitive process) of $443,303,000 to the Great Barrier Reef Foundation, which had been formed in response to an episode of coral bleaching after an El Niño occurrence.

After his defeat, Turnbull continued to call for Morrison to reintroduce the NEG. Alex Turnbull participated in a Twitter campaign, together with Simon Holmes à Court, falsely accusing Angus Taylor of a massive financial impropriety that Greens Senator Sarah Hanson-Young labelled #watergate (Patrick, 2019). This foreshadowed Holmes à Court intervening in the 2019 election, funding candidates favouring greater climate action, a portent of his massive funding of the Teal independents in 2022.

An investigation by the *Australian* found Holmes à Court had a sizable portfolio of family and other businesses focused on making money from any potential boom in clean energy technology. One company,

Decarb Ventures, was established in January 2022, with Holmes à Court and his wife holding 91% of the equity and the balance held by Mitchell Hopwood. Hopwood had established a company called Climate Outcomes Foundation (COF) in April 2019, two days after Climate 200 was registered by Holmes à Court and a month before the 2019 election. COF provided at least $304,000 from unknown sources to Climate 200 independents at the 2019 election (Norrington, 2022).

Holmes à Court claimed that only about 2% of his renewables investments were in Australia, but these would appreciate in value if decarbonisation policies were adopted. For example, he invested in solar energy company 5B Holdings Pty Ltd along with Malcolm Turnbull and the chairman of the Beyond Zero Emissions think tank Eytan Lenko. In November 2021 Lenko said the company could roll out solar farms on a huge scale, but it needed government policy to enforce 'the orderly shutdown of coal-fired power plants' and 'hasten the uptake of renewable energy' before the benefits of solar technology could be 'fully realised' and 'get investors a better return' (Norrington 2022).

Morrison: From Lumps of Coal to Net Zero

Under Turnbull, Morrison as Treasurer in February 2017, appeared in the House of Representatives holding a lump of coal, taunting the Opposition, stating "This is coal. Don't be afraid. Don't be scared. It won't hurt you", and accusing those opposed to the use of coal as having "an ideological, pathological fear of coal" (Murphy, 2017). Morrison was mocking the ALP's commitment to renewable energy after the blackout of the South Australian electricity system on 28 September 2016. Yet he went to COP26 in Glasgow in 2021 committing Australia to Net Zero.

It appears Morrison was not immediately seduced by the international limelight. After he attended the 2021 Leaders' Climate Summit he declined to match other world leaders in setting a net zero or other emissions target, and reportedly requested the removal of climate change targets from a proposed Australia-United Kingdom trade agreement. He initially indicated that he would not attend COP26 in Glasgow, but then changed course and announced that Australia would aim to achieve net zero emissions by 2050 but put his faith in the market to achieve this outcome and adopted no legislation to progress the target. Morrison's damascene conversion appeared genuine. Of all the portfolios into which he had himself secretly sworn in during the Covid pandemic, his role as joint Resources Minister was the only one where he took a substantive policy decision, overruling a decision on gas exploration by the substantive Resources Minister.

Morrison suffered from criticism over the attribution of fires to climate change, when the scope of the disaster had much to do, not with yet another Australian bushfire, but with its impact on increased housing by 'tree changers' in a fire-adapted habitat where hazard reduction burns are now resisted. Similarly, floods – the worst since 1974 – had a worse impact because building had been permitted on floodplains, with no heed paid to warnings that went back to the early days of Australia. Governor Lachlan Macquarie (1817) had warned against building on floodplains back in 1817, writing that "the too fateful Experience of Years has shown the Sufferers the inevitable consequences of their wilful and wayward Habit of placing their Residences and Stock-yards within the Reach of the Floods. . . ."

Conclusion

Despite the Coalition yielding much to the demands of the climate lobby, they were still mortally wounded by the Holmes à Court backed Teals in the 2022 election, and Albanese was able to form government on slightly less than a third of the primary vote. Many have suggested that the Coalition should respond by becoming even more green, but it is arguable that they abandoned the field on climate science and allowed the Teals and others free rein to exploit extreme weather events and the general climate of fear whipped up by activists. It is not that they were thwarted in the Senate; they simply did not attempt to develop genuinely liberal approach to the issue. They thus abandoned a key point of difference that had served them well in 2013 and 2019.

References

Arrhenius, S., "On the Influence of Carbonic Acid in the Air upon the Temperature of the Ground." *Philosophical Magazine and Journal of Science*, 41, 1896, 237-76.

Aston, H., "Liberal Party powerbroker's wife Kristina Photios quits over lack of action on climate change." *Sydney Morning Herald.* 8 December 2016. https://www.smh.com.au/politics/federal/liberal-party-powerbrokers-wife-kristina-photios-quits-over-lack-of-action-on-climate-change-20161208-gt7376.html

Aston, J., "Alex Turnbull's hedge fund 'now a family office'." *Australian Financial Review*, 5 October 2020 https://www.afr.com/rear-window/alex-turnbull-s-hedge-fund-now-a-family-office-20201005-p5626l

Babyak, M.A., 'What you see may not be what you get: A brief, nontechnical introduction to overfitting in regression-type models.' *Psychosomatic Medicine*, 66, 2004, 411–21

Christy, J.R., & McNider, R.T., "Satellite bulk tropospheric temperatures as a metric for climate sensitivity," *Asia-Pacific Journal of Atmospheric Sciences*, 53, 2017, 511-18

Coe, D., Fabinski, W., and Wiegleb., "The Impact of CO_2, H_2O and Other 'Greenhouse Gases' on Equilibrium Earth Temperatures", *International Journal of Atmospheric and Oceanic Sciences*, 5(2), 2021, 29-40.

Coorey, P., "Federal government to pour \$2 billion into major Snowy Hydro expansion,." *Australian Financial Review*, 15 March 2017 https://www.afr.com/politics/federal-government-to-pour-2bn-into-major-snowy-hydro-expansion-20170315-guyo3r

Glasgow, W., and Lacy, C., "Kristina Photios in climate change of heart." *The Australian*, 13 June 2017 https://www.theaustralian.com.au/business/margin-call/kristina-photios-in-climate-change-of-heart/news-story/aae4da2c25b46b021dcfbddbdd43d28c

Hausfather, Z., and Peters, G.P. "Emissions–the 'business as usual' story is misleading", *Nature*, 577.7792, 2020: 618-20.

Karp, P., "Turnbull to announce \$2bn expansion to Snowy hydro-electric scheme." *The Guardian*, 16 March 2017 https://www.theguardian.com/australia-news/2017/mar/16/turnbull-2bn-snowy-hydro-electric-expansion

Macdonald-Smith, A., "Renewable energy set to boom after "two-year drought", *Australian Financial Review*, 1 March 2016 https://www.afr.com/business/energy/renewable-energy-set-to-boom-after-twoyear-drought-20160229-gn6zob

McKitrick, R., and Christy, J., "Pervasive warming bias in CMIP6 tropospheric layers", *Earth and Space Science*, 7(9), e2020EA001281

McKitrick, R., "The important climate study you won't hear about." *Financial Post,* 12 April 2023 https://financialpost.com/opinion/ross-mckitrick-the-important-climate-study-you-wont-hear-about?mc_cid=6d99bd6c90&mc_eid=0d40af115e

Macquarie,Lachlan, "Government and General Orders", 5 March. 1817 https://gallery.records.nsw.gov.au/index.php/galleries/50-years-at-state-records-nsw/1-4/

Manheimer, W., "While the Climate Always Has and Always Will Change, There Is no Climate Crisis", *Journal of Sustainable Development*, 15(5), 2022, 116-134.

Murphy, K., "Scott Morrison brings coal to question time: what fresh idiocy is this?" *The Guardian.* 9 February 2017 https://www.theguardian.com/australia-news/2017/feb/09/scott-morrison-brings-coal-to-question-time-what-fresh-idiocy-is-this

Nicholls, S., "Liberal powerbroker Michael Photios 'took one for the team'", *Sydney Morning Herald.* 26 February 2017 https://www.smh.com.au/national/nsw/liberal-powerbroker-michael-photios-took-one-for-the-team-20170226-gulnlh.html

Norrington, B., "Federal election: Chance of clean-energy windfall for Climate 200 boss if independents get up", *The Australian.* 26 April 2022 https://www.theaustralian.com.au/nation/federal-election-cleanenergy-windfall-for-climate-200-boss-if-independents-get-up/news-story/322e8802a99c48c96a42 3f9b8f85e08b

Ollier, C. "Lysenkoism and 'Global Warming'," *Energy and Environment*, 20 (1&2) 2009, 197–200

Paltridge, G., Arking, A., and Pook, M. "Trends in middle-and upper-level tropospheric humidity from NCEP reanalysis data", *Theoretical and Applied Climatology*, 98(3), 2009, 351-59

Patrick, A., "Taylor didn't invest in 'Watergate' farms: law firm." *Australian Financial Review.* 3 May 2019 https://www.afr.com/politics/federal/ashurst-law-firm-says-angus-taylor-didn-t-invest-in-watergate-farms-20190503-p51jsz

Pielke Jr, R., "It's Time To Get Real About The Extreme Scenario Used To Generate Climate Porn." *Forbes.* 26 September. 2019 https://www.forbes.com/sites/rogerpielke/2019/09/26/its-time-to-get-real-about-the-extreme-scenario-used-to-generate-climate-porn/?sh=9f4bb794af0d

Pielke Jr, R., "How Billionaires Tom Steyer and Michael Bloomberg Corrupted Climate Science", *Forbes*, 2 January 2020 https://www.forbes.com/sites/rogerpielke/2020/01/02/how-billionaires-tom-steyer-and-michael-bloomberg-corrupted-climate-science/?sh=153a3af5702c

Pielke Jr, R., and Ritchie, J. "Distorting the view of our climate future: The misuse and abuse of climate pathways and scenarios", *Energy Research & Social Science*, 72, 2021, 101890

Rasool, S.I., & Schneider, S.H. (1971). "Atmospheric carbon dioxide and aerosols: Effects of large increases on global climate", *Science*, 173(3992), 138-41

Rintoul, S., "Town of Beaufort changed Tony Abbott's view on climate change." *The Australian.* 12 December 2009. https://www.theaustralian.com.au/news/town-of-beaufort-changed-tony-abbotts-view-on-climate-change/news-story/6fe0d32a32e42341a12b999f6da82ec5

Scafetta, N., (2021). "Testing the CMIP6 GCM Simulations versus surface temperature records from 1980–1990 to 2011–2021: High ECS is not supported", *Climate*, 9(11), 2021, 161

Shooters, Fishers and Farmers, "Are 'power-brokers' letting us run out of power?", Press Release. 19 June2017, https://tinyurl.com/5xszusen

Smethurst, A., "How Alex Turnbull is avenging his father ex-PM Malcolm's dumping", *Sunday Telegraph*, 9 December 2018. https://www.dailytelegraph.com.au/news/nsw/how-alex-turnbull-is...m-malcolms-dumping/news-story/c191b8564aa43e6cc08ddeaa3b407a1a

Sturmer, J., "Tony Abbott's department discussed investigation into Bureau of Meteorology over global warming exaggeration claims, FOI documents reveal", *ABC News.* 24 September 2015 https://www.abc.net.au/news/2015-09-24/government-discussed-bom-investigation-over-climate-change/6799628

van Wijngaarden. W.A. and Happer, W., (2020) "Dependence of Earth's Thermal Radiation on Five Most Abundant Greenhouse Gases", *Atmospheric and Oceanic Physics* arXiv: 2006, 03098.

Yandle, B., *The Political Limits of Environmental Regulation*, New York: Quorum Books, 1989

Zou, C.Z., Xu, H., Hao, X., and Liu, Q., "MidTropospheric Layer Temperature Record Derived from Satellite Microwave Sounder Observations with Backward Merging Approach." *Journal of Geophysical Research: Atmospheres*, 2023. e2022JD037472.

8

Managing COVID

David Lee

Introduction

Most of the term that followed the re-election of the Morrison Government in May 2019 was dedicated to the management of the SARS-CoV-2 virus, which caused COVID-19. The novel virus was first identified in the Chinese city of Wuhan in late December 2019. When attempts to contain the virus failed, it spread to other areas of Asia and throughout the world including to Australia (Wright 2021). The World Health Organization (WHO) began referring to COVID-19 as a pandemic on 11 March 2020, and as of June 2023 it had caused nearly seven million deaths, making it one of the deadliest in history (WHO 2023). By the time that the Morrison Government was defeated in May 2022, Australia had had seven million cases and 8000 deaths, with most fatalities occurring after the progressive lifting of health restrictions (Duckett 2023: 87).

As leader of the Liberal Party and Prime Minister in a Liberal–National Party Coalition Government, Morrison was inheritor of a set of principles embodied in the platform of the Liberal Party of Australia. These included a belief in the ideology of liberalism with its emphasis on the individual; a commitment to the federal system and the decentralisation of power; to government being sufficiently responsive so that it could meet its proper obligations to citizens; to equality of opportunity; to parliamentary democracy and the separation and distribution of powers; and to the idea of limited government and maximum encouragement of free enterprise (Liberal Party of Australia 2002; Tiver 1976).

The purpose of this chapter is to examine how a Liberal-National Party Coalition Government responded to the COVID-19 emergency in relation to the broad set of principles and values outlined above. Given the scale of the economic crisis that it confronted, it was inevitable that the Morrison Government would have to jettison, at least temporarily, ideas of limited government by going massively into deficit. This was one of its most significant achievements. It would have been much harder for an Australian Labor Party government to have achieved the same outcome given the reputation for profligacy, fairly or unfairly, that Labor had earned during the earlier Global Financial Crisis of 2007-8.

In managing the pandemic, Morrison took pride in the relatively low number of deaths and in the 40,000 lives that he estimated had been saved during the crisis years of the pandemic, particularly by the swift closure of Australia's international border (Morrison 2022). Also generally successful was the Morrison Government's package of measures to assist businesses and individuals affected by the pandemic. In this the Treasury offered mainly sound advice and the systems of the Australian Taxation Office (ATO) worked efficiently. The assistance measures may be criticised, however, on the ground of party principle that they involved payments to enterprises which did not need them and that they excluded others, like university employees, whose jobs might have continued (equality of opportunity). The Morrison Government performed poorly, too, in its vaccine procurement strategy and management of quarantine and aged care, an argument against the government being responsive to the needs of its citizens. Part of the problem here, however, was that the Morrison Government was let down by Commonwealth agencies, particularly the federal Health Department, that were not fit for purpose following decades of reform. Similar agencies at state level were in much better shape.

From the outset, the Morrison Government accepted that the Commonwealth had to work in concert with the States in managing the pandemic as had been the case a century earlier with the Spanish Flu pandemic. This was in keeping with Liberal Party ideas about federalism although not with the practice of some former Liberal prime ministers, including John Howard and John Gorton. There was, moreover, an inevitability about the need for Commonwealth-State co-operation given the key responsibility of the States over areas such as hospitals, health and schools and the Commonwealth's power of the purse. Nevertheless, despite the initial success of Morrison's machinery for coordination of the Commonwealth and States, relations between the two levels of government frayed with deleterious consequences for management of the pandemic and the Government's prospects of re-election. By not taking actions in areas of Commonwealth power, such as quarantine, the Morrison Government surrendered the initiative to the States in areas such as closures of internal borders and schools. Moreover, Morrison overreacted to the emergency of the pandemic by introducing a practice contrary to all principles of parliamentary responsible government in Australia by secretly swearing himself into several other portfolios (Commonwealth of Australia 2022). Ironically, this only became known through Morrison giving privileged access to information to authors of a book about the pandemic published in 2022 (Benson and Chambers 2022).

Border Closures, the National Cabinet and the Economy

The Morrison Government closed the international border in stages but decisively. On 1 February 2020 it banned the entry of foreign nationals who had been in mainland China and ordered its own citizens who were returning from China to self-quarantine for 14 days. Similar action followed for Iran (1 March), South Korea (5 March) and Italy (11 March). Then, on 20 March, the Morrison Government closed borders to non-Australian residents and made Australian citizens returning from overseas submit to two months of compulsory quarantining in hotels. Morrison and his Treasurer, Josh Frydenberg, did not take these decisions lightly. They understood the impact on the economy and specifically on the likelihood of the Morrison Government being able to deliver the budget surplus it had promised in 2019. Nonetheless, the soundness of the Morrison Government's decisions to close international borders was demonstrated by the fact that, in March 2020, most of Australia's coronavirus cases had been contracted from travellers returning from overseas. The Morrison Government's decisive action on closure of international borders compared favourably with the vacillating approach of the Trump Administration, which at first instituted only a limited travel ban on China (Bollyky and Nuzzo 2020).

In early March 2020, Australia's Chief Medical Officer, Dr Brendan Murphy, was still giving briefings downplaying the impact of the virus and emphasising progressive adoption of social distancing. At the same time, countries such as Italy were introducing drastic measures. In early March, Italian Prime Minister Giuseppe Conte placed more than 60 million people in lockdown and on 11 March prohibited nearly all commercial activity except for supermarkets and pharmacies (Tondo 2020). This was the context in which Morrison developed the idea of repurposing the Council of Australian Governments (COAG) as a "National Cabinet" (Benson and Chambers: 62-5). He proposed to bring together the Governments of the Commonwealth, the States and the Territories, but not their Oppositions, into a "National Cabinet". The National Cabinet became a sub-committee of the federal Cabinet giving its proceedings the same confidentiality that Cabinet and its committees enjoyed. Morrison hoped that by giving the meeting "cabinet" status, he would encourage its members to speak more freely and adhere to agreed decisions (Benson and Chambers: 76).

The National Cabinet functioned well initially and boosted the Morrison Government's stocks after Morrison's misadventures during the bushfire crisis. Journalist Tom Burton wrote in March 2020 that: "Australia's first national cabinet is finally doing what countless reviews, academics and government watches have pleaded for: governments of all colours, and their agencies, working as one, in a form of co-operative federalism many officials had only dreamed of" (Burton 2020). The premiers and territory leaders were happy with Morrison's early handling of the National Cabinet, commending him on chairing it well, and allowing members to speak and receiving pertinent briefings from federal departments including Treasury and the Department of Health (Savva 2022: 89). Establishing the National Cabinet as a vehicle for Commonwealth-State cooperation was both in keeping with Liberal principles and generally the better way to cope with the crisis than the alternative, proposed by some, of the Commonwealth seeking to exert fuller control. Despite the accretion of Commonwealth power over the twentieth and early twenty-first centuries, Australia had not become a unitary state but was a federal polity with States and State leaders enjoying significant popular support.

Establishment of the National Cabinet had consequences, however, for the operation of the Federal Government. It tended to diminish the importance of Cabinet and make its National Security Committee the supreme decision-making body of the government (Savva: 88). This, in turn, meant that the profiles of some of Morrison's ministers outside the National Security Committee were lessened. One of them likened the changes of governance structures to returning to the backbench (Errington and van Onselen 2021: 144). Morrison later developed a "kitchen cabinet", which he used to test ideas which were either submitted to or emerged from the national cabinet. According to Wayne Errington and Peter van Onselen, this kitchen cabinet was essentially the leadership group with the Minister for Health, Greg Hunt, often substituting for Deputy Prime Minister and National Party Leader, Michael McCormack. This had the negative consequence that McCormack sometimes had no place at the National Cabinet table (Errington and van Onselen: 144-5). With the approval of the Attorney-General, Christian Porter, Morrison also carried out a plan to ward against the accretion of powers during the COVID emergency by the Minister for Health. With the knowledge only of Porter and Hunt, Morrison had himself sworn in as Minister for Health and, without the knowledge of his Minister for Finance, Mathias Cormann, as Minister for Finance (Benson and Chambers: 89). In doing so and contrary to Liberal Party principles, Morrison undermined the principles of responsible parliamentary government and the office of Governor-General "as symbol of unity and continuity" (Liberal Party 2022; Commonwealth of Australia 2022).

A political benefit of the National Cabinet was that it helped to draw attention away from the Morrison Government's other political problems and minimised damage from individual backbenchers such as the former Deputy Prime Minister, Barnaby Joyce, and others who could at times be critical of the National Cabinet's vaccination strategy, such as Craig Kelly and George Christenson (*The Age* 2021). The presence on the coalition backbench of opponents of the national vaccination strategy and a slim majority in the House of Representatives made Morrison's task in managing the pandemic and the National Cabinet all the harder. A further political advantage of the National Cabinet was that it made it more difficult for the Leader of the Opposition, Anthony Albanese, to gain traction in the media as he had during the bushfire crisis of 2019-20. The attention paid to the National Cabinet meant that shadow ministers were rarely heard and a campaign to have Albanese installed in the national cabinet was not successful (Errington and van Onselen: 168-9). A negative consequence of the establishment of the National Cabinet for Morrison, however, was that it helped to make the premiers into national figures, and some of them more popular than the Prime Minister himself.

The Morrison Government's greatest success in managing the pandemic was in keeping the economy functioning despite the lockdowns and internal border closures that were put in place by the States and Territories during the pandemic. In this the actions of the Morrison Government compares with similar broadly successful action taken by the Rudd Labor Government during the Global Financial Crisis (Anderson 2013). Frydenberg's pre-election budget in 2019 had forecast a surplus for the 2019–20 financial year. The projected surplus was part of a political strategy either to minimise the scale of the loss of the coalition parties in the 2019 election or to win it, the former being regarded as the less likely option (Errington and van Onselen: 168). Morrison and Frydenberg quickly accepted that, having won the election and with the onset of COVID, the budget needed to go substantially into deficit. While this posed something of a challenge to traditional Liberal principles, it would have been a mistake both economically and politically for the Morrison Government not to have done so given that it was responding to exceptional circumstances.

On 12 March 2020 they introduced the first of three tranches of stimulus spending. The first tranche totalled $17.6 billion and included additional welfare payments, wage subsidies, business cash flow support and accelerated write-downs of assets (Zhou 2020). Barely a week after this announcement, the Reserve Bank of Australia (RBA) signalled that it intended to add "quantitative easing" by purchasing government bonds (Farrer 2020). The second package, totalling $66.1

billion, was announced on 22 March and included a $550 per fortnight Coronavirus Supplement for new and existing recipients of the JobSeeker Payment, which replaced Newstart Allowance and several other payments from 20 March 2020 (Parliament of Australia 2020). This was a notable increase in social welfare payments given that there had been no increase in unemployment benefits in real terms since the Howard years (Errington and van Onselen: 166-67). Moreover, the supplement had the beneficial effect of lifting many welfare recipients out of poverty (Henriques-Gomes 2021). A more controversial element of this second package was the decision to allow Australians affected by the pandemic early access to their retirements savings. Before the end of 2020, nearly three million people had withdrawn a total of $36 billion from their superannuation accounts, well above Treasury estimates that $30 billion would be accessed (Borys and Snape: 2020). Former Labor prime ministers, Paul Keating and Kevin Rudd, were two of the Government's most prominent critics, accusing it of using the COVID-19 crisis to "destroy the superannuation system" (Norman 2020).

On 30 March 2020, Morrison and Frydenberg announced the third and largest stimulus package. This took the form of a $130 billion wage subsidy called JobKeeper and the "biggest single spend on anything in Australian history" (*AFR* 2021). Morrison had initially been reluctant to introduce wage subsidies for workers as some other countries were doing. But he was persuaded otherwise by Frydenberg working in concert with the Secretary of the Treasury, Steven Kennedy. Kennedy offered Frydenberg three options that would keep employees tied to their jobs and their employers. The options were $1000, $1300 and $1500 a fortnight (Savva: 97). Frydenberg chose the third option and arranged for the ATO to administer the payments. Morrison agreed and insisted on a $1500 flat rate, rather than having the support tailored to wages as it was in the United Kingdom (Errington and van Onselen: 170-1).

Under JobKeeper, employers were eligible for a payment of $1500 per fortnight to keep staff employed in cases where the businesses had seen a 30 per cent downturn in revenue in one month. JobKeeper was initially projected to cost the Government $130 billion, but that figure was revised downward to $90 billion by the time of the mid-financial year update in December 2020. The Government prided itself on the simplicity of the scheme, and the ATO performed well in administering it. This was confirmed by the Australian National Audit Office (ANAO) commending the 1160 ATO staff engaged in administering JobKeeper and processing $89 billion to more than one million entities (Ravlic 2022). Frydenberg emphasised this conclusion by pointing to Treasury advice that the unemployment rate would have peaked five percentage points higher and remained above 12 per cent for two years (Khadem 2021).

But despite its overall success and generally efficient administration, the JobKeeper scheme included a significant design fault. It had no mechanism to claw back monies paid to companies that had qualified initially but whose revenues later recovered. In October 2021, the Treasury reported that $27 billion in JobKeeper payments to businesses whose turnover either increased or did not decline as much as required. Because of the absence of a claw-back mechanism, these companies continued to receive JobKeeper payments and in some cases were able to pay executive bonuses and award shareholder dividends (Errington and van Onselen: 171). Although the Government kept its JobKeeper payments secret, *The New Daily* reported in March 2021 that more than 60 Australian Securities Exchange (ASX) businesses had received payments. They recorded combined profits of $8.6 billion over eighteen months, disbursed more than $3.6 billion in dividends to investors since April 2020, paid back just $72 million and awarded $20 million in bonuses to executives (Stacey 2021). Journalist Joe Aston from the *Australian Financial Review* alleged that the amount of money wasted on JobKeeper was closer to $40 billion (Aston 2021) and Labor MP Andrew Leigh judged the scheme "[t]he biggest waste of Commonwealth money in Australian history" (Leigh 2021). This waste was inconsistent with the usual reputation of the Liberal Party for prudent economic management and contributed to the inflationary spiral that Australians experienced after the defeat of the Morrison Government.

Other contentious questions about JobKeeper concerned eligibility, a matter that bears on the commitment of the Liberal Party to equality of opportunity. For example, while making the scheme eligible for private universities, it deliberately excluded public universities, even though the peak universities association, Universities Australia, estimated that 21,000 jobs would be lost from the sector (Moodie 2020). In July 2020, the University of New South Wales criticised the Government after announcing it would have to cut nearly 500 full-time jobs and National Tertiary Education Union president, Alison Barnes, claimed: "[t]ey have stubbornly refused to extend JobKeeper to Australian universities and failed to provide anything close to an adequate support package (McCubbing 2020). On the other hand, higher education expert, Andrew Norton, concluded that the government had been right to exclude public universities, which were partly government entities, partly for-profit businesses and partly charities. Norton found that most public universities received half their income from government sources, giving them a solid financial base that made 2020 relatively stable for them (Hare 2021). The magnitude of the economic challenge brought on by COVID-19 meant that traditional values and past practices of the coalition parties had to make way for new policies to confront the COVID-19 emergency. The situation was like that faced by the United Australia Party government led by the Robert Menzies during the Second World War. The Menzies' Government, despite similar commitment to limited government, perforce had to introduce far-reaching economic controls to manage the economy in wartime. This had seen the Menzies Government, like Morrison's Coalition Government, seek Commonwealth-State co-operation and resist the decision of its Labor successor to use the wartime emergency legislation to monopolise the field of income taxation in 1942.

Vaccination Procurement Strategy and Aged Care

In February 2021 Morrison affirmed at the National Press Club that the first of his priorities was to "suppress the virus and deliver the vaccine" (Savva: 107). In the early part of that year, political analysts could discern signs that the Morrison Government was looking to reap the political advantages of what it hoped would be a successful vaccine rollout. Yaron Finkelstein in the Prime Minister's Office began to arrange pollsters to test public opinion, and other advisers were banking on the Government being able to make a powerful pitch at an election towards the end of 2021 on the back of mass vaccination and the beginning of the return to normality (Errington and van Onselen: 255). Instead, the vaccination rollout, "turned into a bog, full of incomplete, conflicting or inaccurate data that could not even be relied on as a guide to how many vulnerable Australians and their carers had been inoculated" (Savva: 107).

In the early part of 2021, Morrison and his advisers adopted a careful approach to the vaccine rollout. Brendan Murphy, for example, remarked at a doorstop that: "This is not a race. We have no burning platform in Australia. We are taking it as quickly and carefully and safely as we can. We're not like the US, or the UK, or most other countries in the world where they've got people in hospital dying. We can take our time, set up our systems, do it safely and carefully. We are expanding our rollout every day" (Savva: 108). Morrison later echoed Murphy's observations by saying of the vaccine rollout: "It's not a race, right. It's not a competition". This phrase joined other remarks of his, such as "I don't hold a hose mate", delivered during the bushfire crisis, to define Morrison negatively (Savva: 108).

In the circumstances of uncertainty that prevailed in 2020 when vaccines were being hurriedly developed, the optimal procurement strategy for any government was to hedge bets by spreading investments and plans over multiple vaccines. Just such a strategy was recommended to the Government in August 2020 by the consultancy group McKinsey (Farrell and McDonald 2021). But the Morrison Government decided to opt for a two-vaccine strategy with both its preferred vaccines, AstraZeneca and a potential vaccine being developed by the University of Queensland, having strong Australian links. The problem with this strategy was that, if troubles emerged with the narrow range of preferred vaccines, there might be no other vaccine available in sufficient quantities to complete a timely vaccination rollout. This was precisely the scenario that unfolded during 2021.

The Therapeutic Goods Administration (TGA) approved the AstraZeneca vaccine provisionally in February 2021 and finally in March. It had the advantage that it could be stored at normal refrigeration temperatures of between 2 and 8 degrees centigrade, whereas the Pfizer vaccine, the leading vaccine in the United States, required storage at -70 degrees centigrade. Another benefit of AstraZeneca was that CSL Ltd began manufacturing doses locally with deliveries expected to begin in March. These advantages were offset by shortcomings. One was a question about the ability of the AstraZeneca vaccine to bring about "herd immunity", the immunity that occurs when a sufficient proportion of the community becomes immune to the disease (Hyde 2021). Another was the discovery that the AstraZeneca vaccine caused blood clots in a very small number of cases, although a number significant enough to add to vaccine hesitancy (Aubusson 2021). Morrison announced the complication in a late-night press conference along with advice that people under the age of 50 should get the Pfizer vaccine. The Morrison Government's embarrassment was exacerbated when it was later discovered that Hunt and the Department of Health had not taken up Pfizer's offer for early delivery of the vaccine, meaning that the Pfizer vaccine was not available early enough or in sufficient numbers (Martin 2021). Adding to the growing problems was that on 5 March 2021, Italy and the European Union blocked shipment of 250,000 doses from Italy to Australia, citing low case numbers in Australia.

The result of the flawed vaccine procurement strategy was that, although Morrison had been promising that Australia would be "at the front of the queue" in respect of vaccines, 61 other countries began vaccinating their citizens in January 2021. The Australian vaccination program only began on 22 February 2021 with the goal of vaccinating all willing people by 2022. Front-line workers and aged-care staff and residents were accorded priority before a gradual release to less vulnerable and lower risk groups throughout the year. Problems with the AstraZeneca vaccine and not having enough supplies of the main alternative, Pfizer, meant that the vaccination strategy fell behind schedule. Part of the problem was caused by serious structural deficiencies in the Department of Health. Successful policy development and program delivery in the Department of Health requires departmental officers to understand a highly complex sector with services delivered by State governments, thousands of individual doctors and other health professionals and large corporate entities.

But under Hunt as minister, the Department of Health abolished its strategic policy committee. Moreover, staff ceilings had fostered an excessive reliance on consultancies in conjunction with a rapid turnover of managerial officers (Maskell-Knight 2022).

In April 2021 Morrison was forced to abandon targets for the rollout and to concede that not all Australians would get their first jab of the vaccine by the end of the year (Galloway and Bonyhady 2021). Frank Bongiorno, Professor of History at the Australian National University, described the vaccination roll-out as the "worst national public policy failure in modern Australian history, rivalled only by Paul Keating's early-1990 recession we had to have" (Bongiorno 2021) and former prime minister, Malcolm Turnbull, concluded that the rollout was a "colossal failure" because the Commonwealth Government had failed to buy enough vaccines with the result that borders would have to remain closed until at least early 2022 (Reuters 2021). The flawed vaccination strategy also reinforced perceptions of Morrison as a leader who promised but did not deliver (Feik 2020).

In July 2021 Morrison appointed Lieutenant General John Frewen to take control of the faltering vaccine rollout. Morrison gave Frewen "direct operational control of all relevant assets and resources across all Commonwealth government departments and agencies engaged in the direction and operation of the national COVID vaccination program". Frewen was made responsible for "communication around the vaccine rollout, engagement with health providers including hospitals, GPs, Aboriginal Health Services and pharmacies, and engagement with key community stakeholders, business groups and unions" (Anderson 2021). Frewen directly reported to Morrison and Hunt and attended National Cabinet meetings. This appointment was another sign of the obvious deficiencies of the federal Department of Health but, as former Chief of the Army Peter Leahy argued, risked politicising the military (*The Australian* 2021). Guy Rundle claimed that putting a general in charge of vaccines was making Australia look like "one of those landlocked banana republics"; Jon Faine that it was a "mission misfire" and an insult to the doctors and medical practitioners who should be taking the lead; and security export John Blaxland that it was evidence of a "sense of vulnerability" on the part of the

Morrison Government that it had been forced to ask the military to step in (Anderson 2021).

Since 2011 the Commonwealth Government had acquired sole funding and regulatory responsibility for aged care. But in an area that was the exclusive responsibility of the Commonwealth, seven per cent of all COVID-19 cases and 75 per cent of all deaths in the first year of the pandemic occurred in residential aged-care facilities (Duckett: 92). The Commonwealth Government's management of aged care during the pandemic was later subject to withering criticism from a special report from the Royal Commission into Aged Care Quality and Safety (Royal Commission into Aged Care Quality and Safety, 2020). By January 2022, 1198 aged care residences had been affected by COVID-19 with 7861 testing positive and 216 dying. A sign of the failings of the Department of Health in this respect came with the rapid spread of the Omicron variant in late 2021. The Department of Health let a contract to an external provider to provide booster shots for residents in aged care facilities, but the terms of the contract allowed the contractor to stand down over the holiday period (Maskell-Knight 2022). In the areas of vaccine procurement and management of aged care, the Morrison Government demonstrably fell short of being responsive to the needs of Australian citizens.

Commonwealth and States

Although establishment of the National Cabinet briefly boosted the Morrison Government's political stocks, relations between the Commonwealth and the States progressively frayed in 2020 and 2021. For journalist Nikki Savva, Morrison "veered between supporting and opposing lockdowns, closures and mandates. He was caught in a pincer movement between the majority of Australians who supported the tougher measures proposed by state and territory leaders, and a noisy influential minority – which included state and federal Liberals – aggressively attacking governments, and fighting for freedom from vaccines, conventional protection measures and democratically elected leaders they called dictators, whom some of them threatened to kill" (Savva: 87-8). Stephen Duckett saw the problem as coming from a design fault in the National Cabinet, which was set up in haste with no real operational rules. For Duckett: "[a]ny outcome of a National Cabinet meeting was a 'decision' in name only: behind the fig leaf of unity, each state and territory went its own way, while the Commonwealth ran a critique from the sidelines" (Duckett: 89).

This became clear in disagreement between the Commonwealth and States early in 2020 over schools. On 13 March 2020 Morison made clear that he wanted a national policy on schools with his preference that schools should stay open (Duckett: 89). In a social media video, Morrison declared: "We will lose many things in the course of fighting this virus. One thing I know teachers are united on, with their parents is we do not want one of those things to be the loss of a child's education, giving up a whole year of their learning" (Errington and van Onselen: 154-5). By that time, however, policy makers in the States were aware of the unfolding COVID tragedy in Italy (Goodman and Pianigiani 2020). One of them, the Liberal Premier of New South Wales, Gladys Berejiklian, was concerned about the virus spreading through the school system to the community. She contacted the Labor Premier of Victoria, Daniel Andrews, and the two leaders resolved that the schools in their respective States should be closed. After enlisting the support of the Chief Minister of the Australian Capital Territory, Andrew Barr, the trio released a joint statement on 22 March (Murphy and Martin 2020). Morrison had no alternative but to pivot and leave the matter of school closures to the States. When the National Cabinet met again on 18 March, it agreed on a package to ban non-essential gatherings greater than one hundred; to subject other indoor gatherings to social distancing of 1.5 metres; and ban outdoor gatherings of more than 500 with few exemptions (Errington and van Onselen: 148)

The States started closing their borders on 19 March 2020 when Tasmania became the first to impose fourteen days quarantine on non-essential travellers. On 24 March, Western Australia, South Australia and the Northern Territory closed their borders when all inter-state arrivals were required to quarantine for fourteen days. On 11 April Queensland banned interstate arrivals with only Queensland residents and those granted exemptions allowed entry. Then on 8 July, the Victorian and New South Wales governments jointly closed their borders. By December of that year, State border closures and the strains on implementing the hotel quarantining system meant that 30,000 people were registered with the Commonwealth Government as being stranded overseas.

When Tasmania and its Liberal government experimented with State border closure, the Labor Premier of Western Australia, Mark McGowan, began reading about Australian governance during the 1919 Spanish Flu Pandemic and learned that the Government of Western Australia had resorted to impounding the trans-continental train (Savva: 102). This reading informed McGowan's decision not to close down the State internally but to seal off Western Australia's border with the eastern States in addition to imposing two weeks compulsory quarantining for any exemptions. McGowan's action in instituting one of the world's longest border closures (Marcus 2022), lasting 697 days, led to a dramatic upsurge in his popularity but triggered a legal dispute with mining magnate, Clive Palmer, who challenged its legality and called on the Commonwealth to support him in keeping State borders open.

Two of Morrison's senior Western Australian ministers, the Minister for Finance, Mathias Cormann, and the Attorney-General, Christian Porter, persuaded Morrison to have the Commonwealth support Palmer's case. Porter declared that the Commonwealth was acting in the best interests of both the Commonwealth and Western Australia in "having borders which are constitutionally sustainable". This was despite the popularity of the border closure among Western Australians. "If it were as easy", Porter continued, "as going into the High Court and saying 96 percent of people on Western Australia would prefer this, we wouldn't have an issue on our hands, but that is not the question before the High Court" (Cross and Hondros 2020). But two of Morrison's closest political confidants, Alex Hawke and Stuart Robert, tried unsuccessfully to persuade him to drop the action against Western Australia. In Robert's view, the West was lost to the Coalition politically, the moment that Morrison endorsed the challenge (Savva: 102). Hawke and Robert had good reason to be fearful. Most Western Australians thought McGowan's decision to be the right one. Thus, although there was an argument of principle for the Commonwealth to take a stronger stance against State border closures, politically and practically it was disastrous for the Morrison Government to have done so.

In another area, although it was one of the enumerated powers of the Commonwealth in the Constitution, the Morrison Government was content to leave quarantine to the States. In doing so Morrison declined to take the advice of former Secretary of the Department of Health, Jane Halton, who recommended purpose-built quarantine centres. The only one on mainland Australia was at Howard Springs in Darwin. Its potential to manage returning travellers without leaking infection was clear, but it was not big enough to handle the large number of Australians who wanted to come home. Morrison accepted advice from others that Commonwealth-constructed quarantine facilities would become "white elephants" after the end of the pandemic. While not initiating extensive Commonwealth action on quarantine, Morrison and his ministers nonetheless frequently criticised Labor States, such as Victoria, following an outbreak from state-administered quarantine hotels. The bad blood between the Commonwealth and Labor States, Victoria, Queensland and Western Australia on administration of quarantine, border closures and lockdowns contributed to the progressive unravelling of the national cabinet.

 Borders reopened internationally in February 2022 (Knaus 2022) as the States also progressively reopened their borders with Western Australia the last to do so. But a wave of the Omicron variant of the coronavirus in the summer of 2021–22 occurred while there was a lack of supplies of rapid antigen tests to allow those affected to test whether they had the virus (Ward 2022). This meant that there could be no return to normality of the kind that Morrison and his advisers were hoping for in the months preceding the federal election, delayed until May 2022, but rather a self-imposed lockdown in many States. In this situation, Morrison urged that Australians should now embrace a "culture of responsibility" that placed the onus on individuals to take protective action against COVID-19 rather than a "culture of mandates" by government (SBS News 2021). Journalist Paul Daley commented: "I also get a distinct feeling I'm not alone in finding thoroughly galling a PM who accepts liability for so damned little (not the delayed vaccine and now booster roll-out) ... hectoring me about what we want while urging us to take personal responsibility" (Daley 2021).

Conclusion

The Morrison's Government's record in handling the pandemic was mixed. On the positive side, it acted swiftly and decisively to close the international border and was prepared to suspend economic orthodoxy to go massively into deficit to keep the economy functioning during border closures and lockdowns. On the other hand, it erred in not ensuring greater equity among potential recipients and in making payments to some enterprises that had no need of them. In this respect, trying to keep more in step with traditional political values of fiscal prudence may have led to a better long-term outcome for Australia.

Taking the route of Commonwealth-State co-operation in the crisis was consistent with party ideals, although not always with previous coalition practice. Moreover, a completely Commonwealth-led approach was never a viable alternative given the division of powers and responsibilities in Australia's federal polity. Morrison did not have the advantage, as wartime Commonwealth leaders had, of the defence power of the Constitution. Morrison's establishment of the National Cabinet was therefore a commendable attempt to encourage Commonwealth–State co-operation as the means of ensuring the best national response to the COVID-19 emergency. It was the practical management of relations between Commonwealth and States in the National Cabinet that let the Morrison Government down in areas such as school and border closures and State lockdowns. Moreover, the swearing in of Morrison into multiple ministries was unnecessary and contrary to the principles of responsible parliamentary government. The Morrison Government's vaccine procurement strategy and action on quarantine were inadequate, its management of aged care tragic and it did not secure sufficient supply of essential materials such as Personal Protective Equipment (PPE) and tests (Senate 2022). In all these areas, a Liberal–National Party Government was not responsive to the needs of Australian citizens. Finally, Commonwealth–State relations progressively deteriorated over issues such as school and border closures and state-administered lockdowns. This not only hindered management of the pandemic but was a large contributing factor to the Morrison Government's election loss in May 2022. Emblematic of this was that Western Australian provided the Australian Labor Party with the seats it needed to win majority government (Towie 2022).

References

The Age, Editorial, "The real confusion about vaccines comes from the Morrison government's own ranks", *The Age*, 14 January 2021

Anderson, D., "How Australia weathered the global financial crisis where Europe failed", *The Guardian*, 28 August 2013

Anderson, W., "When the General Calls: Military Tactics Against COVID-19 in Australia", *Arena*, December 2021

Aston, J., "JobKeeper wasted $40 billion, not $27 billion, but who's counting?", *Australian Financial Review*, 12 October 2021

Aubusson, K., "NSW hospitals hunt for rare blood clots linked to AstraZeneca vaccine", *The Sydney Morning Herald*, 8 April 2021

The Australian, 'Don't Politicise the Military or Hide Behind Them', *The Australian*, 8 July 2021

Australian Financial Review editorial, "Too few strings was JobKeeper's success and failure", *Australian Financial Review*, 6 October 2021

Benson, S., and Chambers, G., *Plagued: Australia's Two Years of Hell—the Inside Story*, Neutral Bay: Pantera Press, 2022

Bollyky, T., and Nuzzo, J., "Trump's 'early' travel 'bans' weren't early, weren't bans and didn't work", *The Washington Post*, 1 October 2020

Bongiorno, F., "A little jab now and then: the federal government's handling of vaccinations shows how much damage has been done to the public sector", *Inside Story*, 9 July 2021

Borys, S., and Snape, J., "Super release slows but almost 3 million Australians have sucked billions from retirement savings", ABC, 31 December 2020

Burton, T., "National cabinet creates a new federal model", *Australian Financial Review*, 18 March 2020

Commonwealth of Australia, *Inquiry into the Appointment of the Former Prime Minister to Administer Multiple Departments*, Canberra, Commonwealth of Australia, 2022

Cross, C., and Hondros, N. "'I think he's the enemy of Australia': McGowan ramps up war of words with Palmer on WA border battle", *The Sydney Morning Herald*, 31 July 2020

Daley, P., "It's an Australian summer of self-imposed lockdown. Bring on the 2022 election", The Guardian, 31 December 2021

Duckett, S., "The (mis)management of the COVID-19 pandemic" in McCaffrie, B., Grattan, M., and Wallace, C., (eds), *The Morrison Government: Governing through Crisis, 2019–2022*, Sydney: NewSouth Publishing, 2023, 87-101

Editorial, "Clear Message is the Best Ammunition for General in the Vaccine Rollout", *The Sydney Morning Herald*, 30 June 2021

Errington, W., and van Onselen, P., *How Good is Scott Morrison?* Sydney: Hachette, 2021

Farrell, P., and McDonald, A., "A consultancy firm was paid $660,000 to advise on Australia's COVID-19 vaccine strategy. But a government official said they provided no 'specific advice'", ABC, 3 June 2021

Farrer, M., "What is quantitative easing and why is the Reserve Bank of Australia using it?", *The Guardian*, 3 November 2020

Feik, N., "The announcement artist", *The Monthly*, October 2020

Galloway, A., and Bonyady, N., "Vaccine targets dumped: Morrison concedes all Australians may not be vaccinated by end of the year", T*he Sydney Morning Herald*, 11 April 2021

Goodman, P., and Pianigiani, G., "Why Covid Caused Such Suffering in Italy's wealthiest Region", *The New York Times*, 19 November 2020

Hare, J., "Decision to keep unis out of JobKeeper Justified, analysis finds", *Australian Financial Review*, 6 July 2021

Henriques-Gomes, L., "Covid supplement end will mean being pushed further into poverty, Australia's jobless warn", *The Guardian*, 9 March 2021

Holden, R., and Leigh, A., "The race that stopped a nation: Lessons from Australia's vaccine failures", *Oxford Review of Economic Policy*, 2022

Hyde, Z., "Herd Immunity is the end game for the pandemic, but the AstraZeneca vaccine won't get us there", *The Conversation*, 15 February 2021

Khadem, N., "Treasury confirms it knew government was paying out billions in JobKeeper to firms that 'may not need support'", ABC, 11 October 2021

Knaus, C., "Australia to reopen international border on 21 February", *The Guardian*, 7 February 2022

Leigh, A., "Jobkeeper: "The biggest waste of Commonwealth money in Australian history", *Pearls & Irritations*, 5 September 2021

Liberal Party of Australia, *The Federal Platform of the Liberal Party of Australia*, 2002

Maskell-Knight, C., "Why the Department of Health has proven tragically inept", *Pearls & Irritations*, 29 January 2022

Marcus, L., "Western Australia ends one of the world's longest border closures", CNN, 3 March 2022

Martin, S., "Pfizer asked to meet with Greg Hunt about 'millions of doses' of vaccine but was offered bureaucrat instead", *The Guardian*, 8 September 2021

McCubbing, G., "Jobkeeper could have prevented cuts: UNSW", 16 July 2020

Moodie, G., "Why is the Australian government letting universities suffer?", *The Conversation*, 19 May 2020

Morrison, S., "Why I Love Australia" Liberal Party of Australia on YouTube 2022

Murphy, K., and Marton, S., "Confusion reigns over Australian coronavirus school closures after Morrison press conference", *The Guardian*, 22 March 2020

Norman, J., "Paul Keating and Kevin Rudd unite to pressure Scott Morrison on superannuation guarantee increase", ABC, 31 August 2020

Parliament of Australia, "COVID-19 Economic response—social security measures part 1: temporary supplement and improved access to income support", 23 March 2020

Reuters, "Australia's vaccine rollout 'a colossal failure', ex-PM Turnbull says", 27 July 2021

Ravlic, T., "ANAO Reports on ATO's JobKeeper Performance", *The Mandarin*, 7 April 2022

Royal Commission into Aged Care Quality and Safety, Aged Care and COVID-19: A Special Report, Royal Commission (Canberra), 2020

Senate, Final Report of the Select Committee on COVID-19, Commonwealth of Australia, April 2022

Savva, N., *Bulldozed: Scott Morrison's Fall and Anthony Albanese's Rise*, Brunswick: Scribe, 2022

SBSNews, "Scott Morrison urges 'personal responsibility' instead of mask mandates and lockdowns", 21 December 2021

World Health Organization (WHO), "Weekly Epidemiological update on COVID-19", 1 June 2023

Stacey, L., "The Big Grift: How the Top End of Town Rorted JobKeeper", *MichaelWest Media*, 5 March 2021

Tiver, P., 'The Ideology of the Liberal Party of Australia: A Sketch and Interpretation', *Politics*, 11(2), November 1976, 156-64

Tondo, L., "Coronavirus Italy: PM extends lockdown to entire country", *The Guardian*, 10 March 2020

Towie, M., "Western Australia goes all in on red—and it could deliver Labor majority government", *The Guardian*, 22 May 2022

Ward, R., "'This is deplorable': Australians furious as rapid tests run out, stalling work, family plans", *Sydney Morning Herald*, 4 January 2022

Wright, L., *The Plague Year: America in the Time of COVID*, New York: Knopf, 2021

Zhou, N., "Australian government unveils $17.6 bn stimulus package as coronavirus hammers stock market", *The Guardian*, 12 March 2020

9

Religious Freedom was left at the Altar

Mark Spencer

Introduction

Few people, if any, would claim to make their best decisions at 3:30 am after working all night. If any members of the 46th Commonwealth Parliament made that claim, the debate on the *Religious Discrimination Bill 2022* (Cth), and associated legislation,[1] on the morning of 10 February 2022 is the evidence to prove them wrong. This chapter reviews the Coalition Government's ability, or rather inability, to confirm religious freedom in Australia during its nine years in office, and the drivers which made this such a failure of policy direction and political nerve. For a party that is "dedicated to political liberty and the freedom and dignity of man" this reflects a significant disappointment.[2]

Background

But the failure of the Morrison Government to pass this legislation has its origins much, much earlier. It was the passage of *Discrimination Amendment (Sexual Orientation, Gender Identity and Intersex Status) Act 2013* (Cth) under the Gillard Government that laid the seeds of the tragedy that unfolded nearly a decade later. This act inserted "sexual orientation" and "gender identity" into the *Sex Discrimination Act 1984* (Cth) as protected characteristics. In accordance with the drafting practices of the day, these characteristics were also included amongst the attributes for which exemptions were provided to religious bodies, including religious educational institutions.[3] This was a deliberate recognition of the government of the "importance of the right to freedom of religion" and the legislation itself was so non-controversial that it was dealt with by the Federation Chamber. These exemptions remained non-controversial for the next five years, until weaponised during the Wentworth by-election campaign in 2018.

Despite being clearly and unequivocally recognised as a fundamental human right in modern international law, from the *Universal Declaration of Human Rights* in 1948 through to the *International Covenant on Civil and Political Rights* ("ICCPR") ratified by Australia in 1980, religious freedom has patchy protection in Australian domestic law. Constitutional protections, Section 116, have been found to be very narrow in application, not creating any "individual rights", and there has never been any stand-alone legislation prohibiting religious discrimination at the federal level. Historically, many church groups have opposed attempts to legislate religious freedom, most notably in the 1988 referendum where the proposed amendment to Section 116, was "strongly opposed by many church representatives and by independent schools, both fearful of the future of state aid to such schools" (Bennett and Brennan 1999: 29).

This position shifted dramatically following the passage of the, provocatively named, *Marriage Amendment (Definition and Religious Freedoms) Act 2017* (Cth) in December 2017. This act amended the *Marriage Act 1961* (Cth) to allow any two people to marry, regardless of sex, and followed 23 bills dealing with same-sex marriage being introduced into the Federal Parliament since 2004 (Neilsen 2017: 5). The religious freedoms protected in the Act were very narrow, allowing ministers of religion and certain existing marriage celebrants to refuse to solemnise a marriage, and allowing bodies established for religious purposes to refuse to provide facilities, goods and services for marriages on religious grounds. Faith groups across many religious traditions opposed this change to what is a core tenet of their faith and practice.

The Prime Minister, Malcolm Turnbull, had made his support for the Act clear, but it remained contentious within the government. It was at this time that many conservatives and religious leaders sought to ensure that religious freedoms would be protected, not merely in relation to marriage ceremonies, but more broadly, in anticipation that once this act was passed activists would move on to target other areas where religious freedoms were protected more aggressively (Newton 2017).[4] During the debate on the Act, now Opposition Leader Peter Dutton, then a "[l]eading conservative cabinet minister", is reported to have indicated that " ... a new 'religious protections' bill may be introduced in 2018" (Massola 2017). It is clear that the political compact made around the *Marriage Act* involved a strengthening of protections for religious freedom, however these protections were never legislated.

Expert Panel review of religious freedom

Instead, in December 2017 an expert panel chaired by former MP Phillip Ruddock was charged with reviewing whether Australian law adequately protected freedom of religion. The Expert Panel would report to the Prime Minister by, following an extension, 18 May 2018. The establishment of this review was described as "a thought bubble designed to solve a political problem" (Koziol 2017). This aptly characterised the role of this review, because at the same time there was, in fact, already a review underway into religious freedom.

On 29 November 2016 the Human Rights Sub-Committee of the Standing Committee on Foreign Affairs, Defence and Trade was asked to inquire into and report on the status of the human right to freedom of religion or belief in Australia.[5] An interim report had already been tabled the month prior to the announcement of the Expert Panel review, in November 2017 (Fawcett 2017). The Expert Panel review, as a political fix introduced by Prime Minister Turnbull to resolve the concerns flowing from the changed definition of marriage, proved to be a political time-bomb, with people of faith, and LGBT students in faith-based schools, still paying the price.

The subsequent failure to release the Expert Panel's report proved to be another political miscalculation. According to one of the report's authors, Father Frank Brennan (Wesselinoff 2023):

The delay in release of the report and the shambolic handling of its publication highlighted the political problem with our recommendations. The Turnbull wing of the Liberal Party favoured the tweaked tightening of the Sex Discrimination Act provisions but not the introduction of a Religious Discrimination Act. The Morrison wing of the Liberal Party were troubled by the former but attracted to the latter.

The failure of the Turnbull and Morrison governments to swiftly find an internal consensus position proved to be a kiss of death for any prospect of a rapid and decisive legislative response. Despite some feeble attempts to drive the narrative and control the media cycle on these issues, the genie very quickly came out of the bottle – with a life of its own.

Morrison makes promises for 2019 election

Following a leadership spill in August 2018 the new Prime Minister, Scott Morrison, came out strongly and "... vowed to change laws to protect religious freedom ..." (Crowe 2018). This commitment was quickly embroiled in controversy following the selective leaking of aspects of the Expert Panel's report in October 2018 during the Wentworth by-election (Topsfield 2018). The leaks, thought by many to be political pay-back, focussed on the exemptions provided to religious bodies so un-controversially and with bi-partisan support in 2013. The reporting took these exemptions, which would allow schools to expel LGBT students and claimed, with no evidence, that schools were, in fact, expelling these students.

Under political pressure from the Opposition, Greens and minor parties the Prime Minister, within days of the leaking of the report, had "... promised discrimination law amendments to make clear no student at a private or religious school should be expelled on the basis of their sexuality" (Karp 2018). The rot had set in and the fate of protections for religious freedom became inexorably tied to amendments to the *Sex Discrimination Act*. No other fundamental human right has been shackled in this way.

This promise by Prime Minister Morrison began a debate that continues to this day regarding the exemptions that have now been in the *Sex Discrimination Act 1984* (Cth) for nearly a decade. The Morrison Government took policies to the 2019 federal election to introduce a religious discrimination bill, if re-elected, and refer the amendment of the exemptions in the *Sex Discrimination Act 1984* (Cth) to the Australian Law Reform Commission. Many faith groups valued these clear commitments, with a wide range of commentors, including key ALP figures (Vistonay 2019) recognising the impact of religious voters on the outcome of the May 2019 election.

Draft legislation 2019-22 – delays and compromises

With this clear mandate for a religious discrimination bill, and an Opposition acutely aware of the cost of not protecting religious freedom, then Attorney-General, Christian Porter, released an exposure draft legislative package in August 2019.[6] It was not a good start to the legislation, with talk of a boycott by "blindsided" faith groups (Chambers and Brown 2019), reports that it was "… met with a distinct lack of enthusiasm by religious leaders and law experts." (Rodrigues 2019), and claims that it was "… hostile to fundamental democratic freedoms" (Phillip 2019).

To have released an exposure draft legislative package without extensive consultation with those groups most affected is inexplicable. Aware of the intense public interest in this legislation, it is confounding that faith groups were not brought into the tent and their views sought, even on a confidential basis, to ensure a more positive reception for the bill when proposed publicly. Was this political hubris or, as some legal scholars opined privately, fundamentally flawed legal analysis and understanding of religious freedom rights within the public service? Certainly, there was robust criticism of the application of international human rights law and jurisprudence in many of the submissions on this initial exposure draft.

While the expectations from faith leaders for a religious freedom bill enshrining a positive right to such freedoms were dashed, that did not stop opponents of the bill from raising a suite of bizarre and extreme examples of what the bills were purported to allow (Towell 2019). In many cases the scenarios raised would not have been unlawful under the existing legislative regime, but such a dispassionate assessment did not reduce their political impact. In the light of such opposition, from all sides it seemed, it came as no surprise that within a matter of months, on 10 December 2019, the Prime Minister and the Attorney-General released second exposure drafts of the three bills.

This second exposure draft legislation was a substantial improvement on the initial tranche and welcomed by Christian schools (Christian Schools Australia 2019). In many ways the second exposure draft reflected what the initial package could have been if the government had undertaken preliminary consultations with faith groups. While some fine tuning was recommended by faith groups and others, this second exposure draft reflected the core of the bills finally introduced to the Parliament. This false start on the religious discrimination bill would prove costly as the COVID-19 pandemic hijacked the government's legislative agenda.

It would be nearly two years after the release of that second exposure draft before the Prime Minister, Scott Morrison, himself introduced the *Religious Discrimination Bill 2022* (Cth) and associated legislation into the Parliament on 25 November 2021. The following day the Attorney-General, Senator Michaelia Cash, referred the bills to the Parliamentary Joint Committee on Human Rights for inquiry and report to both Houses of Parliament by 4 February 2022. On 2 December 2021, the Senate referred the bills to the Legal and Constitutional Affairs Legislation Committee for inquiry and report by the same deadline. Both of these committees recommended the passage of the bills, albeit with some minor amendments accepted by the government.

Before the Senate even referred the bills to the Legislation Committee, there were media reports of a deal with a group of Liberal 'moderates' to amend the *Sex Discrimination Act* by removing the exemptions which allows religious schools to discriminate against another person on the grounds of sexual orientation, gender identity, marital or relationship status or pregnancy (Martin 2021). The blunt instrument of removing all exemptions was opposed by Christian schools, who indicated to the Attorney-General in response to these claims that should this be the case support would be withdrawn for the package of bills, other faith groups indicated similarly. Amendments were proposed by the government that would prohibit the expulsion of students on the basis of sexual orientation, but not gender identity (Visentin 2022a), with the government reported to be concerned about single-sex schools (Visentin 2022b).

While the government was reported as having secured party room support for the bills (Visentin 2022b), this was to quickly unravel when a previously secret letter from the Prime Minister was revealed (Patrick and McIlroy 2022). The letter from the Prime Minister to the Opposition Leader from 1 December 2021 offered to remove the exemptions in the *Sex Discrimination Act* relating to both sexual orientation and gender identity, far more than was included in the government's proposals before the Parliament. The *Religious Discrimination Bill 2022* (Cth) itself was actually passed by the House of Representatives, however five government MPs crossed the floor, with Labor,[7] to support crossbench amendments that removed the exemptions in the *Sex Discrimination Act* relating to both sexual orientation and gender identity as offered by the Prime Minister in his secret letter (Evans 2022a). The Morrison Government then shelved the bills rather than taking the amended package to the Senate for debate (Coorey and McIlroy 2022).

Whether the Prime Minister was "misled" through this process as some have indicated (Evans 2022c), or the final bill package "flawed" (Evans 2022b), and deserving of being abandoned, those Coalition MPs who crossed the floor certainly paid a price at the subsequent election, with only one retaining her seat, and with a reduced margin. Both major parties vowed to introduce a religious discrimination bill in the lead up to the 2022 federal election, with stronger commitments from the ALP than they had provided in 2019.

That in 2024 there are no comprehensive federal protections against religious discrimination is a blight on all of those in the Australian Parliament. While the *Sex Discrimination Act* was controversial in 1984, it is staggering to think that 40 years later similar protections for religious discrimination have not been provided. The clear mandate for religious freedom protections in the 2019 federal election provided the golden opportunity for such legislation to be passed.

While the COVID-19 pandemic might be claimed to be an 'act of God' that hijacked the passage of the legislation, the failure by the former Attorney-General to more actively pursue legislation in the early days of the parliament has proven costly. Prime Minister Morrison's secret letter that served to undermine the government's own legislation and empower internal opponents, proved to be the final twist in this almost Shakespearian tragedy. Both of these errors though, were a result of the trying to deal with the poisoned chalice left by Malcolm Turnbull's failure to resolve the politics around same-sex marriage. The 'triumph' around same-sex marriage proving a 'tragedy' for people of faith, as well as those students in faith based schools now continuing to live in, unfounded, fear of expulsion as a result of the political campaign to block religious discrimination protections.

Conclusion

Comparing different governments is like comparing sporting heroes of different eras, the rules and techniques have often changed significantly, and the opposition players or teams are of varying quality. The Australian Democrats of the Howard era, who "found support in the centre ground of Australia's political landscape" (Moore, 2021) and were critical in the introduction of the GST, have been replaced with a far more left-leaning Senate crossbench of Greens and independents. At the same time the development of social media and the impact of 'X', formerly known as Twitter, on the daily news cycle introduces a dynamic unknown in the times of Menzies or Howard.

Former Prime Minister John Howard understood though, "on cultural issues, symbols and attitudes are important", arguing for "a simple and vigorous response" to challenges in these areas (Kelly 2017). Such a simple and vigorous response to the foundational falsehood of schools expelling LGBT students would have created a profoundly different political context. While some within the Government accepted and took up this challenge there was no unifying narrative, no overarching commitment that held together the party that has always being a "broad church". This almost existential search for meaning seems to have characterised much of this Government's term. As it says in the gospel of Mark, "If a house is divided against itself, that house cannot stand" (Mark 3:25), or at least not deliver religious freedom.

References

Bennett, S., and Brennan, S., *Constitutional Referenda in Australia*, Canberra: Department of the Parliamentary Library, 1999

Chambers, G., "Stronger protection in new religious freedom bill", *The Australian*, 10 December 2019

Chambers, G., and Brown, G., "Religious groups 'blindsided' by Porter draft bill", *The Australian*, 29 August 2019

Christian Schools Australia, "Attorney-General in the Christmas Spirit", Media Release, 10 December 2019

Coorey, P., and McIlroy, T., "Defeated Morrison shelves religious freedoms until after the election", *Australian Financial Review*, 10 February 2022

Crowe, D., (2018), "Scott Morrison vows to change laws on religious freedom but won't be a 'culture warrior' PM", *Sydney Morning Herald*, 7 September 2018

Evans, J., "The government lost a dramatic showdown on religious discrimination laws overnight. So what happened?", *ABC News Online*, 10 February 2022a

Evans, J., "Government shelves religious freedom bill indefinitely, leaving election promise hanging in uncertainty", *ABC News Online*, 10 February.2022b

Evans, J., "Prime Minister Scott Morrison 'misled' by moderate Liberals on religious discrimination vote, Dutton says", *ABC News Online*, 11 February 2022c

Fawcett, D., (Chair), Joint Standing Committee on Foreign Affairs, Defence and Trade, *Legal Foundations of Religious Freedom in Australia: Interim Report*, Canberra: Commonwealth of Australia, 2017

Karp, P., "Scott Morrison will change the law to ban religious schools expelling gay students", *The Guardian Australia*, 12 October 2018

Kelly, P., "The crisis for conservatism", *The Australian*, 25 February 2017

Koziol, M., "Philip Ruddock review into religious freedom fails to deter conservative MPs from attack on marriage bill", *Sydney Morning Herald*, 22 November 2017

Martin, S., "Religious discrimination bill: moderate Liberals strike deal to protect gay students", *The Guardian*, 1 December 2021

Massola, J., "Peter Dutton, Scott Morrison flag push for 'religious protections' laws once same-sex marriage is legalised", *Sydney Morning Herald*, 16 November 2017

Moore, T., "Australian Democrats pledge to 'keep the bastards honest' one more time", *Sydney Morning Herald*, 6 October 2021

Neilsen, M.A., BILLS DIGEST NO. 54, 2017–18 - Marriage Amendment (Definition and Religious Freedoms) Bill 2017. Canberra: Department of Parliamentary Services, 2017

Newton, M., "Shelton warns of erosion of rights in wake of SSM result", *The Courier Mail*, 15 November 2017

Patrick, A., and McIlroy, T., "The night God, sex and the backbench humbled a prime minister: The untold story of a pivotal event in the history of the Morrison government: a bitter struggle between Liberals over religious and gay rights", *Australian Financial Review*, 20 February 2022

Phillips, D., "ScoMo's religious freedom plans may be worse than doing nothing", *The Spectator Australia*, 2 October 2019

Rodriguez, M., "Faith law doesn't go far enough", *The Catholic Weekly*, 4 September 2019

Topsfield, J., "Religious freedom review enshrines right of schools to turn away gay children and teachers", *The Age*, 9 October 2018

Towell, N., "'Sinful and dirty': Fears for women under new religious freedom laws", *The Age*, 4 October 2019

Visentin, L., "Gay students protected, but trans students could still be expelled", *Sydney Morning Herald*, 8 February 2022a

Visentin, L., "'Think about our team': PM pressures moderates as party backs religious laws", *Sydney Morning Herald*, 8 February 2022b

Vistonay, E., "Votes lost in religion backlash, says Bowen", *The Australian*, 23 May 2019

Wesselinoff, A., "Religious freedom debate yet to strike the right balance: Brennan", *The Catholic Weekly*, 13 July 2013

Endnotes

1   The *Religious Discrimination Bill 2022* (Cth) was part of a legislative package that also included the *Religious Discrimination (Consequential Amendments) Bill 2021* (Cth) and *Human Rights Legislation Amendment Bill 2022* (Cth).

2   The Liberal Party of Australia, Federal Constitution as adopted by the

Federal Council in 2017, Objectives, clause 2(a).

3   The Act also inserted into the *Sex Discrimination Act 1984* (Cth) protections against discrimination on the basis of "intersex status". No exemption for discrimination on this basis was sought by religious groups in relation to this ground as outlined in the explanatory memorandum to the bill.

4   Matthew Newton, "Shelton warns of erosion of rights in wake of SSM result", The Courier Mail, 15 November 2017. 7

5   See full details here: https://www.aph.gov.au/Parliamentary_Business/ Committees/Joint/Foreign_Affairs_Defence_and_Trade/Freedomofreligion

6   This legislative package contained exposure draft legislation and explanatory memoranda for the *Religious Discrimination Bill 2019* (Cth), *Religious Discrimination (Consequential Amendments) Bill 2019* (Cth), and the *Human Rights Legislation Amendment (Freedom of Religion) Bill 2019* (Cth).

7   These Liberal MPs were Dr Katie Allen, Mrs Bridget Archer MP, Dr Fiona Martin, Mr Dave Sharma, Mr Trent Zimmerman

10

Welfare Reform: Lost Opportunity

Patrick McClure

Introduction

In April 2012, Hon Joe Hockey, then Coalition Shadow Treasurer, delivered in London an address entitled "The End of the Age of Entitlement". He stated that government spending on social programs such as health, housing, education, income support and retirement benefits had reached extraordinary levels as a percentage of GDP across western nations. Inadequate taxation revenue had forced nations into levels of debt that were unsustainable. Hockey argued that the only solution was to rebuild fiscal discipline and restore budget surpluses until debt was repaid. This could be achieved by cutting expenditure (Hockey 2012).

The themes of fiscal sustainability and reducing expenditure became one of the goals of the Abbott Coalition Government elected on 7 September, 2013. A National Commission of Audit chaired by Tony Shepherd was formed in October 2013 to make recommendations to return the budget to a sustainable surplus. Its aim was to review government expenditure (Shepherd 2014).

I had previously chaired a Reference Group on Welfare Reform in 2000 for the Howard Coalition Government. Its final report and recommendations had received strong public and government support at the time. Consequently, I was viewed by the new Abbott Government as an experienced social policy expert who would produce a balanced report to assist the new Coalition Administration in its future policy drive in this vital area. There was also a sense of continuity with the successful Howard Government (*Canberra Times* 2015; McClure 2000; McClure 2021).

Consequently, I was appointed on 13 December 2013 as Chair of a Reference Group to advise the Department of Social Services on options to "ensure Australia's welfare system is sustainable, effective and coherent and encourages people to work". The Minister for Social Service, the Kevin Andrews asked for advice on "reforms that can be implemented within the existing welfare payments system structure to improve the sustainability of the system and enhance participation. This advice should also provide broad direction for future reform of the welfare system" (Andrews 2013).

Members of the Reference Group were Patrick McClure as Chair, Sally Sinclair, CEO of the National Employment Services Association and Wesley Aird, Indigenous Consultant. Paul McBride, Deputy Secretary of the Department of Social Services led the Welfare System Taskforce of staff from the Department that supported the review.

The Reference Group was specifically asked for advice on how Australia's welfare system can:

- provide incentives to work for those who are able to work;
- adequately support those who are genuinely not able to work;
- support social and economic participation through measures that build individual and family capability;
- be affordable and sustainable both now and in the future and across economic cycles;
- be easy to access and understand able to be delivered efficiently and effectively.

Interim Report and Consultation

The Reference Group produced an *Interim Report* which Minister Andrews and I launched on 29 June 2014. Its aim was to encourage public debate and discussion (Andrews 2013).

There was a six-week period of public consultation which included a call for public submissions and comments. There was also hosting of roundtables with key stakeholders in capital cities to discuss the future directions and questions identified in the *Interim Report*. A portal for online submissions and statements was also available.

The Reference Group received a total of 271 public submissions from individuals and organisations. It also received 231 online comments from individuals.

Thirteen roundtables were held in Sydney, Melbourne, Adelaide, Brisbane, Perth, Hobart and Cairns during July - August 2014 with a total of 175 representatives from key stakeholder organisations.

Five individual roundtables were also held with 55 income support payment customers in Brisbane, Sydney and Melbourne during August 2014. The five customer groups were sole parents, job-seekers, carers, students and people with disability.

Case for Reform

The *Interim Report* outlined a clear case for reform across several areas. These included:

Complexity

There were currently around 20 income support payment types and 55 supplementary payments. The many payments and supplements have resulted in a system that is difficult to navigate and administer. Existing means testing add to this complexity and result in a system that is confusing to income support recipients.

System Coherence

The effect of different indexation measures, changing priorities and ad hoc policy responses have led over time to a "patchwork quilt" income support system that is inequitable and lacks coherence.

People with similar living costs and incapacities to work receive different levels of income support and different participation requirements. For example, pensions and allowances are indexed differently which has created a widening gap between the two.

Benefits of Work

Most people gain health benefits associated with employment, both physical and mental. Work can be a vital part of recovery for people with mental health conditions. Intergenerational benefits of work accrue as children who grow up in employed households have better social, emotional, physical development and learning outcomes.

Meeting Future Economic and Social Challenges

The Australian economy has undergone major structural changes in recent decades. These changes include increasing skill levels, an ageing population, higher participation among women and older Australians and increases in the part-time and casual workforce. There is also a need for early intervention for groups at risk of long-term welfare dependence.

Final Report

The *Final Report* entitled *A New System for Better Employment and Social Outcomes* was launched on 23 February 2015. It outlined four Pillars of Reform (McClure 2015).

Pillar One: A Simpler and Sustainable Income Support System

Simpler Architecture

In the new system a major redesign of the payment architecture is the centrepiece of reform. In place of the 20 current payments there are 5 primary payments:

- Working Age Payment – a means tested payment for adults who are expected to work now or in the future, with three tiers to reflect the varying needs and capacity of individuals to work:

- The Upper Tier should be for people who have a limited capacity to work and due to this are more likely to stay on payment for a longer duration;
- The Middle Tier should be for people with a moderate capacity to work and parents and primary carers of dependent children and dependent young people under the age of 22 years;
- The Foundation Tier should be for people with full capacity to work or study;

- Supported Living Pension – a means tested payment for individuals over 22 years who are permanently and severely restricted in their capacity to work;
- Child and Youth Payment – a means tested payment for parents of dependent children and dependent young people under the age of 22;
- Carer Payment – a means tested payment for individuals over 22 with caring responsibilities;
- Age Pension – this payment was outside the scope of the Reference Group.

The current 55 supplements should be reduced to four main categories:

- Housing – to assist with costs of rental accommodation
- Child and Family – to assist with specific extra costs related to children
- Education – to assist with specific additional costs of children and young people, when they need to live away from home to work or study
- Care and Disability – to assist in caring for children and adults with disability or people who are frail and aged

A Passport to Work should be developed that supports people to transition from income support to work. This removes the fear people have of taking a job, by making it easier to understand the financial rewards of work. It provides a safety net that enables them to return to their income support payment if a job ends.

In transitioning to the new system no person moving from a payment under the old system to a payment under the new system should have a reduction in their rate of payment.

The *Final Report* recommended a twin tracked approach to payment adjustments across all income support payments:

- A community living standards adjustment following a periodic review undertaken by a panel of experts
- An automatic cost of living adjustment every six months, following a process to determine the most appropriate cost of living index for the new payment structure

Pillar Two: Strengthening Individual and Family Capability

Pillar Two focuses on how the social support system can strengthen individual and family capability.

The new social support system should identify and invest in groups at greatest risk of remaining on income support for the long term. An actuarial approach should be used to identify these groups. Mainstream services should then be used to support these people on their path to self-reliance through work.

Some of the skill sets that individuals need to succeed in the workplace include technical skills, language, literacy and numeracy, social interaction and ability to do work.

There is a need for access to affordable childcare which provides parents with the opportunity to find a job or participate in education or training.

Mental health conditions are becoming more prevalent in Australia. About 30 per cent of people receiving the Disability Support Pension have psychiatric or psychological conditions. There are different degrees of work capacity within various groups. Some people with episodic mental health conditions will have periods of relative wellness where they are able to participate in activities that are part of a recovery plan including work.

The vocational rehabilitation approach to mental health services is supported by leading experts in the mental health sector. There is strong evidence that being able to work to capacity is a high priority for people with mental health conditions. Individual Placement and Support is one model of employment support for people with severe and persistent mental health conditions.

Affordable housing with access to jobs and services is essential to allow people to participate socially and economically.

Australian Investment Approach

An investment approach targets resources upfront to build capability and pathways to jobs for disadvantaged groups. This reduces the future liability associated with group members becoming long-term dependent on income support.

Early intervention is a critical feature of an investment approach and involves targeting services and interventions to people at risk of becoming long term dependent. There is strong evidence across the OECD that early intervention is effective in preventing social problems, breaking the cycle of intergenerational disadvantage and making long-term savings in public spending.

A key issue in targeting investment is identifying those people most at risk of long-term disadvantage.

Key features of an Australian investment approach should be:

- Valuation and revaluation – annual valuations will calculate the lifetime liability for people on income support. It will determine the return on investment through the reduction in liability. It will also identify groups most at risk of welfare dependence;
- Evidence-based interventions and locally designed services – a broad range of support services will be available to provide tailored services for at-risk groups;
- Flexible funding pool – this includes the ability to cut funding of programs with poor outcomes and invest in new programs;
- Monitoring and evaluation – ongoing monitoring of service

outcomes for individuals will contribute to the data and evidence.

The valuation identifies groups most at risk of life-term welfare dependence, for example, teenage parents. The Government then funds providers to deliver early intervention services targeting those groups. The funding is based on key outcomes. The actuarial valuation can then assess the life-time savings to Government from assisting groups such as teenage parents into training and jobs (McClure 2015).

Pillar Three: Engaging with Employers

The new social support system should have a strong employment focus with business and government playing key roles supporting people disadvantaged in the job market to find jobs.

Australia's labour market has changed over the past few decades with more highly skilled jobs, increasing casual and part-time work, flexible working arrangements and growing and emerging industries.

Industries that employ the most people are Health Care and Social Assistance, Education and Training, Retail Trade, Professional, Scientific and Technical Services, Construction and Accommodation and Food Services.

Groups disadvantaged in the labour market such as people with disability, those with mental health conditions, young people and mature aged job seekers will benefit from employment growth in some of these industries.

Investment in training and education should be better targeted to both current and future jobs to ensure people have the best opportunity to secure sustainable employment. Higher education and training levels improve employment prospects for job seekers. Bachelor degree or higher qualification, Advanced Diploma or Diploma and Certificates III and IV improve employment prospects for job seekers.

Key occupations that will increase in demand in the Australian economy are carers in the aged, disability and child-care sectors. This growth reflects an ageing population and the demand for carers in aged community and home-based services as well as nursing homes. The total expenditure of the Commonwealth, states and territories on the National Disability Insurance Scheme is estimated at over $30 billion per annum. There is strong demand for carers of people with disability. Strong growth is also projected for carers in child care centres and in-home settings.

Many employers are committed to a diverse and inclusive workforce including people with disability and mental health conditions, mature age workers and young people. They recognize that employing a diverse workforce leads to a competitive edge, as their employee profile better reflects their customer base. It also enhances a company's reputation and brand. Large companies such as the Westpac Group, Telstra, Toll, IBM, Woolworths, Bunnings, ANZ and NewsCorp Australia support diverse and inclusive workforces.

Jobs Plan

A Jobs Plan with initiatives that increase workforce participation for disadvantaged groups is needed to ensure that all Australians gain the benefits of employment growth. In the first instance a Jobs Plan for people with disability and mental health conditions should be developed.

The key components of the Jobs Plan include:

- awareness raising and education campaign to promote the benefits of employing people with disability and mental health conditions;
- a leader's group bringing together key leaders in the disability sector, business and government;
- industry led awards to recognize best practice;
- tailored support services such as the Individual Placement and Support (IPS) model;
- setting targets cross government for employment of people with disability and mental health conditions;
- government and business consider procurement from organizations that employ people with disability and mental

health conditions;

- promotion of wage subsidies for small to medium enterprises to employ people with disability and mental health conditions (McClure 2015: 127-30).

Pillar Four: Building Community Capacity

The new social support system should include a role for civil society to forge partnerships, enhance philanthropy, create investments in a social purpose capital market and support social enterprises as a means of providing opportunities for economic and social participation.

Civil society includes organizations with a social purpose. Their purposes include health, social services, education, research, culture, arts, sport, recreation, religion, community development, employment and training, housing, ageing, disability, environment, law and advocacy.

There are around 600,000 social purpose organizations in Australia. They mainly operate in education and research (31%), social services (19%) and health and hospitals (18%). The sector contributes close to $55 billion to GDP, receives $100 billion in income and holds $175 billion in assets. The organisations employ over 1 million Australians (McClure 2015: 159-62).

Partnerships between civil society organizations have a proven track record of building the capacity of communities and individuals and families. One example is Foyer Oxford which arose out of partnership between Anglicare WA, Foundation Housing and the Central Institute of Technology. The Foyer model includes an early intervention approach to prevent young people becoming long-term homeless; wraparound services that support young people with transitional housing, combined with personalized social supports to access employment, education and training; and a focus in counselling on individual strengths and capacities rather than problems and deficits.

Australian philanthropy giving provides around $11 billion to civil society per annum. This comprises about $8 billion from individuals and $3 billion from businesses. Private and Public Ancillary Funds (PAFs) allow individuals, families and associations to make tax deductible donations to their own charitable foundations. The income earned from the funds invested is in turn distributed to charities. In June 2014 there were 1,246 registered PAFs with around $4 billion in donated funds under management (McClure 2015: 166)

A social purpose capital market should facilitate investments with social impact through Social Impact Bonds (SIB). This is an investment model where government pays for agreed social outcomes that result in better outcomes for individuals and families, as well as longer term savings to Government. The first NSW Government SIB, the Newpin program, involving UnitingCare and Social Ventures Australia, raised $7 million from investors. The results are encouraging with the restoration of out of home care children to their families and support services and capacity-building for parents (McClure 2015: 168-9).

Social enterprises are organizations led by an economic, social, cultural or environmental mission consistent with a public or community benefit. They can be non-profit or for-profit entities and derive the bulk of their income from trading activity to fulfill their mission. There are an estimated 20,000 social enterprises in Australia, with trading activity of around $20 billion per annum (McClure 2015: 169-72).

The Australian Government is supporting social enterprise development through its Social Enterprise Development and Investment Fund (SEDIF). It has provided $20 million in seed grants matched by private investment. Social Traders is an organization that provides social enterprises with resources, access to networks, investment and markets. Australia would benefit from a long-term strategy to support social enterprise development.

Corporate Social Responsibility (CSR) is a concept that involves businesses ensuring their conduct is legal, ethical and sustainable. When properly adopted, CSR is beneficial for local communities including disadvantaged individuals and groups. Social procurement, where a social outcome influences the purchasing of goods or services, is another way business can demonstrate CSR.

Micro businesses (less than five full time employees) are responsible for employing around 20 percent of the workforce in Australia. These businesses are often embedded in their local communities and are active contributors to community capacity building. There is a need for programs to support entrepreneurs to establish micro businesses.

Microfinance is another example of the role of business and investment in community capacity building. Financial independence and access to loans are important elements of building individual capacity and community participation.

Launch and Media Response

I launched the Final Report on 23 February 2015 with the Hon Scott Morrison, the new Minister for Social Services, in a presentation to Parliament House Press Gallery newspaper editors and journalists.

I then gave studio and door-stop interviews to news radio and television journalists in the Parliament House Press Gallery including David Speers, Kieran Gilbert and Laura Jayes of Sky News, Chris Uhlmann of Channel 9 and Michael Brissenden of the ABC. I also had interviews with Paul Kelly and Peter van Onselen on Sunday Agenda and with Paul Murray Live on Sky News Australia. He did interviews with Alan Jones and Ray Hadley on 2GB Radio as well as Patricia Karvelas on ABC Radio National.

Editorial, *The Canberra Times* (25 February 2015) stated:

> The Federal Government chose wisely in selecting Patrick McClure to conduct a review of the welfare system focussed on improvements that will lead to better employment and social outcomes.   McClure, with extensive experience in welfare issues in the non-government sector, has long been an advisor to governments on both sides of the fence, open to ideas from all parts of the political and social spectrum and, if sometimes likely to shape his ideas in directions he thinks politicians might be inclined to follow, unlikely to alter them simply to meet the personal, political or economic agendas of others...

Editorial, *The Australian*, (25 February 2015) stated:

> Mr McClure who has decades of experience in social policy and service delivery, showed he had the best interests disadvantaged families at heart when he pointed out that long-term reliance on income support increases the risks of poor health, low self-esteem and isolation...He has rightly acknowledged that a properly functioning income support system should be focussed on encouraging people to work to their capacity...

Article, *The Australian* (2015b) observed:

> The report by community sector reformer Patrick McClure focuses on increasing the workforce participation of welfare recipients but recommends that no-one be worse off under the new system ...

Patricia Karvelas (2015) wrote that:

> Patrick McClure has delivered the most ambitious, courageous and transformative blueprint for welfare reform the nation has seen. If adopted these reforms have the potential to revolutionize the safety net and provide better incentives for work. The welfare system has become unwieldy, ad hoc, inconsistent and fundamentally unfair. The chief recommendation, a tiered working-age, would reflect the capacity of people to work now or in the future. The Disability Support Pension would be provided for people with a permanent impairment and no capacity to work.

Rick Morton (2016), *The Australian*, writes:

> An explosion in welfare payments have prompted the architect of the federal government's social security review to warn of a moral obligation to intervene and move the young into work. Mr McClure said 'there is a need for government to intervene if you are thwarting a young person's career and job opportunities because they have caring responsibilities. Young carers have the worst outcomes. They are similar to young people who come from out-of-home care – they are more likely to end up homeless, on welfare for the rest of their lives, not in jobs.

Government Response

The Report, *A New System for Better Employment and Social Outcomes* offered the Coalition Government a platform to take a leadership role in welfare reform in Australia. As the media commentary indicated, it was a "transformative blueprint for welfare reform." The Report had strong media and public support.

The newly elected Abbott Government was focussed on reducing debt and cutting expenditure across government programs. Joe Hockey had delivered his headland speech, "An End to the Age of Entitlement" which emphasised fiscal responsibility and reduction in government expenditure. Hockey had also become Treasurer in the Abbott Government. The National Commission of Audit had, as noted, recommended cuts to social programs. It therefore seemed that there was considerable policy and political alignment for many of the recommendations of the Final Report to be accepted by the Coalition Government.

There was, however, a seeming a lack of commitment within the Coalition Government, to invest in and implement the reforms and recommendations of *A New System for Better Employment and Social Outcomes.* In an initial meeting with the Chief of Staff of the Prime Minister's Office of the Abbott Administration, there appeared to be limited interest in welfare reform and investment in early intervention and capacity building. This was in contrast to the Howard Government where I had a close working relationship and support from John Perrin, the Social Policy Advisor in the Prime Minister's Office (see McClure 2021).

In the Howard Government there was continuity and commitment to welfare reform in the Minister for Social Services, Hon Jocelyn Newman. There was also continuity in the Prime Minister's Office. In contrast in 2015 there was also a great deal of turmoil and division within the Coalition Government. The incumbent Prime Minister Tony Abbott was defeated in a leadership spill and Malcolm Turnbull became Prime Minister in September 2015. There were changes in the Minister for Social Services from Kevin Andrews to Scott Morrison and then Christian Porter. This contributed to a loss of commitment and momentum in the leadership of welfare reform. It required a minister to champion the case for welfare reform in Cabinet and for the Coalition Government leadership team to navigate legislation through Parliament. The changes in Prime Minister and Minister for Social Services led to different government priorities. Welfare reform became a lost opportunity for the Coalition Government.

Since the 2015-16 Budget the Australian Government has implemented the Priority Investment Approach contracting PWC to complete annual actuarial valuations and implementing a $100m million Try, Test and Learn Fund. It has introduced the Job Seeker Payment to replace or consolidate seven existing payments in the income support system. It has also established a Social Impact Investment Taskforce to develop a strategy for the Commonwealth Government in the Social Impact Investing market in Australia.

Priority Investment Approach

The Priority Investment Approach (PIA) is a new way of addressing welfare dependence. It involves actuarial analysis to identify groups with the highest future, life-time cost of welfare dependence. Funding of early intervention strategies with these disadvantaged groups achieves better outcomes for them and also saves billions of dollars in future costs (McClure 2015).

The actuarial model predicts the future income support use of the Australian population. People are grouped into 12 broad welfare classes: 6 for income support recipients, 3 for people receiving payments but no income support and 3 for the rest of the population. Each year the model is enhanced to take account of changes to the economy and the unemployment rate.

The evidence indicates that teenage parents, youth on disability support and young carers are three groups with the highest average future lifetime welfare costs.

The Australian Government invested $100 million in the Try, Test and Learn Fund to fund early intervention projects for young carers, teenage parents, working aged carers, students, mature aged people, at risk youth and refugees.

The latest Priority Investment Approach baseline data for future lifetime cost of welfare shows a ten percent reduction in future lifetime costs of $700 billion from 2015 to 2018. There have been significant reductions in the number of people on Disability Support Pension, Parenting Payment, Youth Allowance and Family Tax Benefits A and B. (*The Australian* 14 Octover 2019).

Commentator Paul Kelly (2016) concluded:

> The new policy, the Priority Investment Approach, is driven by path-breaking analysis by PricewaterhouseCoopers that documents shocking failures in three tested areas: young students, young parents and carers. It reveals long-run welfare traps not being rectified and offers the platform for a new method. By seeking to change individual lives, the Coalition government is changing the direction of welfare policy... Minister Porter stated that as a nation we have a moral obligation to help people live fulfilling lives by gaining sustainable employment and breaking from the cycle of intergenerational welfare dependency.

Universal Basic Income

We examined a Universal Basic Income. A Universal Basic Income (UBI) is a guaranteed income paid to all adult citizens. There is no income or asset test and no obligation for individuals to be looking for a job or in training.

During the Covid pandemic in 2021 the Australian Government introduced a temporary JobKeeper payment as a subsidy to businesses to pay employees. The payment was set at a higher rate than the current JobSeeker Payment. The Government feared that during the pandemic jobs would be lost and people would be without any income. This intervention by the Australian Government in the market was viewed as fulfilling the social contract between the Australian Government and its citizens during an unprecedented pandemic. It also led to revived interest in a Universal Basic Income.

Most UBI proposals share three features. Firstly, it is a universal payment, that is, the same rate is paid to all adult citizens regardless of income or need. It is paid to people who are employed or unemployed, single or in relationships and people with or without disabilities.

This is the major difference from the income support system in Australia. Australia has one of the most targeted income support systems in the world. It is means-tested in terms of income and assets and is also targeted towards different categories of people in need, that is, people who are aged, people with disability, unemployed, sick, carers or students. Over 5 million Australians receive income support either as a part or full pension or payment.

Secondly, a UBI is unconditional, that is, it is paid to all adult citizens without any mutual obligations. This is different from the Australian income support system which has obligations for eligible job seekers to look for jobs and participate in education or training.

Thirdly a UBI level of payment is adequate, that is, it is at a high enough level that individuals can meet their basic needs without additional income. The UBI replaces existing income support payments. The issue in Australia is the level of payment. There is a major difference between the rates of the Age Pension, Disability Support Pension and the JobSeeker Payment. If no one is to be worse off it would mean a massive increase in the Commonwealth Government budget to pay people at the higher level.

It is not possible to create a UBI without major reform of the taxation system. Its advocates recommend increased government revenue from a range of taxation proposals including increased mining, corporate and carbon taxes. A major challenge for any Australian government is to gain public support to fund a UBI at an adequate rate of payment. A UBI will become increasingly relevant if the labour market changes and large numbers of Australians lose their jobs and income.

Conclusion

The challenge of welfare reform continues. The income support system at the time of the review was $150 billion of annual government expenditure. It is difficult to get cross-party support for welfare reform. It is also hard to find a balance in providing an adequate level of income support, simplifying a complex system of payments, funding early interventions to prevent lifetime welfare dependence and developing pathways for people to access training and jobs.

The Coalition Government, while it had some achievements in reshaping our complex welfare system, could have done more. It lacked, however, a clear vision of what it wanted to achieve, the principles on what they should be based, and a consistent strategy on how its prime goals could be achieved. The change in prime ministers and ministers also meant the Coalition was unable to articulate a convincing narrative to gain public and interest group support that is necessary to achieve successful reform. The result was a patchwork of changes that lacked consistency and missed tackling some of the major flaws that bedevil the Australian welfare system.

References

Andrews, K., Minister for Social Services, Letter to Patrick McClure, 9 December 2013

The Australian, "Welfare overhaul: Fairer, simpler and sustainable: McClure's revolution from 20 payments to 5", 25 February 2015

The Australian, Editorial, "The welfare overhaul Australia has to have", 25 February

The Australian, "Welfare reform saves millions", 14 October 2016

Canberra Times, Editorial "Welfare review a good start", 25 February 2015

Hockey, J., Shadow Treasurer, The End of the Age of Entitlement", Address to Institute of Economic Affairs, London, April 17, 2012

Karvelas, P., *The Australian*, 10 June 2014

Kelly, P., "Coalition target set on ending lifelong welfare", *The Week-End Australian*, 17-18 September 2016

McClure, P., "Hearts and Heads: The Challenge of Welfare Reform", in Frame, T., (ed), *The Desire for Change, 2004-2007: The Howard Government Volume V*, Sydney: UNSW Press, 2021, 177-193

Mclure, P., Chair, Reference Group on Welfare Reform, *Final Report*, Participation and Support for a More Equitable Society, Canberra: Commonwealth Government, July 2000

McClure, P., Chair, Reference Group on Welfare, *Interim Report*, A New System for Better Employment and Social Outcomes, Canberra: Commonwealth Government, June 2014

McClure, P., Chair, Reference Group on Welfare, *Final Report*, A New System for Better Employment and Social Outcomes, Canberra: Commonwealth Government, February 2015

Morton, R., "Nation must face moral obligations to break carer welfare cycler", *The Australian*, 5 September 2016

Shepherd, A.F., Chair, National Commission of Audit, *Towards Responsible Government*, Canberra: Commonwealth Government, 2014

11

Aboriginal Affairs
– not even holding the line

Gary Johns

Introduction

Aboriginal poet Kath Walker wrote in the 1960s, "White men had to learn civilised ways, now it is our turn" (*New Dawn*). Liberal MP Bill Wentworth persuaded Prime Minister Robert Menzies to agree to a Commonwealth referendum held under Prime Minister Harold Holt in 1967. The referendum was a means to assure Aborigines that they would be treated as equals. No doubt there were varied reasons for voting yes in the hearts of the 92 per cent of those who did, but it is safe to say that it was an act of equality and unity. However, separation has been a dominant theme since.

Prime Minister William McMahon was the first to appoint a Minister for Aboriginal Affairs. William Wentworth was appointed to this post in 1971, with Peter Howson, the junior minister, assisting. Hewson was subsequently president of the Bennelong Society, dedicated to integrating Aboriginal people into the open society. In 1971, Liberal Senator Neville Bonner was the first Aborigine to become a member of parliament. The Coalition, in later years, having sponsored the march to equality, wilted in the face of an assertive university-educated, wholly integrated Aboriginal elite. Equality, the surest means of offering better lives, proof of being university-educated Aborigines, was overrun by identity politics. An evaluation of the performance of the Coalition in Aboriginal affairs in 2013-2022 has to be viewed in light of these two almost mutually exclusive philosophies, equality versus identity.

The Hon Senator Nigel Scullion and The Hon Ken Wyatt MP were the two ministers for Aboriginal affairs during the Abbott, Turnbull and Morrison governments. Judging from the initiatives, expenditure and statements from the two Coalition ministers and their prime ministers, evidence is scarce that Coalition policy rose above being "practical" instead of Labor's propensity to the "symbolic". The missing piece in Coalition policy in this field is that they never understood, and therefore never articulated, the destination they envisaged for Aboriginal policy and people. They were, as a result, unable to resist the siren call of identity politics and demands of an Aboriginal elite for special treatment.

The first principle in good policy making is understanding the facts with which policy is to deal. Constant repetition in the ministers' statements during these governments about Closing the Gap between Aborigines and non-Aborigines was factually incorrect. There was only a gap between some Aborigines and all other Australians. The Coalition did not make this distinction clear or explain why it existed. Had they done so, they would have had to point out how some Aborigines live about as well as other Australians and others do not. They would have had to point out that the pathway for successful Aborigines was paved with Western values and any consistent, or not inconsistent, Aboriginal values. The Coalition were too afraid to do so. Not since The Hon Senator John Herron in the Howard Government has the Coalition had a Minister for Aboriginal affairs who stood up to the Aboriginal leadership, at that time, encamped in the Aboriginal and Torres Strait Islander Commission.

The Coalition misunderstood that Labor and the Aboriginal leadership were being very practical in their symbolism – each was pursuing an ideological path of separatism, ensuring that an Aboriginal elite accumulated more power and appropriated more taxpayers' money to that end. The Coalition failed to understand the politics because they had no alternative philosophy. The obvious alternative philosophy was equality of citizenship, achieved through integration. Had the Coalition explicitly proselytised integration, it could have enhanced most Aborigines' chosen course. The Coalition could have provided a defence against the course that the minority of Aborigines have chosen, that is, to remain dependent on their Aboriginality.

The best that could be said of the Coalition efforts in 2013-2022 is that they held the line against the most extreme proposals of the Aboriginal industry but failed to win any substantive battles. In the period, more people identified as Aboriginal, more money was spent on programs, and more Aborigines were employed in the public service, probably drawn from the ranks of recent identifiers. However, the Gap between a minority of Aborigines (those who have been to gaol) and all other Australians did not close.

Main changes in the period

The main administrative change was the establishment of the National Indigenous Australians Agency (NIAA) in 2019, which is responsible for whole-of-government coordination of policy development, program design, and service delivery for Aboriginal Australians and Torres Strait Islander people. The public servants operating the NIAA were drawn from the Department of Prime Minister and Cabinet and other agencies, consolidating those already undertaking these services.

The significant societal changes in the period were not aspects of the Gap between some Aborigines and others, but in the numbers who identified as Aboriginal, which increased significantly. At the beginning of the period, perhaps 550 000 identified; by the end of the period, it was closer to 800 000. The increase was among those who lived in regional and major urban Australia, and likely children attributed to parents where only one was of Aboriginal descent. For example, of the Aboriginal births registered in 2017, 27 per cent were births for which both parents identified as Aboriginal, 43 per cent were births where only the mother was Aboriginal, and 30 per cent were births where only the father was Aboriginal. The Northern Territory had the highest proportion of births where the mother and father were Aboriginal (43 per cent). Tasmania had the lowest proportion of Aboriginal births (12 per cent) where both mother and father were Aboriginal (ABS 2019). The new identifiers probably accounted for the few positive elements of Closing the Gap – for example, success at year 12 completion and possible child morbidity decline. Nothing much changed: different people with different outcomes ticked the box.

Family formation is one of the significant indicators of stress among

Aborigines. However, Aboriginal families were rarely mentioned in any speech or policy document during the period. For example, in the period 2013-2022, on average, paternity was not acknowledged in four per cent of all Australian births. Among Aboriginal mothers in the Northern Territory, paternity was not acknowledged in 44 per cent of Aboriginal births. In Victoria, paternity among Aboriginal mothers was not acknowledged in nine per cent of births, and in Tasmania six per cent of births (ABS: *Explore data*). Ninety-five per cent of all Aboriginal and Torres Strait Islander births in the Territory were ex-nuptial, including traditional marriage. There is a significant problem in Aboriginal family life, but not in all Aboriginal families. State-based figures do not accurately reflect the regional nature of the crisis. Northern, remote Australia, arguably the most recognisably Aboriginal people, are in dire straits in terms of family malformation.

Intermarriage, the change in the characteristics of those identifying as Aboriginal, and the breakdown of the Aboriginal family (not necessarily related) were two significant events in the period and more generally. No prime minister mentioned either of these trends during the period. A failure of the Coalition in the period was not knowing the facts. At a basic level, they should have pressed agencies like the Australian Bureau of Statistics to clarify the Aboriginal population's different lives.

What did Coalition leaders say?

Since the initiation of Closing the Gap in 2008, each successive prime minister has delivered a report on outcomes and efforts by the Australian Government against multiple targets. Each year, the prime minister has delivered the message that the targets are not on track.

Prime Minister Abbott was the first of the Coalition prime ministers of the period to speak to the Closing the Gap Report. His 2014 speech commenced without acknowledging elders (Closing the Gap 2014). His 2000 words reflected on a theme, "our tendency was to work 'for' Aboriginal people rather than 'with them'" that was gaining traction. His journey featured heavily; indeed, Abbott was the most experienced and engaged prime minister in Aboriginal affairs. The report on targets for Closing the Gap was not fulsome; the target to halve the gap in child mortality, the target to have 95 per cent of remote children enrolled for preschool and the target to halve the gap in year-12 attainment were given some glimmer of achievement. Abbott's second annual speech on Closing the Gap 2015 was 1800 words and reflected very mild success, again on year 12 attainment, child mortality and attendance (Closing the Gap 2015). There was no substantive discussion of why the Gap existed or which segment of Aboriginal society lagged.

Prime Minister Turnbull's 2016 2500-word speech commenced in an Aboriginal language, which was not identified. For the first time, the acknowledgments appeared – "Today we are meeting together on Ngunawal country, and we acknowledge and pay our respects to the elders". Moreover, "I pay my deep respects to the Aboriginal and Torres Strait Islander custodians who have cared for this country, and to the elders who continue to hold the knowledge of their rich and diverse cultures" (Closing the Gap 2016: 1171). Turnbull accepted the post-modern identity theme, "A person's right to shape their own identity, and for that identity to be respected, is central to the wellbeing of all people". In 2017, Turnbull continued the acknowledgments of "the seed from which hope and healing grow" and took nearly 3000 words to expound on modest gains in Closing the Gap (Turnbull 2017: 2). As it was the 50th anniversary of the 1967 referendum, he stated that "we are united in our determination to ensure that our Constitution is amended once again to recognise our First Australians".

Perhaps one of the worst moves in the period was to expand the Productivity Commission to include a new Indigenous Commissioner to lead the Commission's policy evaluation work. The Productivity Commission was handed the task of tracking expenditure and programs following Prime Minister Rudd's apology to the so-called stolen generations – Aborigines removed from their families and taken into care throughout the twentieth century. The Commission has performed the task professionally, except in one regard. No doubt, under pressure to suggest a "path forward", it has inserted in each Overcoming Indigenous Disadvantage (OID) report "stories of success" without proof that these stories, or programs, were successful. It has also published the Indigenous Expenditure Reports (IER), which suggested enormous costs for little return.

Consequently, the government asked it to create a methodology for evaluations of Aboriginal programs, a belated recognition that "evidence about what works and why remains thin". (Productivity Commission 2020: 4).

The problem in Aboriginal affairs sits right here. Like the stories of success in the OID reports, the Indigenous Evaluation Strategy (IES), was to be hemmed in by two large ideological constructs: that culture (and "knowledges") must be recognised, and that Aborigines must own the process. In other words, evidence and options that regard culture and Aboriginal ownership as problems will be disregarded. Cultural re-creation and self-determination are central to the industry (Johns 2022: 177)

Turnbull's 2018 speech, presenting the 10th Closing the Gap Report, moved further into the language familiar to the referendum campaign. 'Galarrwuy' Yunupingu describes his culture as a "gift"; a gift to the nation.' (Close the Gap 2018: 1) The subtle threat of refusing the gift would be an insult. This concept has the ring of having been workshopped by pollsters and sits behind the grab for power implicit in the Voice.

Nevertheless, a rare dose of common sense was injected into Prime Minister Turnbull's 2018 speech. "Indigenous Australians either directly own or have legal rights to most of the North: 66 per cent of Queensland, 80 per cent of the Northern Territory and 94 per cent of Western Australia is communal freehold Aboriginal land or claimed or determined Native Title land" (Closing the Gap 2018: 3). Unfortunately, there was no suggestion of how to make native title work for title holders. An excellent place to start would have been some basic facts that few native title body corporates make money other than funds gifted by the government to administer their organisations.

Prime Minister Scott Morrison's first Gap speech, in 2019, was 4000 words and had a touch of weariness in the acknowledgements: "As we always do in this place, we meet on the land of the Ngunawal people" (Morrison 2019: 432). Perhaps he was weary because he had to report that only two of the seven Closing the Gap targets were on track. Looking for a way out, he pivoted to the next iteration in the industry arsenal, hinting in his predecessor's speech that the government "did not truly seek to partner with Aboriginal and Torres Strait Islander peoples". Morrison intoned, "Today, I'm calling that out". It was a signal that Prime Minister Morrison had swallowed the line that the only good program was one managed by Aboriginal organisations.

On a positive note, Morrison said, "Every Indigenous child that gets into school and stays in school is a victory that should be claimed" (Morrison 2019: 434). Indeed, it should, but the Coalition had no way of achieving that goal while refusing to understand what such a journey entailed and the vast cultural changes that Aboriginal people had to make to achieve it. Instead, they were words without substance, and by default, the separatists would nod and use them to accumulate more control. Morrison's second and final speech in the Closing the Gap series in 2020 was 1,500 words (Morrison, 2020). He showed incredible frustration, "For 12 years, I have sat in this chamber and listened to Closing the Gap speeches. It is a tale of hope, frustration and disappointment—a tale of good intentions and, indeed, good faith" (Morrison 2020: 969).

He made the extraordinary and wholly inaccurate statement, "Our Aboriginal and Torres Strait Islander children in Australia today do not have the same opportunities as all other children growing up in Australia. They never have in Australia. Never" (Morrison 2020: 969). Only some do not have opportunities, and those are not for lack of "access" to resources. He fell into the victim "truth trap" that only victims can know how to solve their problems: "It was the belief that we knew better than our Indigenous peoples. We don't. We also thought we understood their problems better than they did. We don't. They live them" (Morrison 2020: 970). This is an aspect of identity politics. It bears no relationship to problem-solving.

He at least gets it right in the following statement: "We all have in our own way sought to grapple with the consequences of 2 1/4 centuries of Indigenous disempowerment. What I know is that to rob a person of their right to take responsibility for themselves, to strip them of responsibility and capability to direct their own futures, to make them dependent, is to deny them their liberty, and slowly that person will wither before your eyes" (Morrison 2020: 970). Liberty is not achieved by "empowering" Aboriginal controlled services to monopolise Aboriginal victims. He reverts to standard Aboriginal industry ideology "building the Aboriginal and Torres Strait Islander community controlled services sector" (Morrison 2020: 972).

Referring to Indigenous Minister Ken Wyatt, "Think about a life where even the most basic decision-making is stripped away from you—by governments thinking they know better" (Morrison 2020: 972). This is precisely where the Morrison Government was heading, to recreate old masters in new ethnic splendour. They are corralled by their own; there is no agency in this control, just as there was a limited agency under control orders. Morrison made the wholly unchallenged and inaccurate statement, "We know that when Indigenous people have a say in the design of programs, policies and services, the outcomes are better—and lives are changed" (Morrison 2020: 972).

An important Rubicon was crossed in this statement by Morrison (2020: 974), "We also support recommendations about truth-telling" shades of what was to come, the Uluru Statement – Voice, Treaty and "Truth" a shocking retreat into identity politics from which Aborigines will not recover. The Coalition let it happen. In the long tradition of government relabelling programs, 2019 marked the final report against the Closing the Gap framework established in 2008. In March 2019, a Partnership Agreement on Closing the Gap 2019-2029 between all Australian governments, the Coalition Peaks and the Australian Local Government Association, was signed. The new agreement stemmed from the belief that when Aboriginal and Torres Strait Islander people have a genuine say in the design and delivery of services that affect them, better life outcomes are achieved. There was no evidence for this statement.

Practical action? – Cashless Debit Card

The only definite actions in the period unrelated to "recognition" or Aboriginal control by Aboriginal services were the Cashless Debit Card (CDC) and the defunding of the National Congress of Australia's First Peoples budget under the First Abbott government. The Card is the best illustration of a Coalition initiative that, while "practical", lacked a rationale sufficient to withstand the forces of separatism lying in wait in the Aboriginal and welfare industries. This should not have been difficult, as welfare quarantining in income management was first introduced in 2007 under a previous Coalition Government as part of the Northern Territory National Emergency Response. Income management aimed to assist income support recipients in managing their fortnightly payments — such as Newstart/Youth Allowance, parenting or carer payments, and the Disability Support Pension — for essentials like food, rent and bills.

In 2016, the Turnbull Government agreed to trial a new approach to income management — the Cashless Debit Card, in Ceduna and the East Kimberley. The Cashless Debit Card trial aimed to test whether social harm caused by alcohol, gambling and drug misuse could be reduced by placing a portion (up to 80 per cent) of a participant's income support payment onto a card that could not be used to buy alcohol or gambling products or to withdraw cash. It was also meant to trial a lower-cost welfare quarantining solution to replace current income management arrangements. The latter was necessary as the arrangements were not entirely new.

In 2017, the trial was extended in Ceduna, the East Kimberley, the Goldfields region of Western Australia, Bundaberg, and Hervey Bay Region in Queensland. The cashless debit card differed from the BasicsCard in that it was meant to be useable at all retailers (except those that sold alcohol or gambling products) rather than just government-approved stores. This meant the Card could not be used at outlets that sold a mix of excluded and non-excluded goods, such as hotels, bistros and supermarkets, or retailers that sold gift cards that could be used to purchase alcohol or gambling products.

The welfare sector vigorously opposed the card; for example, the St Vincent de Paul Society argued that there was no evidence that it improved the well-being of individuals or communities, either by reducing substance abuse or by increasing employment outcomes. Further, it carried a risk of "social exclusion and stigmatisation", increased "financial hardship", and the "erosion of individual autonomy and dignity". St Vincent de Paul Society argued that it was a "punitive and paternalistic measure" driven by ideology rather than evidence (St Vincent de Paul Society 2019: 1).

Researchers from the University of Adelaide assessed the trial. The university found primarily positive responses to the trial. Alcohol consumption had reduced; however, it was not possible to attribute these changes to the Card alone. They concluded that they could be attributed "to the full complement of relevant policies in the trial areas" (Mavromaras 2021: 65). They found a decrease in the use of illicit drugs but no definitive conclusion about whether the Card influenced "the personal or social harm caused by the use of illicit drugs". It helped to reduce gambling "with positive impacts, especially in the context of family and broader social life" (Mavromaras: 2). They found that the Card made financial planning and money management better for those who were probably the most vulnerable and who needed it most. However, it "introduced hurdles to those who felt that they needed the Card the least" (Mavromaras: 2). Safety improved, although safety improvements could not be attributed to the Card alone.

About half the Card participants reported that their control over their lives and their money had improved, and half that their control had been reduced since the introduction of the Card. Aboriginal participants essentially reported improvements. By contrast, a large majority of non-Aboriginal participants in one site reported reduced control over their lives and their money.

Feelings of discrimination, embarrassment, shame and unfairness due to being on the Card were reported across all trial sites. Employment outcomes remained the same. The main reasons were disability, ill health or care responsibilities among the participants.

This review was subject to an audit by the Commonwealth Auditor General. The objective of the audit was to assess the Department of Social Services (DSS) implementation and evaluation of the Card Trial (ANAO 2019). It was not an audit of the trial's success per se. For example, it was an audit of whether appropriate arrangements were established to support the implementation of the Trial and whether the Trial was adequately monitored, evaluated and reported. The audit report concluded that the DSS had established mainly appropriate arrangements to implement Card Trials; however, its approach to monitoring and evaluation needed to be revised.

DSS agreed to Auditor-General Report No.1 2018-19 recommendation that it undertake a second evaluation of the CDC program because of the limitations of the University of Adelaide review. This audit focused on DSS' management of the second impact evaluation. A follow-on audit concluded that DSS's administrative oversight of the Card program was practical; however, "DSS had not demonstrated that the CDC program is meeting its intended objectives" (ANAO 2022: 6). The main issue was the difficulty of attributing changes in behaviour to the trial. The tragedy of the allegedly relative paucity of evaluation, which cost $2 million, was that it left the door open to the welfare lobby, whose main concerns were "inclusiveness" and "paternalism". Consequently, the Card program ended in March 2023 following a change in government. In the grand tradition of new government relabelling programs, participants who had a Card when the program ended were moved onto enhanced Income Management.

Conclusion: Sobering thoughts for when next in government

It is too simple to blame the February 2023 riots and looting in Alice Springs and other remote locations at the end of the trial. However, again, the Coalition could not call on a solid philosophical base, thus leaving the gate open to those forces whose ideology suited the end of the trial, which was only ever a staging post, a stabiliser, on the path to integration. The present view is to exclude "cultural" Aborigines from a "tainted" modern Western world. Who excludes whom from what seems to be in the eye of the beholder. Being "practical" does not even hold the line against separatist ideology, and Aboriginal kids are paying for it with their lives.

Prime Minister Morrison stated in the foreword to the Partnership Agreement, "Every improvement will be done side-by-side, with respect for the wisdom and capabilities of Aboriginal and Torres Strait Islander people, and an appreciation for their grace towards their fellow Australians" (Commonwealth of Australia 2021: 1). The Coalition had been fed, and had swallowed, the line that all the government had to do was listen and all would be well. However, in listening, it was listening to an Aboriginal industry whose interests were to talk to anyone with money who would listen. Moreover, the Aboriginal industry said, "Give us the money". No one was talking about an alternative pathway to address the needs of Aborigines: integration. Integration implies that any provider, not only Aboriginal-controlled organisations, could help. Integration means being free of government programs and investing in self-development.

Too much of the time and energy of the Coalition in the period was consumed with recognition of Aboriginal people in the Constitution. Plans for a referendum only advanced to the stage of repeated inquiries and parliamentary committees. The bipartisan appointed Referendum Council endorsement of the Uluru Statement from the Heart's call for a constitutionally entrenched "Voice to Parliament" was rejected by the Turnbull Government. The Morrison Government supported a legislated but not entrenched "Voice to Government" and deferred constitutional recognition indefinitely.

Too little time was invested in a Liberal philosophy. Most Aborigines are doing about as well as all other Australians; only a minority suffer. The answer to alleviate their suffering lies in the pathways followed by those who have integrated, yet Liberals failed to understand this truth. Instead, they meekly held the line against an industry hell-bent on control, accumulation and separatism.

References

Abbott, T., MP, House of Representatives Ministerial Statements *Closing the Gap: Prime Minister's Report 2014 Speech* Wednesday, 12 February 2014

Abbott, T., MP, House of Representatives Ministerial Statements *Closing the Gap*, Wednesday, 11 February 2015

Auditor-General Report No.1 2018–19 Performance Audit. *The Implementation and Performance of the Cashless Debit Card Trial*, Canberra: Commonwealth Government, 2019

Auditor-General Report Performance Audit. *Implementation and Performance of the Cashless Debit Card Trial – Follow-on*, No. 29, 2021–22, Canberra: Commonwealth Government

Australian Bureau of Statistics, *Estimates and Projections, Aboriginal and Torres Strait Islander Australians*, Canberra: Commonwealth Government, 2019

Australian Bureau of Statistics (accessed November 2023) explore.data.abs.gov.au

Commonwealth of Australia 2021 *Commonwealth Closing the Gap Implementation Plan*, foreword

Johns G., *The Burden of Culture*, Sydney: Quadrant Books, 2022

Mavromaras K., Moskos M., Mahuteau S., Isherwood L., *Evaluation of the Cashless Debit Card in Ceduna, East Kimberley and the Goldfields Region Consolidate*, Report Future of Employment and Skills Research Centre, University of Adelaide, 2021

Morrison, S., MP Prime Minister, House of Representatives Ministerial Statements, *Closing the Gap Speech*, Thursday, 14 February 2019

Morrison, S., MP Prime Minister, House of Representatives Ministerial Statements, *Closing the Gap Speech*, Wednesday, 12 February 2020

NSW Department of Child Welfare and Social Welfare, *New Dawn: A Magazine for the Aboriginal People of NSW*, Sydney: NSW Government, April 1970.

Productivity Commission, *Indigenous Evaluation Strategy*, Canberra: Commonwealth Government, 2020

St. Vincent de Paul Society, *Policy Briefing: Cashless Debit Card*, 2019

Turnbull, M., MP, House of Representatives Official Hansard, *Ministerial Statements Closing the Gap*, Wednesday, 10 February 2016

Turnbull, M., MP Prime Minister, *Closing the Gap Report Statement to Parliament* House of Representatives, Parliament House, 14 February 2017

Turnbull, M., MP Prime Minister, *Closing the Gap Report 2018*, House of Representatives, 12 February 2018

Part 4: Conclusions
– where to for the Coalition?

12

The Disestablishment of the Liberal Party

Michael Sexton

Introduction

The concept of the "establishment" was first identified by the English journalist, Henry Fairlie, in the 1950s. He was referring to those individuals and groups in Britain who, although not in the main politicians, exercised most of the power and influence that directed the affairs of the nation. Identifying these individuals and groups was not a particularly difficult exercise in the case of Britain where, even now, much of that power and influence is still wielded by those who attended the great public schools, such as Eton and Harrow, and then Oxford and Cambridge Universities.

In Australia, for the first four decades of the post war years, the establishment broadly included the corporate sector, the Protestant churches, the medical and legal professions, senior public servants, the ABC and university administrators and academics. These groups largely supported the Liberal party and, up to the election of Whitlam government in 1972, Labor had spent almost a quarter of a century in opposition, although this period had been somewhat artificially extended by the party's split in 1955. Many of these establishment forces did not accept the change of government in 1972 and their obstruction of its policies was an important factor in the events that led to the government's removal from office in November 1975.

During the 1980s, however, a cultural change came over many public and private institutions in Australia. As they subscribed to the new doctrines of political correctness, they inevitably found themselves alienated from the Liberal Party, given the character of those doctrines, which included:

- portrayal of Australian society as essentially racist
- hostility to the resources industry in the context of climate policy
- antipathy to all forms of the Christian religion
- transference of power from parliaments to courts by way of a bill of rights
- advocacy of open borders without any restrictions on unauthorised immigration
- suspicion of the activities of law enforcement bodies
- governance by international bodies, such as the UN, when they disagreed with an Australian government

In a development that would no doubt have bemused Sir Robert Menzies, Labor and the Greens have become the parties of this transformed establishment. None of this means, of course, that the Liberals cannot win elections in the future in Australia, although they are currently out of office in every jurisdiction except Tasmania – where the government has no majority in the lower House and depends on the support of cross-benchers – and, in most cases, by a margin of seats that would preclude a return to office at the next election in these jurisdictions. But their task is far from easy and it may be useful to look in a little more detail at some of the institutions that comprise the new establishment and the problems they have caused for the Liberals.

The media world

Overall, although there are some exceptions, the Australian media is largely supportive of the policies of Labor and the Greens. This is particularly true of the ABC where most staff are fiercely hostile to the Liberals. Liberal governments at the federal level have occasionally tried to address this problem by the appointment of board members but, even if it wished to, the board is powerless to influence the staff and senior management appears unconcerned with the organisation's tenor, perhaps considering that most of its audience approves of this tenor in any event.

The same can largely be said about the Nine newspapers, particularly the *Sydney Morning Herald* and the Melbourne *Age*. If the published letters to the editor in these two journals were surveyed over a long period of time, one might be forgiven for thinking that there was not a single Liberal voter in their readership. Presumably this is not the case but opinion pieces by their own journalists and third party contributors are generally directed to a readership that has little time for the Liberals. Even more hostile are *The Guardian*, *The Saturday Paper*, *The Monthly*, *Quarterly Essay*, *Crikey*, *New Matilda* and *New Daily*.

The only alternative views can be found in the News Corp publications, particularly its metropolitan tabloids such as the *Daily Telegraph* in Sydney and the *Herald Sun* in Melbourne. These journals, however, are not especially supportive of the Liberals but are certainly less politically correct then their many rivals. In the case of *The Australian* there is quite a degree of diversity in its opinion pages and amongst its journalists. Even on Sky television's current affairs programs there is a range of regular commentators from both sides, although the presenters are generally hostile to Labor and the Greens.

It is true that most members of the electorate in Australia do not share the media's obsession with political events but this overall distain for the Liberals has no doubt had some impact over a lengthy period of time and there is certainly no indications that this situation is likely to change in the immediate future.

Universities

Given the explosion in the number of school-leavers moving on to tertiary institutions over the last two decades, there is an obvious problem for the Liberals in that most academic and administrative staff in universities share a politically correct agenda and a significant proportion of academics are strongly antipathetic to the Liberals. There are no figures available but it might safely be assumed that the political views of Australian academics largely reflect those of their American colleagues where various studies of college professors have found Democrat voters outnumbering Republican supporters by over 10 to 1.

The American historian, Richard Hofstadter, said of the concept of a university in 1968:

> A university is a community, but it is a community of a special kind – a community devoted to inquiry … Its presence marks our commitment to the idea that somewhere in society there must be an organization in which anything can be studied or questioned – not merely safe and established things but difficult and inflammatory things, the most troublesome questions of politics and war, of sex and morals, of property and national loyalty.

Hardly the role of universities in Australia at this time! In keeping with a lack of any spirit of inquiry, Sydney University in 2018 rejected a proposal by the Ramsay Centre for Western Civilisation to initiate a course on this subject at the university. This rejection came after a group of its academics engaged in a public protest. They issued a statement claiming that "the only people who invoke 'Western civilisation' in anything other than a critical spirit are members of the racist right" adding that "Western civilisation is a favourite umbrella term sheltering all manner of toxic and paranoid prejudices."

There are presumably still some students who attend university and would like these institutions to be, as they once were to some extent, places for the exchange of ideas with scope and disagreement on political, social and economic questions. But they would know that any public contradiction of what John Kenneth Galbraith first termed in the 1960s the "conventional wisdom" would be highly detrimental to their academic progress and possibly even to their future career after university.

Schools

In somewhat the same way as the spirit of political correctness pervades universities, it now looms large in school curriculums. This would only be a problem for the Liberals, of course, if they were seen as opponents of political correctness and, if this were once true, there may be some doubt as to their stance today. In a desperate – and futile – effort to appeal to various groups holding these views, quite a number of Liberals have tried to accommodate these groups and in the area of economic policy, for example, Liberal administrations have embraced ever-increasing government expenditure and ever-higher taxation to almost the same extent as their opponents.

Nevertheless, the Liberals still have in some quarters an historical reputation for balanced budgets and lower taxation so that they are hardly suited by the National Curriculum. In years 9 and 10, for example, students read and watch the film adaptation of Naomi Klein's *This Changes Everything* – a rather febrile anti-capitalist manifesto. It may be, of course, that if, the curriculum contained a range of views on this subject, Klein's work could be included but, as in most areas, no alternative views are provided.

The same kind of selectivity can be found in studies of history and literature in the National Curriculum. As in the case of universities, there may be school students who hold contrary views but they would know that to express them would simply be an invitation to the examiner to mark down their work with all the consequences that this might have for advancement at school and afterwards.

Community bodies

The welfare sector, exemplified by its peak body, the Australian Council of Social Services, is hardly an area that has changed its political direction over recent times. It has always been part of Labor's constituency and, while required to work with Liberal governments, does not do so with any great enthusiasm. The object of these bodies is increased government expenditure for the groups they represent and they do not see the budgetary process as the allocation of finite resources. This is not, however, to single them out for criticism because the same attitude prevails amongst almost all sectors that depend in whole or in part on government funding.

One federal agency that showed little enthusiasm for working with a

Liberal administration was the Australian Human Rights Commission which, over the period 2013-2022, was consistently at odds with the government over issues such as freedom of speech and border protection. There are many who would say that this is an entirely healthy form of opposition to government policies but it is interesting that the government was unable, either by appointments to the Commission or in any other way, to influence the exercise of its functions. The Commission starts with the advantage, of course, that any questioning of its views can be portrayed as an attack on human rights – a term that resists clear definition but has become ubiquitous in national and international legal circles.

Corporate sector

In its establishment days the Liberals were strongly supported by both big and small business. Overall small business still sees its interests as best protected by a Liberal administration but the situation has become more complicated with respect to the corporate sector. Its position can be contrasted with that of the union movement which is a part, perhaps the major part, of the Labor Party, either formally or at least informally. This means that the union movement, led by the ACTU, campaigns against the Liberals whether they are in government or in opposition and provides very substantial funds to Labor but none to the other side of politics.

The corporate sector, particularly the boards of major public corporations, on the other hand, is much more cautious about its political involvement. Many large corporations make donations to both sides of politics as some form of insurance. One of the understandable reasons for caution on the part of the corporate sector is that, while there is really nothing that a Liberal government can do in retaliation to the campaigns of the union movement, a Labor administration can make life difficult for particular areas of the business sector and even for individual corporations.

It has been obvious in recent federal election campaigns, that, while the union movement vigorously supports Labor with funds, personnel and public comments, the peak business organisations have been largely silent, seemingly unwilling to risk offending what may be an incoming Labor government, even though Liberal policies may, albeit only marginally in many cases, be more beneficial to their members.

Another reason for caution on the part of many board members of major corporations is their embrace of the doctrines of political correctness, given that this phenomenon is a product of the new and not the old establishment. There may be some question as to how sincerely these views are held in private by many board members but publicly they want the approval of the new establishment and are also aware that open disapproval by that group might well be damaging to the reputation of their organisation and to themselves as individuals.

Legal professional bodies

Each State and Territory has a body representing solicitors – often called the Law Society, and a separate body representing barristers, usually termed the Bar Association. There is also an Australian Bar Association, and more particularly in terms of resources, the Law Council of Australia which is the peak body containing the various State and Territory organisations as members. With a few exceptions all these bodies were consistently critical of the last federal Liberal administration on issues such as border protection and human rights.

This is not a recent development. In 2002, for example, the NSW Labor government proposed changes to the existing sentencing legislation to set out standard non-parole periods for a range of offences, including murder and armed robbery. The trial judge would still have had considerable discretion to move from the standard figure in any particular case. This legislation, which was ultimately passed, was opposed by every section of the NSW legal establishment – the Bar Association, the Law Society, Young Lawyers, the Legal Aid Commission and even the Director of Public Prosecutions.

The previous year the Bar Association had released a public statement on sentencing laws that referred to the "fate of the unpopular and oppressed in countries such as South Africa under apartheid, Chile and Argentina under military rule and Nazi Germany". It can be assumed that not everyone in the legal profession around Australia shares these kinds of views but, as in many other areas, the cost of publicly disagreeing with these professional bodies is a severe deterrent to the expression of a contrary opinion.

In a 1981 book, by Laurence Maher and myself, *The Legal Mystique*, we noted the largely traditional views of judges and the legal profession in general. In the four decades since the publication of that work there has certainly been a profound change in the views of the various legal bureaucracies in Australia.

Cultural events

The various aspects of the cultural world – literature, music, film, arts – are largely strongholds of political correctness and there are few friends for the Liberals in these areas. The most visible manifestation perhaps of this position is the range of literary festivals held every year around the country that take place not only in the major cities but also in regional centres. It might be thought that these events would provide an opportunity for discussion and debate about current political, social and economic issues but there is seldom any disagreement between the participants and a politically correct consensus is very much the rule. This does not seem to be a problem for the audiences who seem to largely share the views of the writers and journalists who take speaking roles at the festivals. There seems little appetite in the audiences to have their views challenged in any way and they can usually be confident that their opinions will only be reinforced by the contributors.

It would be easy to complain about this lack of any exchange of ideas but it needs to be recognised that both contributors and audiences are essentially drawn from a segment of society that subscribes to the doctrines of political correctness and has no interest in debating these issues. It would, of course, be possible to invite to these festivals some from amongst the relatively small group of writers and members of the media who reject the conventional wisdom and ask them to put forward these dissenting opinions. But there is little danger of that happening in the immediate future and literary festivals will continue to be an echo chamber as they have been in the past.

Back to the future

What is striking in political terms about the Liberals' loss of support from many public and private institutions is that it has happened in a relatively short space of time, perhaps about 40 years. This does not mean, of course, that they cannot win a federal or State election in the immediate future, although, as already noted, in all eight Australian polities where they are in opposition, except possibly Queensland and New South Wales, the gap in parliamentary numbers in the lower House would make this very difficult at the next election in each of those jurisdictions. To this must be added the fact that the Liberals need to gain an absolute majority in those lower Houses because otherwise Labor would almost certainly be able to form government with the support of the Greens and any Independents. It is also true that, even when in government, the Liberals face severe difficulties in implementing their policies because they do not have a majority in the Senate or in the five State upper Houses. The same is true for Labor, given that neither of the major parties has been able to obtain such a majority in recent times, but Labor is normally able to rely on the Greens and Independents to enact their legislative proposals, albeit often after considerable negotiation with these groups.

Arguably more serious than any of these factors is the low level of support for the Liberals in voters agreed between eighteen and mid-thirties. There are a number of factors contributing to this, including the climate in universities that has already been discussed and the attraction of the Greens to a group of voters who have never known even the mildest of economic recessions and appear to believe that economic growth can never falter. This kind of Panglossian attitude was reflected in a Lowy Institute poll last year that indicated that more than half of the electorate supported the reduction of coal exports and the banning of new coal mines – this in a country that is the world's largest coal exporter and where export earnings from mining exceeded all other sectors of the economy.

Optimists on the Liberal side would say that there have always been political cycles in Australia and both of the major parties have experienced periods in the wilderness at both the federal and State levels. They would add that the electorate is likely to react quickly to any significant downturn in the national economy. As already noted, however, the Australian economy has had a stable pattern of growth for several decades. And, as to the notion of political cycles, the two-party system that operated for most of the country's political history has certainly been destabilised by the advent of the Greens and Independents. A pessimist on the Liberal side might think that the norm in the immediate future would be Labor governments, even if on some occasions minority administrations in formal or informal coalition with the Greens and some Independents.

13

What was it all for?

Scott Prasser

Introduction

This concluding chapter asks the question, given the dismal record of the Coalition in office recounted in this volume and other critical analyses – what were nine years of Coalition government all for? What was its legacy, if any, notwithstanding some sterling efforts by individual ministers across a range of different portfolios where some successes were achieved. Yet, these do not constitute a government triumph. They are akin to a platoon that wins a skirmish while the army of which they are a part loses the battle because of disconnected leadership, inept strategy, poor generalship, and lack of commitment and drive.

Failure all round

Sadly, this is not a story of a government that strove to implement genuine reforms – actions to make society better (Banks 2012:106-8). Nor did the Coalition, with a few exceptions, as noted, fight the "good fight" as Austin Holmes, chief economist at the Reserve Bank of Australia once described the battle to get "good sense" into policy outcomes (1981: 1). Rather, as the chapters in this volume recount, the Coalition so much of the time did not even know what they were fighting for except to cling onto office, and to keep the other mob out.

Using Keating's criterion mentioned in the Introduction that, "When the government changes, the country changes" (Keating 2014: 207), the problem was that after nine years in office, the Coalition did not change the country very much. It can even be argued that its unwillingness to fight the "good fight" left the country worse off.

The Coalition failed at all levels – in policy, in politics, and in overall governing, in managing the ship of state.

The Coalition failed to develop policies that reflected not just its principles, but also those that reignited the reform momentum. Report after report from the Productivity Commission reminded us all that reform had long run out of steam (Banks 2019; Banks 2023; Productivity Commission 2017). In so many areas while some worthwhile initiatives were started too often they ended in confusion, half-baked compromises or were just quietly abandoned altogether. Many examples spring to mind – taxation reform, federalism, deregulation, of the university sector, and even school funding after success in having amendments passed to the legislation, was then abandoned.

Politically, the Coalition failed on several counts. First it failed to articulate an alternative, accessible and modern narrative to frame its policies, counter prevailing orthodoxies, provide a point of differentiation from its opponents, give voters real choice and those disaffected ones a voice (see Chapter 2). It is recognised that public opinion will follow the latest fads unless alternatives are heard (Westin 2008: 21-3). Too often under the Coalition, policy field after policy field was abandoned too easily and too often to the other side (Chapters 7, 8, 9). Too often the Coalition looked like bystanders watching the political game being played rather than being active participants. Over and over, the Coalition just reacted to events and the media.

Even when the Coalition wanted to fix a problem, its goals were unclear and worse, they lacked the political strategies and skills to achieve success. The Coalition complained about ABC bias but during its nine years in office articulated no policy to address the problem, proposed no new administrative arrangements and developed no strategy in how to implement any proposed reform. This was a problem repeated over and over across most policy areas.

In terns of governance the Coalition had firm control of the levers of power, the public service, key appointments, and other bodies and happily engaged in a rabid form of politicisation as is detailed in Chapter 4. This, however, hardly reflected any principles of governing as such, of the role and limits of government, of where the different institutions like parliament and the public service fit in the architecture of government, and how they might be modernised to better reflect democratic practice in a changing society. The Coalition, and in particular, the Liberal Party, once the party of respectability, became the party of avarice in both personal behaviour of some of its members and its treatment of public offices as part of the prize of winning. It accepted too unquestioningly the growing politicisation of our institutions, adopting a "now it's our turn approach" rather than tackling its underlying causes and being exemplary in its own actions. Reforms of a sort happened to different institutions and practices but so often these were in reaction to events and problems exposed than any thought about how institutions might work better. It is interesting to note that no Liberal prime minister has given the Garran Oration to the Institute of Public Administration Australia since John Howard in 1997 (Federal Liberal Health Minster Greg Hunt gave the Oration in 2020).

What's the Liberal Party's (Coalition's) problem?

So why did Australia's most successful political party, the Liberal Party and most successful and long-lasting political partnership, the coalition with the Nationals, fail so dismally between 2013-2022 in not just losing office but in failing to leave a lasting mark?

The Liberal Party's failing may be a result of its own endogenous features – poor recruitment and candidate selection, growing factionalism, weak untrained staffing, declining membership, outdated branch structures, limited networking abilities, unclear philosophy, and inept policy development. The issues Starr mentioned in Chapter 3.

This is not to deny the wider system drivers at work that is affecting all major parties – a declining primary vote, low party membership, apathy, the increasing pluralisation and fragmentation of society, growth of post materialist values, changing work structures and the disconnect between inner city educated elites and singles with those in outer suburbia. The issue is these are affecting the Coalition more decisively (Kelly 2018; Lesh 2018; Marsh 1995). Unlike Labor, the Coalition has no organised network into the wider community. Labor has the unions, and though the trade union movement overall is in decline it remains strong in critical areas like education, health and the public service. These are important for their on the ground connection to issues that affect large parts of the electorate. They are also a source of recruitment. This has been accompanied by demographic shifts to central urban areas, increased tertiary education, more singles, more renting and more fluidity in movement. Cumulatively, these trends partly explain why so many institutions are captured and are disowning the Liberal Party (Chapter 12). It partly explains the Liberal retreat from the inner urban seats and lack of inner urban seats after the 2022 federal election (Loughnane and Hume: 2022).

So, is the Coalition's time past? Is the inherent conservative orientation of the Liberal Party (a contested label) and its National Party partner, out of joint with current social trends and values that cannot be reverse and therefore the Coalition is doomed (Kelly 2018)?

At present it seems that the Labor Party, in contrast to its experience in the 1950s and 1960s, has been better able to adapt to some of these trends which are not transitory but reflect permanent shifts in social structures, values and expectations. For the Labor Party the test will be whether in seeking to deflect the Greens and thus adopting a more left of centre policy agenda, whether the policy consequences will be politically damaging and Labor will unable to sustain itself in office for long.

The challenge for the Liberal Party is whether it can adjust to these trends without tearing itself apart as its "progressives" rush to accommodate too easily the latest fad and its conservatives seek to react rather too unthinkingly without acknowledging the veracity of numerous social and economic changes to provide an electorally attractive response. Adding to the challenge is that the Liberals are in coalition with the

National Party which is electorally even more detached from some of these movements although contradictorily continues to perform and hold its own because its seats are less affected by these different electoral vicissitudes.

References

Banks, G., "Successful Reform: Past Lessons, Future Challenges", in Banks, G., (ed), *Advancing the Reform Agenda: Selected Speeches*, Productivity Commission: Canberra: Commonwealth of Australia, December 2012, 103-20

Banks, G., "The politics of productivity: Success and failure down-under", Conference Dinner Speech, OECD Global Forum on Productivity, 20 June 2019

Banks, G., "Australia's Productivity Malaise: Reflections on the 'Debate'" *Edward Shann Memorial Lecture*, UWA, Perth, 16 August 2023

Holmes, A., "The Good Fight", *Economic Record*, March 1981, 1-11

Kelly, P., "Bricks are falling from the Conservative fortress", *The Australian*, 21 February 2018

Kelly, P., "Flawed frailty of the middle class", *The Australian*, 2-3 February 2019

Lesh, M., *Democracy in a Divided Australia*, Redland Bay: Connor Court Publishing, 2018

Loughnane, B., and Hume, J., *Review of the 2022 Federal Election*, Liberal Party of Australia, December 2022

Marsh, I., *Beyond the Two Party System: Political Representation, Economic Competitiveness and Australian Politics*, Melbourne: Cambridge University Press, 1995

Productivity Commission, *Shift the Dial: 5 Year Productivity Review*, Inquiry Report No 84, Canberra; Commonwealth of Australia, August 2017

van Onselen, P., "Coalition can't expect to coast back into office", *The Australian*, 22 April 2023

Warhurst, J., "Patterns and Directions in Australian Politics over the Past Fifty Years", *Australian Journal of History and Politics*, 50(2), 2004, 163-77

Westin, D., *The Political Brain: The Role of Emotion in Deciding the Fate of the Nation*, New York: PublicAffairs, 2008

About the Contributors

Robert Carling is a retired senior Commonwealth Treasury official and is currently Senior Fellow at the Centre for Independent Studies, Sydney, NSW. He writes regularly in the national media on economic and budget issues.

John Halligan is Emeritus Professor of Public Administration and Governance in the Faculty of Business, Government and Law, University of Canberra. His research interests are comparative public administration and governance in Anglophone countries, including the Australian public service, public sector reform, performance management, and currently a comparative study of digital government. Recent books: *Reforming Public Management and Governance: Impact and Lessons from Anglophone Countries*, Edward Elgar, 2020; *Policy Advice and the Westminster Tradition: Policy Advisory Systems in Australia, Britain, Canada, and New Zealand*, Cambridge University Press, 2020 (with Jonathan Craft).

Gary Johns served in the House of Representatives and was Special Minister of State and Assistant Minister for Industrial Relations in the second Keating Government. He served as an Associate Commissioner of the Commonwealth Productivity Commission and was the Australian Charities and Not-for-profits Commissioner 2017-2022. He received the Centenary Medal for "service to Australian society through the advancement of economic, social and political issues" and the 2002 Fulbright Professional Award in Australian-United States Alliance Studies, served at Georgetown University Washington DC. He is the author of *The Burden of Culture* (Quadrant) and chair of *Close the Gap Research*.

Aynsley Kellow is Professor Emeritus of Government at the University of Tasmania. He is a former Expert Reviewer for the Intergovernmental Panel on Climate Change, and his recent books include *Negotiating Climate Change: A Forensic Analysis* and *The OECD: A Decade of Transformation. 2011-2021* (with Peter Carroll).

David Lee is Associate Professor, School of Humanities and Social Sciences, University of New South Wales, Canberra, having been Director of the Historical Publications and Information Section, Department of Foreign Affairs and Trade, from 1997 to 2019. His research interests include the history of Australian politics and public administration, economic, business and mining history, Australian biography, and the history of Australian diplomacy and strategic policy. His publications include *Stanley Melbourne Bruce: Australian Internationalist*, (2010), *The Second Rush: Mining and the Transformation of Australia* (2016) and *Stanley Melbourne Bruce: Institution Builder* (2020). He is the Chair of the Commonwealth Working Party of the Australian Dictionary of Biography.

Malcolm Mackerras AO is Distinguished Fellow of the PM Glynn Institute, Australian Catholic University. Malcolm is Australia's veteran election watcher, having become a public psephologist as long ago as May 1953. In January 2006 his "distinguished service" to Australia's democracy caused him to be honoured by being made an Officer in the Order of Australia, AO.

Greg Melleuish is a Professor in the School of Humanities and Social Inquiry, University of Wollongong. He has written widely on Australian liberalism and Australian political ideas. Greg's most recent publication (with Stephen Chavura) IS *The Forgotten Menzies* (MUP 2021). "The Whitlam Narrative", in Scott Prasser & David Clune (eds) *The Whitlam Era*, (Connor Court 2022), 'Menzies: Democracy, Spirit and Education,' in Zachary Gorman (ed) *The Young Menzies*, (MUP 2022) (with Stephen Chavura); and most recently, "Newspaper Leaders as Moral Exhortation: Understanding the Rhetoric of Civil Religion in Colonial Australia", *Religions* 14(4), 2023.

Patrick McClure AO has worked in leadership roles in the social purpose sector over many years and was also CEO of the Society of St Vincent de Paul (NSW/ACT). Patrick chaired the Australian Government's *Reference Group on Welfare Reform* reviewing the income support system for both prime ministers John Howard and Tony Abbott. He also chaired the *Review Panel of the Australian Charities and Not-for-Profits Commission* and was a member of the Prime Minister's Community-Business Partnership Board and the Board for a New Tax System. Currently he is a member of the NSW Treasury Social Impact Investment Expert Advisory Group. Patrick was awarded an Officer of the Order of Australia (AO) and an Australian Centennial Medal. He has a Master of Arts (Public Policy), Bachelor of Social Work (Distinction) and Diploma of Theology.

Scott Prasser has worked in federal and state governments in senior research and advisory positions and several academic posts. He has written extensively on Australian government. His recent publications include: *Royal Commissions and Public Inquiries in Australia* (2021 2nd ed); *The Whitlam Era* (2022 co-edited), *New directions in royal commissions and public inquiries: Do we need them?* (2023) and co-edited *The Art of Opposition* (2024). Scott is currently Senior Fellow at the Centre for Independent Studies.

Graeme Starr held academic positions at New England and Newcastle universities and was visiting fellow at the Public Policy Institute of the Australian Catholic University. A graduate of Sydney University, he completed his masters' degree Carleton University in Canada, and his doctorate at West Virginia University in the United States. Graeme was Research Officer for the Liberal Party's Federal and NSW secretariats, later NSW Liberal Party State Director, and Chief of Staff to the former Federal Minister Ian Sinclair AC, and for John Howard in opposition. His publications include: *The Liberal Party of Australia: A Documentary History* (1980); *Policy and Change: The Howard Mandate* (1997); *Carrick: Principles, Politics and Policy* (2012).

Michael Sexton SC is Solicitor General for New South Wales and the author of several books on Australian politics and history, including *Illusions of Power: The fate of a reform government* published in 1979. This was reissued in 2005 as *The Great Crash: The short life and sudden death of the Whitlam government*.

Mark Spencer is currently serving as the Director of Public Policy with Christian Schools Australia. Mark is responsible for advocacy on behalf of Christian schools in a wide range of educational policy as well as areas relating to religious freedom and equal opportunity and discrimination law, both at the Commonwealth and State or Territory level. Mark has qualification in accounting, governance and law, and has also been involved in politics in a variety of roles. Mark is married to Melanie, a Christian school leader, and they have three adult children.

Andrea Wallace is a Lecturer at the School of Business, University of New England. Andrea holds an undergraduate and postgraduate qualifications in politics, history, and economics from the University of Canterbury, New Zealand. In 2019 she completed her PhD focusing on local government structural reform. In addition to her ongoing research in local government, other research interests include public policy and social and economic issues.